D1238252

Reprints of Economic Classics

FRANCIS HUTCHESON

Also published in

REPRINTS OF ECONOMIC CLASSICS

BY WILLIAM R. SCOTT

ADAM SMITH AS STUDENT AND PROFESSOR [1937]

FRANCIS HUTCHESON

HIS LIFE, TEACHING AND
POSITION IN THE
HISTORY OF PHILOSOPHY

BY

WILLIAM ROBERT SCOTT

M.A. (TRIN. COLL. DUB.): D.PHIL. (ST ANDREWS): F.R.S.A. (IRELAND):

ASSISTANT TO THE PROFESSOR OF MORAL PHILOSOPHY AND LECTURER IN
POLITICAL ECONOMY IN THE UNIVERSITY OF ST ANDREWS

THE ADAM SMITH LIBRARY

REPRINTS OF ECONOMIC CLASSICS

AUGUSTUS M. KELLEY · PUBLISHERS
NEW YORK · 1966

FIRST PUBLISHED 1900
REPRINTED 1966 BY PERMISSION OF
CAMBRIDGE UNIVERSITY PRESS

PRINTED IN THE UNITED STATES OF AMERICA
by SENTRY PRESS, NEW YORK, N. Y. 10019

TO THE
MOST REVEREND

WILLIAM ALEXANDER, D.D., D.C.L., LL.D.,

LORD ARCHBISHOP OF ARMAGH AND PRIMATE OF ALL IRELAND,
A PRELATE JUSTLY RENOWNED ALIKE FOR THE ORATORY
THAT MOVES, AND THE TOLERATION THAT BINDS TOGETHER
CHRISTIANS OF DIFFERENT CREEDS—

THIS RECORD OF THE LIFE AND WORK
OF A PRESBYTERIAN THINKER, KNOWN IN HIS DAY FOR
ELOQUENCE AND BROADMINDEDNESS, WHO WAS ASSOCIATED
WITH ARMAGH AND BEFRIENDED BY A FORMER
ARCHBISHOP OF ARMAGH

IS DEDICATED,

BY ONE WHOM HIS GRACE HAS ENCOURAGED
BY "MEASURED WORDS" OF RIPE WISDOM.

PREFACE.

As a rule a book dealing with the work of a single thinker is often intended to establish some favourite thesis of the writer. No such claim is made for the following account of Hutcheson's life and position in the History of Philosophy. Indeed any definite conclusions arrived at have been ascertained incidentally. They formed no part of the original plan of the work, which was exceedingly modest, being in fact an endeavour to collect information as to the main facts of Hutcheson's life in Dublin prior to his appointment as Professor at Glasgow. Of this part of his life very little was known and yet it seemed that a man who had been a friend of the Lord-Lieutenant and who had enjoyed the confidence of both Irish Primates should have left some trace upon the social history of his time. The search for such traces of his personality was exceedingly disappointing. Sources from which information might reasonably have been expected gave very small results; and, just when one was ready to despair, new facts were discovered in quite unexpected quarters. This apparent elusiveness of Hutcheson's life appealed to that hunting disposition, which according to evolutionists, is a legacy from remote and non-literary ancestors; and, finally, I decided to endeavour to run the quarry to earth by examining contemporary history, memoirs and letters in the hope of making an exhaustive search after the necessary material for an account of Hutcheson's life in Ireland. I had intended to reduce the results to some kind of narrative in the form of a magazine article during the year of the 150th anniversary of Hutcheson's death. However, after making a rough draft, I found the material had grown beyond these limits and that the account would have been necessarily incomplete. Besides, I had accumulated a considerable amount of information upon Hutcheson's life at Glasgow; and, when Miss Drennan of Belfast had kindly placed the valuable series of letters written by Hutcheson to her great-grandfather at my disposal, I determined to make a fresh beginning and write a biography which would be complete as far as possible. Such an account of Hutcheson's activities let in much new light upon his general mode of thought, and it became necessary to collate these facts with the internal evidence afforded by his writings. Consequently an analysis of his books is added to the life— not as a mere summary of his Philosophy but rather as an attempt to trace out its origin and to follow step by step the various forms it assumed in the mind of Hutcheson himself. In this exposition no attempt has been made to force him to be self-consistent nor yet to emphasize his inconsistencies. I had intended to end the book at this point, leaving it to the reader to draw his own conclusions from the facts, but it was suggested that, in such a form, the volume would appear unfinished and I have therefore added two chapters, summarising the general conclusions, which appear to me to be deducible from the material contained in the earlier chapters. Such being the growth of the book it will be seen that it is not intended to prove any position and that the place assigned to Hutcheson in the

History of Philosophy is really that which he himself sought to gain, though this fact has been lost sight of through lack of knowledge of several important aspects of his life and work.

I am much indebted to Miss Drennan for the loan of the valuable collection of letters already mentioned. There are twenty of these, one of which has not been printed as it deals with business matters, but the remaining nineteen have been reproduced practically in full, with the exception of a few sentences, which repeat in a condensed form what has been elsewhere detailed more fully. Owing to the fact that most of these letters deal with heterogeneous subjects, it was necessary to divide them into parts and assign each to its proper chapter in the biography. I am also indebted to the following persons and institutions for permission to print MS. material— Sir Edward Reid; Advocates' Library, Edinburgh; Magee College, Londonderry; Public Record Office, Dublin; Registry of Deeds Office, Dublin; Royal Irish Academy, Dublin; Royal Society, Edinburgh; Town Council, Edinburgh; Trinity College, Dublin; and the Senatus of the University of Glasgow. I have to thank the editor of *Mind* for permission to reprint some paragraphs from an article which appeared in that publication, dealing with James Arbuckle.

During the composition of the work I received many valuable suggestions, which have cleared up doubtful points, or enabled me to avoid certain errors I might otherwise have made. Thus, in reference to the first seven chapters, I beg to thank the Rev. Alex. Gordon, M.A., of the Memorial Hall, Manchester; Rev. W. T. Latimer, B.A., of Eglish, Dungannon; and Mr Pillow of Armagh for information upon special points; and also, for many hints and improvements in the more philosophical portion, Profs. Knight, Ritchie, and Herkless of the

University of St Andrews, and Prof. L. C. Purser of Trinity College, Dublin. To Prof. Ritchie I am specially indebted for reading the whole work in MS. and also the greater part of it in proof.

My thanks are due to the Syndics of the Cambridge University Press for their liberality in publishing the volume.

St Andrews.
July 26, 1900.

CONTENTS.

CHAPTER III.

Hutcheson one of fortune's favourites, his introduction to Lord Carteret, the Lord-Lieutenant; the learning of his Court and his patronage of Scholarship; offers made to Hutcheson of preferment—the report concerning the Provostship of Trinity College, uneasiness of John Hutcheson, Francis Hutcheson's reply, points of difficulty in this explanation; a restatement of the argument; Hutcheson's honesty of purpose but want of sufficient firmness under the circumstances. Carteret's respect for his disinterestedness and its results.

Hutcheson's meeting with Archbishop King, who protects him from prosecutions in the Ecclesiastical Courts.

Criticisms of the *Inquiry*; Burnet's Letters in the *London Journal*; influence of Butler and Wollaston; attacks of the orthodox.

Publication of the *Essay on the Passions*. Hutcheson's introduction to Primate Boulter; his father's death. The contest for the Professorship of Moral Philosophy at Glasgow.

CHAPTER IV.

The state of the University—two parties—the party of Progress and the party for Conservatism; the change from "Regents" to Professors; the Commission of 1728. Hutcheson a member of the Progressive party.

His revival of academic discipline—lectures in English and with eloquence. He was in fact a Professor-preacher of a two-fold gospel. The effects of his teaching. The recognition of this in the traditions of Scottish Chairs of Moral Philosophy and in the superior finish of Scottish University lectures generally.

Hutcheson's influence on his pupils. He was their banker, guardian and friend; his care of "wild Irish teagues"; his missionary efforts amongst them. Letters relative to Bob Haliday. Various opinions of the value of his educational work.

CHAPTER V.

Hutcheson a member of numerous Committees upon College business; the Boulter benefaction; the "Professors' Manses"; friction with the Town Council; Hutcheson's aid to the foundation of the publishing house of Foulis; Clothworthy O'Neil's degree.

Hutcheson's "heresy"; the effect of this attack upon his policy in the University; his counter-attack upon the reactionary party, which begins with the support of Leechman for the Chair of Divinity—Leechman's character; incidents and results of the contest; the final contest over the election of a Professor of Greek and triumph of the "Forward policy."

CHAPTER VI.

The revived interest in Shaftesbury's works due to success of Hutcheson's writings. Butler and Hutcheson, Berkeley and Hutcheson, Pope's *Essay on Man*, Voltaire. The interval from 1728–1735, exceedingly fruitful in minor works; Tindal, Peter Brown, Dr Watts, Samuel Colliber, Conyers Place. The Clarke controversy, John Balguy, Archibald Campbell's 'Αρετὴ Λογία, his criticism of Hutcheson, and his Hedonistic Calculus, the latter repeated in the *Enquiry into the Origin of the Human Appetites and Affections* &c., sometimes attributed to John Gay, who had criticized Hutcheson in the *Dissertation concerning the fundamental Principles of Virtue or Morality*, Thomas Johnston, Joseph Foster, John Clarke, John Brown, Thomas Chubb and other writers.

Effects of criticism upon Hutcheson, additions and alterations in the new editions of his early works, and the composition of the *System of Moral Philosophy* from 1734–1737. Letters explaining the peregrinations of the MS., the additions of friends. Hutcheson appears to have, by 1740, outgrown the ideas of the *System of Moral Philosophy*, and hence rather than rewrite it he starts afresh, as a result the *Metaphysicae Synopsis* and *Philosophia Moralis Institutio Compendiaria* were published in 1742, Hutcheson's own opinion of these works.

Hume's introduction to Hutcheson in 1739; Hume's Letters, Hutcheson's suggestions and criticisms and Hume's replies. Hutcheson introduces Adam Smith to Hume, the relations of the three, Hutcheson's influence upon Reid, Hume's criticism of Hutcheson's *Inst. Mor. Comp.*, Hutcheson's approximation to Butler.

Hume suspects Hutcheson of being unfavourable to his candidature for the Chair of Ethics at Edinburgh; probable grounds of Hutcheson's opposition; his own refusal of the Chair.

CHAPTER VII.

Hutcheson's friends, particularly Drennan; portraits and descriptions of Hutcheson; his attention to the business concerns of his friends; correspondence with the Presbytery of Pennsylvania; his sympathy and help for poor Presbyterian Clergy in Ireland.

Hutcheson on the Rebellion, his last visit to Ireland, his death. Reasons for delay in the publication of the *System of Moral Philosophy*; Hutcheson's descendants; editions of his works, and the prices.

CHAPTER VIII.

Hutcheson's life his strongest argument; his strength lay in speaking, not in writing; contrasted, in this respect, with Butler.

Hutcheson and Shaftesbury. Shaftesbury's Philosophy supplied two

great national needs. First the need for Beauty of, and in, life. The
Puritans and the Æsthetic sense. The degradation of Beauty extends
further back than Puritanism. The exotic character of Art in England.
The Puritans and Children of Israel, the hostility of the former to
Greek Literature. Therefore the need for the completion of the Re-
naissance in the reinstatement of Beauty and the Hellenic ideal of life.
Secondly the need for a reply to Hobbist and Theological Egoism.
Theological "blasphemy" of man. Shaftesbury's reply. Consequences
of Egoism, its moral atomism, individualism, mechanism and determinism.

Priority of Shaftesbury's answers to these two needs investigated,
the reinstatement of Beauty prior and more important. Shaftesbury's
return to Hellenism, compared with Cambridge Platonists. The Greek
ideal of life, its artistic sense, completeness, serenity, harmony. The
Cosmos or "System" of the Universe and Man—the artistic point of
view. The validity of the return to the Hellenic ideal investigated.

Shaftesbury's answer to Egoism. Criticism of Egoism carries him
beyond the Hellenic to a Christian Ideal—that of unselfishness. Shaftesbury's treatment of the "good, kind affections," and its difficulties.
Reconciliation with the Æsthetic view of life. The moral man uses his
"self-affections" as a trustee for the social organism. From this point
of view man is a "Microcosm" and the harmony of this with the
Macrocosm is beautiful. Inconsistency of this transition, the æsthetic
standpoint being merged in the teleological, hence the existence of an
"Intelligent Artificer." Shaftesbury's "better self" compared with
Green's Ethics.

Shaftesbury and Leibniz. Pre-established Harmony and Optimism.
Shaftesbury and Locke. Shaftesbury indebted to Locke for his terminology in dealing with "reflex senses." If Shaftesbury follows Locke in
thought, as well as language, he is doubly an egoistic hedonist. His
double point of view explains his language. From the first standpoint
moral approval is an intuitive judgment of taste by a spectator upon the
excellence of the lives of others. But from the other standpoint, Beauty
has been resolved into teleology, and how is the congruity of the ends
of the Microcosm and Macrocosm to be determined? It is known
intuitively and objectively. The "Pre-conceptions." The capacity for
cognising identity of ends "natural," i.e. φύσει, how cultivated.

The *Quid Juris* of this power, in the Consciousness, objectively, of
unity with the Cosmos; and, subjectively, in a consciousness of Dignity
or Worth.

Shaftesbury's form of expression aristocratically esoteric. This exclusiveness inconsistent with the brotherhood of man. Its artificiality.
This reflected in Shaftesbury's style. Mr Stephen's criticism of it,
which is too strong: his comparison of Shaftesbury and Matthew
Arnold, the qualifications to be added to it; similarity between Shaftesbury and Mr Ruskin.

CHAPTER IX.

Arbuckle and Hutcheson "incomplete followers" of Shaftesbury;
their relation to Shaftesbury and to each other. Difficulties arising
from later additions to the *Inquiry*. First edition represents a distinct
phase of thought. Hutcheson modified Shaftesbury's theory and expression of it (*a*) by refusing to attack Revealed Religion, (*b*) by introducing
democratic elements, (*c*) endeavouring to reconcile external and internal
Harmony. Hence a corresponding division of Internal Sense, which is
hedonistic, and so Hutcheson misses Shaftesbury's hints regarding
"Egoity," moral perception and Virtue as objective.

The *Sense of Beauty* refers to "Uniformity amidst variety." Hutcheson's want of appreciation for Colour—uniformity tends to increase,
variety to decrease; but this tendency should not be pushed too far.
Anticipation of Kant's disinterestedness, Universality and Necessity of
Judgments of Taste.

The *Moral Sense*—it is hedonistic, disinterested, refers to character;
its object Benevolence, as "greatest happiness of greatest number."

Though the two senses are apparently separated, they are closely
related. Uniformity involves End or Design, and hence an Intelligent
Artificer of the Whole Universe; further, Beauty involves a Benevolent
designer, hence Æsthetics pass into Divine Ethics and so the object of
the Sense of Beauty is the regularity of Divine Benevolence, as the
object of Moral Sense is the regularity of human Benevolence.

Ethical Idealism of this view contradicted by the Lockian nature of
Hutcheson's Psychology—whence comes the idea of End and how is it
hedonistically perceived? The doubtful objectivity of Primary Qualities
and the subjectivity of Secondary Qualities. How this effects the objects
of Internal Senses—there is no *certain objective* uniformity, therefore
no proof of the "intelligent designer" and the whole theory remains
subjective. This, criticised by followers of Clarke; Hutcheson borrows
material from Butler. Butler's relation to Shaftesbury.

CHAPTER X.

Hutcheson, in endeavouring to give content to the idea of the Microcosm, borrows from Butler. Egoistic Propensions and Particular
Affections and Self-love; altruistic Propensions, Affections and Benevolence. But Benevolence is a superior principle to Self-love, both in
its object and genesis, since it controls all particular Affections *and*

Self-love. Benevolence a "universal calm desire"; how Desire differs
from Passion and Affection, Desire differs from the preceding uneasiness
and subsequent pleasure.

Universal calm Benevolence is generated by the application of
reason to a particular affection, under the ideal of the good of the
Macrocosm—it "*commands*" and "*disciplines*" the particular affections
and ascertains the "tendency" of actions. Does "tendency" only
mean "motive"? Important though vague position of Reason, in
"assisting" and "governing" the moral Sense, and if so, Reason can
reach ultimate ends, though this is denied.

Universal Benevolence now becomes the condition of the uniformity
of the Moral Sense, but if so, it *is* the Moral Faculty; how this view is
borrowed from Butler. Benevolence now occupies part of the position
assigned to the Moral Sense, in the *Inquiry*, and Benevolence takes the
place of Butler's Conscience—the Moral Sense being a supernumerary.

The rational elements in the genesis of Benevolence might have
aided in overcoming the difficulty in the relation of the *Microcosm to the
Macrocosm*; further Reflection is introduced as "a source of Ideas"
and more prominence given to Primary Qualities; but at the same time
the objectivity of "ideas of Relation" is emphatically denied, and,
therefore, implicitly, "relations" of cosmic or moral order and further
the variability of the Moral Sense is admitted, consequently there is no
outlet to the Macrocosm. The reason of this inconsistency—the uniformity of moral rules justified by the rational element in Benevolence,
the "pleasures of Virtue" guaranteed by the Moral Sense, and Hutcheson cannot give up either of the two.

CHAPTER XI, PART I.

Why the *System of Moral Philosophy* represents a distinct stage of
thought. The great output of controversial literature and contact with
Dunlop's revival of Greek Literature explain the transition from the
second period to the third.

The introduction of the idea of Perfection, as an element in the
Summum Bonum, and the idea of ἀρετή and ἐνέργεια, borrowed from
Aristotle, hence inconsistency with "Reflection." The internal senses
derived from both.

1. The General *Sense of Beauty* subdivided (*a*) into Beauty proper,
(*b*) "Imitation," (*c*) Harmony, (*d*) Design, and possibly (*e*) Novelty and
(*f*) Grandeur. 2. Sense of Sympathy. 3. Moral Sense or Faculty.

4. Sense of Honour. 5. Sense of Decency or Decorum. Each of the last three "Senses" has for its object an excellence of mental activity, therefore what is the characteristic of *moral* excellence? It is cognitive and practical activity, in the highest degree of efficiency, directed towards the good of the Macrocosm. Moral Excellence passes to individual perfection—the difficulty of this view. Hutcheson's reply still leaves the Moral Sense a supernumerary. Hence he changes the object of the Sense which is (a) moral excellence recognised by a bare Consciousness without necessarily involving any hedonistic element; (b) in reference to "immutable" natural laws of reason, hence, there is, in the Moral Faculty, a *Conscientia antecedens*, or Moral decision, followed by a *Conscientia subsequens* of moral feeling; (c) but the Moral Sense is also understood as wholly hedonistic, and not the consequent, but the prophetic anticipation of moral reasoning; (d) besides approving Calm Benevolence it has also for its object particular altruistic affections.

The Internal Senses adjusted to the order of the Microcosm only through the distinction between Self-love and Benevolence. The addition of "Perfection" to Self-love and its difficulties.

The Macrocosm in the third Period. The Moral Faculty added to Teleology as a connecting link; these two sum up all human activities and powers in the highest potency. Teleology proves (a) the existence of one or more intelligent artificers, (b) of one. (c) The Moral Faculty tends to establish optimism, (d) which is proved by the addition of individual immortality, therefore the intelligent artificer is benevolent, and (e) ontologically he is one, perfect. Further the Macrocosm is to be conceived as a social organism·and hence the importance of the theory of rights. The matter is largely borrowed and the main interest is the affiliation of it to the general happiness theory. The "state of nature" a golden age of Benevolence, therefore natural rights depend upon their conduciveness to social good. The inconsistency in the admission of natural rights of the individual and further in the "adventitious" right of Property.

CHAPTER XI, PART II.

Smith's indebtedness to Hutcheson in Economics not sufficiently recognised. Smith follows Hutcheson in the arrangement of his subject-matter and also in his treatment of division of labour, value in use, labour and value, money and coinage. Significant silence of both the *System* and Smith's *Lectures on Police* with regard to Distribution, and hence the conjecture that for the latter theory Smith is indebted to the Physiocrats, while much of his earlier work is traceable to the influence of Hutcheson. Smith's Naturalism is due to Hutcheson—the "Fructification Theory"—Hutcheson and taxation.

CHAPTER XII.

The three "Compends" contain a later revision of Hutcheson's
Philosophy than the *System*, because (*a*) there is an increase in the
number of Internal Senses, (*b*) incidental expressions of the *System* are
developed systematically, (*c*) there are traces of Stoicism, due to the
translation of Marcus Aurelius in 1741.

Hutcheson's previous indebtedness to Cicero makes the transition to
Aurelius easy. General principles of Stoicism, and special views of
Aurelius incorporated in the "Compends." The reaction from the
Utilitarianism of the Third Period to a new intuitionalism and to a
fresh identification of Virtue and Beauty.

The Summum Bonum—" to follow Nature." " Nature" used partly
in the Stoic, partly in the Ciceronian Sense. It is the Macrocosm, as
social; reduced to its simplest terms; further, since the Macrocosm is ruled
by a Benevolent God the *vox naturæ* is the *vox Dei*; hence Hutcheson
approximates Malebranche in holding that the cause of Sensations is the
Divine power—they are either *marks* or *signals*. There is little trace of
the Stoic φαντασία καταληπτική, rather the criterion of the "natural" is
the *consensus gentium* or an appeal to the heart; this possibly due to
Hutcheson's æstheticism, and hence the "natural" becomes the teleological. Hume's notice of this—the three classes of ends and their
"naturalness," and therefore the criterion of the "natural" in its
teleological character; how Hutcheson here approaches Butler.

Secondly "Nature" is not only mental data in their lowest terms but
also in their highest or as the ideal. No "Golden Age," as State of
Nature, rather the social organism is progressive—the "seeds" of virtue
are due to nature as the "original," the culture of them to Nature as the
ideal. The function of Reason in this transition.

What is Hutcheson's ἡγεμονικόν? It is partly appreciative, partly
directive, the former is Conscience, the latter "Right Reason." Right
Reason is the source of Law, which is both Law of Nature and Law of
God. τὸ ἡγεμονικόν is Conscience in reference to the Beauty of Virtue;
and Right Reason in reference to Law and obligation. There is again
an æsthetic confusion in the use of the word "order"—which is either
categorical or teleological.

Further, Conscience has categorical powers and as such passes into
the idea of *will*. Therefore the ἡγημονικόν leaves a dualism between
"understanding" and will. This reintroduces the former difficulty of the
rational elements in Calm Benevolence and thus there is a doubt both
as to what is the moral faculty and what is its object. This is disguised
by æsthetic references.

Is the Will free? Determinism of the *Inquiry*. The inconsistencies
of the *Passions* prepare the way for "Liberty of Suspense." The

position of the *System* and "Compends." The mind as *tabula rasa* and *res actuosa*—but from the former we cannot reach the latter nor *vice versa*. This theoretical difficulty absorbs the practical one of the second period. Hutcheson's Eclecticism.

CHAPTER XIII.

HUTCHESON'S GENERAL INFLUENCE UPON THE "ENLIGHTENMENT"   257

Hutcheson the leading figure of the "Enlightenment" in Scotland. His Philosophy was (*a*) popular, (*b*) eclectic. The resemblances and differences between the Scottish and the French and German Enlightenments.

The bearing of Hutcheson's Puritanism upon his work—it leads to a departure from Shaftesbury's Hellenism, for which is substituted the Classicism of the Roman Empire.

This explains the increase of Eclecticism in Hutcheson's work, which made it more of a popular Philosophy : and also the precedence he gives Benevolence (following the later Stoics). Hence Hutcheson is a "Pseudo-Classic," and Monboddo—the last of his followers of this tendency of his system—is hostile to Roman Literature.

Was Hutcheson the founder of the "Scottish School"? 1. If this term means "Philosophy produced by persons connected with Scotland" it is unjust to Hutcheson's predecessors there. McCosh understands it in this sense, yet he excludes Kant and includes Shaftesbury. McCosh's further "test" for admission to the school would exclude many whom he admits. As applied to Hutcheson, it is doubtful whether he would conform to it, and, even if so, his thought being borrowed from the later Stoics, they, not he, would be the founders. 2. If "Scottish School" be taken as equivalent to Natural Realism, Hutcheson was not the founder of it as he was not a Natural Realist. Prof. J. Seth's claim, that Hutcheson was original, discussed.

Hutcheson's true place in the History of Philosophy—both logically and chronologically he was earlier than Hume. He is really a leader of the British Enlightenment, an eclectic and popular thinker, who prepared the way for Hume's Scepticism—thus he not only trained those who succeeded him, but found an audience for them.

Hutcheson was influenced by the English Enlightenment through Butler, and in turn, he influenced the Enlightenment in Germany. His influence upon the next generation was considerable, an instance of this deduced from his Naturalism, e.g. "*Natural* Signs" (Reid): "*Natural* Realism" (Hamilton): *Natural* Faculties (Dr Martineau). Naturalism, from his historical origin (with the Stoics), involves an apparent contradiction, as defined by Prof. Sorley, the reason of this and hence Hutcheson's point of contact with a portion of the Enlightenment in France.

CHAPTER XIV.

1. Was Hutcheson's Intuitionalism a positive contribution to Philosophy? His indebtedness to Cicero here, and, what is new is chiefly the emphasis with which he repeats Cicero's ideas.

2. *His relation to Universalistic Hedonism.* The third period is Utilitarian.

> (*a*) Hutcheson originates the expression "greatest happiness of the greatest number," its history from Hutcheson to Bentley through Priestley and Beccaria.
>
> This formula traceable from Hutcheson to the latter Stoics. Instances from Cicero.
>
> Hutcheson uses several variants.

> (*α*) "The general good of *all*" or "common interest of *all*," instances from Simplicius, Seneca, Cicero, Epictetus, and Marcus Aurelius.

> (*β*) "The good of the *greatest whole*" or "*system*"—anticipations from the same authors.

> (*γ*) The greatest good of *all rational* agents.

> (*δ*) The greatest good of all *sensitive* beings. Anticipations of these. The logical order of the different variants, which are all traceable to Stoic influence and hence the paradox that the Stoics have provided the formula for Hedonism. Utilitarianism starts from one variant, Adam Smith from another, Hume from a third. How Hutcheson's rational Beings are related to those of Kant.

> (*b*) By an inconsistency, Hutcheson's anticipates both Bentham's and Mill's valuations of "pleasures."

> (*c*) He also anticipates the distinction between motive and intention.

> (*d*) A suppressed Premiss in Mill's Proof of Utilitarianism supplied by Adam Smith and Hutcheson, in the Economics of the former as a postulate, which, again, is deducible as a Metaphysical thesis from the teaching of the latter.

> (*e*) Hutcheson and Association of Ideas.

3. *His relation to Æsthetics and Teleology.* His *Inquiry concerning Beauty*, the first modern æsthetic treatise. The definition of Beauty. Hutcheson's Beauty is really a teleological conception. His share in the renaissance of teleology and more especially his contribution to the doctrine of Final Causes.

INTRODUCTORY.

In many respects Francis Hutcheson is an interesting, if somewhat mysterious, figure in the History of Modern Thought. Almost all writers upon the development of Philosophy in Britain assign him an important share in its growth, yet there is no little uncertainty, when any attempt is made to specify his exact sphere of influence.

From his arrival at Glasgow, in 1730, until his death, in 1746, he published nothing of moment; so that, it has been generally assumed, that his mode of thought was fully formed during his residence at Dublin, before his removal to Scotland. The influences to which he was subjected, in the earlier period, constitute a lost chapter in the history of Philosophy, and therefore an attempt is made, in the first three chapters of the following narrative, to supply the blank. If Hutcheson had any share in the renaissance of speculative activity in Scotland—and many writers assign him a most important one—the whole course of thought after him is divorced from its historical continuity until this question has been investigated.

Yet it will be found that Hutcheson's life in Ireland, while interesting in itself, is little more than a preparation for his activities in Scotland. The former is the promise of youth, the latter its fulfilment. In fact, with Hutcheson, more than most thinkers since Socrates, his life was his best legacy to

posterity; and, therefore, such data as can be recovered
are recorded to enable the reader to form some picture of
his personality (Chapters IV—VII). This was at once his
strength and the source of the power he exercised over his contemporaries. All high aims in life, any practical activities, even
though apparently trivial, that tended towards the "common
good," commanded his sympathy and support; and, therefore,
his ideal of academic teaching was exceptionally stimulating
both to pupils and those who fell under his influence. The
Classicism he received from Shaftesbury, as he modified it,
opened a new horizon to university-men in Scotland; while his
exposition of it secured continuity between his successors and
the past. His eclectic type of thought was what the country
required to transplant Philosophy from the region of "dry-as-
dust" academicism to the hearts and lives of the people. Thus
he may not inaptly be termed a leader in the Scottish Enlightenment. More than this, his intense interest in the
elevation of life, his passion for the improvement and advancement of mankind made him a pioneer of the movement, which
is generally attributed to Utilitarianism. To modify a phrase
of Mr Austin Dobson's, he was a paladin of Philosophic Philanthropy.

Hutcheson's life being his strongest argument—full as it is
of noble aims, and disinterested endeavour—one can scarcely
avoid feeling that there is a certain injustice to him in any
investigation of his thought as published. It will be shown
that his books are but incomplete reproductions of his actual
teaching. Yet, since they constitute all that is left of it, they
need to be investigated in the light of the additional information upon his life—for his biography is the best commentary
upon his books.

Since there is much that is common to Shaftesbury and
Hutcheson, some account is required of the virtuoso-cult
of the former. This will be found in Chapter VIII. Then
both from internal and external considerations there are
reasons to believe that Hutcheson's works are far from being
a homogeneous whole. Quite apart from fundamental inconsistencies, inherent in his Eclecticism, he passed through

four distinct "periods," and these are characterized in Chapters IX—XII.

Finally it only remains to sum up his position as a writer upon philosophic subjects, and an estimation of his place in the "Enlightenment" is contained in Chapter XIII; and, in Chapter XIV, some of his positive contributions to the thought of his successors are noted.

CHAPTER I.

EARLY YEARS.

From the time of the Plantation of Ulster by James I, there had been a steady immigration of Scotsmen to the North of Ireland, who brought with them their native frugality and perseverance, "their love of education and desire to have an educated ministry; their attachment to the Bible and the simple Presbyterian worship[1]." Many ministers, too, came from Scotland to attend to the spiritual wants of the Scottish colony in Ireland, and amongst these was Alexander Hutcheson, a member of a reputable family of Monkwood, in Ayr-shire, and the grandfather of Francis, the future philosopher. He came to Ireland temporarily, and was soon " called " to the congregation of Saintfield in Co. Down[2]. It was not long before "his pleasing manners, social disposition and excellent talents" won him friends[3], amongst whom he was proud to number the Hon. Brigadier Price of Hollymount[4] and the Earl of Granard[5]; by the latter acquaintance, forming a connection with County Longford, which was destined to influence his descendants materially for the next two generations. Still stronger ties arose by marriage and the acquisition of landed property, for he became possessed of the townland of Drumalig (or Drummalig)[6] in Co. Down, a considerable estate, which, in the

---

[1] *The Scottish Philosophy*, by James M⁰Cosh, LL.D., London, 1875, p. 49.

[2] *History of Armagh*, by Stuart, Newry, 1819, p. 486.

[3] *Ibid.*

[4] Will of Alex. Hutcheson in the Public Record Office, Dublin.

[5] Wodrow's *Analecta*, iv. p. 231.

[6] *Belfast Monthly Magazine*, xi, volume for 1813. Will of Alex. Hutcheson, *ut supra*.

disturbed state of the country during the closing years of the seventeenth century, brought him many cares owing to the "Tories" or robbers who preyed upon landholders, in the country districts[1]. However he had, doubtless, some compensation in the future prospects of his property, which at the time of the Ordnance Survey was described as containing 78 houses, 81 families, and 386 persons, the land being of the best quality and fetching from 20s. to 30s. an acre[2].

Alexander Hutcheson had only one surviving son[3], who was named John, and who was also a Presbyterian minister. John Hutcheson partly from his father's position, partly from his "good understanding and reputation for piety, probity and all virtue[4]," was a success in the Church. His first charge was at Downpatrick, whence he was called to Armagh. From Armagh he went to the congregation of Capel Street, Dublin, in 1690; but Dublin did not suit his health, and he returned to Armagh in 1692, where he remained until his death. John Hutcheson was prominent amongst his brother ministers, first by the part he took in politics, enrolling men to bear arms in favour of the "protestant succession" during the years of trouble before the Rebellion of 1715[5]; and secondly in ecclesiastical controversy, in which he evinced a warm interest. After the dispute of the Seven Synods, or the "Seven Years War" of the Irish Presbyterian Church, which began in 1720, John Hutcheson was asked to answer the "Narrative" of the Non-Subscribers, and members of his own party quote his account with high commendations[6].

John Hutcheson was thrice married; his first wife bore him three sons, the eldest being named Hans and the second Francis. His second wife was a Miss Wilson of Tully in Co.

[1] MS. Minutes of Presbytery of Down in Library, "Magee College."

[2] MS. Reports of the Survey (Co. Down) in the Library, Royal Irish Academy.

[3] Or, at least, one son who was alive in 1711, as Alex. Hutcheson, in his will, speaks of "his only son, John." There were two daughters.

[4] Account of the Life of Francis Hutcheson, by William Leechman, prefixed to the System of Moral Philosophy, London, 1755.

[5] Wodrow's Analecta, iv. p. 233.

[6] Wodrow's MS. Letters, vol. xxii. No. 104. Witherow's Memorials of the Presbyterian Church, First Series, p. 343.

Longford, and from this marriage there resulted a large second family[1].

Francis was therefore the second son. He was born on August 8th, 1694. It is related that the birth took place at Drumalig (not at Armagh), a fact that is explained by the supposition that John Hutcheson, having returned from Dublin two years before, was probably engaged in building his house at a place called Ballyrea, about two miles from Armagh[2]— a situation somewhat historic owing to its vicinity to "The Navan," an immense earthen mound surrounded by the remains of a high embankment or wall. This tumulus is similar to the more celebrated examples at Newgrange and Dowth (near Drogheda), but it has never been excavated. Archaeologists believe that this was the site of the residence of one of the Celtic royal families of the North of Ireland.

Soon after the family settled at Ballyrea, Francis was brought there, and he remained with his parents until he was eight years old, when the question of his education was debated[3]. Possibly Armagh, the seat of the Irish Primate, afforded few facilities for the training of a Presbyterian child, or it may have been that the grandfather, now an old man, longed for the company of his grandson in the lonely manse at Drumalig. It is known that Alexander Hutcheson had conceived an old man's partiality for the child, almost while in long clothes. Seeing him, when three years of age, the old man is reported to have said—"Francis, I predict, thou wilt one day be a very eminent man[4]"—and, for once, the future did not falsify the prophecy of affection. So Francis, with his elder brother, Hans, went to their grandfather in the adjoining

---

[1] Stuart's *Hist. of Armagh, ut supra.* · *Belfast Monthly Magazine, ut supra.* The MS. Register of Baptisms of the First Armagh Congregation contains the following entries:

"Sept[r] 30th 1714 Rhoda, dau. of John Hutcheson, Bap[d]
        March 5 1716–17 Margaret d. of John Hutcheson Bap[d]."

[2] Stuart's *Hist. of Armagh, ut supra.*

[3] Another possible cause of the child being sent from home so young may have been the presence of a step-mother and a second family. However without the aid of the marriage certificate this is mere conjecture.

[4] Stuart's *Armagh, ut supra.*

county, where both attended a school, kept by John Hamilton, in a disused Meeting House near Saintfield[1], where a good classical education was obtainable, and was probably more prized, inasmuch as it had a flavour of the contraband. At this time the Established Church jealously guarded the monopoly of education and viewed all teaching by Dissenters with suspicion, even if the statutory penalties were not enforced. When this furtive character of education amongst Dissenters is remembered, as well as the general neglect of external aids to culture, which, indeed, seem to have been especially ignored in this district—so much so that a Church of Ireland school, in the same village nearly a century later, is officially described as " Saintfield Old School, existing from time immemorial, a small cabin, with clay floor, unceiled, and very much out of repair[2]"—it will not be difficult to imagine that Francis Hutcheson acquired the "rudiments" without having opportunities of cultivating the taste for luxury. At this school he gained the basis of his classical education, which proved serviceable to him, not only in his literary and professional work, but also in the society he mixed with, as a young man, in Dublin, where the making of an epigram or the capping of a quotation was a ready road to favour and patronage.

At this period, too, we gain a brief glimpse of Hutcheson's character. The grandfather was partial to his favourite and over-valued his progress as compared with that of his less-gifted elder brother. Francis is recorded to have been pained by this preference and he found no joy in any praise his brother did not share, so that he employed " all means and innocent artifices in his power to make his brother appear equally deserving of his grandfather's regard[3]." Meanwhile the boys were growing up, and, when Francis was about fourteen, the problem of his higher education arose. The Ulster Presbyterians were in a difficult position in this matter, as no University was open to them nearer than Scotland, and to meet this difficulty private "academies" were established to provide teaching in the

---

[1] *Belfast Monthly Magazine, ut supra.*
[2] MS. Survey of Co. Down, R. I. A. Library.
[3] Leechman; Stuart, *ut supra.*

"higher branches." These were in fact small denominational Colleges—little side-currents in the advanced education of the time, necessarily fleeting individually, but accomplishing valuable work as a whole. Members of other Churches admitted that there "was a great deal of philosophical knowledge amongst the Dissenting teachers[1]," and the reputation of some of the pupils (as for instance Butler) is high in the annals of philosophy. It was one of these academies that Hutcheson himself founded, at a later date, in Dublin.

The quaint little town of Killyleagh in Co. Down had been fixed upon as a site for one of these seminaries as early as 1697[2]. When Hutcheson attended it, the teacher was the Rev. James MacAlpin, who enjoyed a considerable local reputation amongst Presbyterians as a learned teacher of philosophy. He appears to have had classes in Classics, Scholastic Philosophy[3], and probably Theology. Here Hutcheson, no doubt, received early and lasting impressions of the beautiful pastoral landscape around, which inspired many passages in his early works. Here, too, he probably made the acquaintance of his cousin William Bruce, son of the minister of Killyleagh, who became his lifelong friend. At this Academy Hutcheson made rapid progress, and he was certified to be able "to stand the test of the most severe examinations, and his intimate acquaintances are satisfied that the most severe scrutiny into his character and conduct would tend to his advantage[4]."

At the age of sixteen Hutcheson was taken from the Academy; his grandfather was now in failing health, and he may have desired the presence of his favourite grandson. Probably family matters were discussed and the old man must have expressed an intention to provide handsomely for Francis. Leechman says that " when his grandfather made an alteration of a prior settlement of his family affairs in his [i.e. Francis'] favour, though many arguments were used by his relations to

---

[1] MS. Letter of Lord Monboddo to Horsley.

[2] *Christian Moderator*, I. p. 429.

[3] Leechman, *ut supra*. MᶜCreery's *Presbyterian Ministers of Killileagh*, p. 110.

[4] *Belfast Monthly Magazine, ut supra.*

prevail with him to accept of it, he peremptorily refused and insisted to the last that the first settlement should actually take place[1]." Inasmuch as the "final settlement" is a will dated a few days before the testator's death[2], and, as it provides for Francis beyond the expectations of a second child, it may be worth while to trace the disposition of the property, especially as an exact statement of Hutcheson's pecuniary position throws light on a remarkable crisis in his later career. Alexander Hutcheson had given before his death one half of his landed property in the townland of Drumalig to the elder brother Hans[3]; and the other half is willed to John Hutcheson, (the father of Hans and Francis) for his life, and then is strictly entailed to Francis. John Hutcheson besides is residuary legatee, and the personal estate is bequeathed to fifteen grandchildren, the issue of the two daughters of the testator. Further the lands entailed to Francis are charged with an annuity to the third son by John Hutcheson's first marriage. It will, therefore, be seen that Francis obtained absolutely no benefit under this will during his father's lifetime, and that he could not interfere with the disposition of the property, owing to the entail. When he actually came into possession of the property, he was freed from responsibility regarding his elder brother, Hans, who was without children, and whose half of the Drumalig estate eventually returned to the only surviving son of Francis[4]. Several of the other brothers were well-to-do, and there only remained one full and one half brother for whom he was anxious to provide. The means by which he endeavours to secure them an interest in his properties are exceedingly complicated[5], and any account of the perplexing legal devices would be beyond the scope of this narrative; but they suffice to prove that the disinterestedness, manifested by Hutcheson as an inexperienced youth, continued

[1] Leechman, p. ii.

[2] The will is dated Sept. 5th, 1711. This will as well as others referred to below are preserved in the Public Record Office ("Four Courts"), Dublin.

[3] Wills of Hans and Francis Hutcheson.

[4] Will of Hans Hutcheson, *ut supra*; Stuart's *Armagh*.

[5] Will of Francis Hutcheson, dated June 30th, 1746, *ut supra*. (He died in Dublin on August 8th of the same year.)

up to the close of his life and that experience of the world had
not weakened the dictates of his early enthusiasm.

The death of Alexander Hutcheson in 1711 deprived
Francis of a warm and indulgent friend, but the same event
secured easy circumstances to John Hutcheson, who might
otherwise have experienced some difficulty in educating his
large family. The descendants of the Scottish settlers in
Ulster have always proved their appreciation of the advantages of education for their children, and it is probable
that John Hutcheson would have made sacrifices for the son
who already showed such brilliant promise, but the legacy of
Alexander Hutcheson made matters easy[1]; indeed it may have
been that the old man expressed a wish that some of the
income accruing from the life-interest in Drumalig should
be spent in educating Francis[2].

However this may be, Hutcheson matriculated at the University of Glasgow in the year 1711, being then in his seventeenth year. He is described as "Scotus Hibernus," and he
probably had many friends amongst his fellow-students, as
more than half of those entered under J. Loudon, the Regent,
were similarly designated[3]. The change from the humble
"Academy" at Killyleagh must have been great—indeed it
was Hutcheson's first acquaintance with a large town, since, in
all probability, his previous experience was confined to villages
and his native city of Armagh, which from its antiquarian and

[1] John Hutcheson has been called "a poor Presbyterian minister"—an
assertion true enough if he had had only his stipend to depend upon; but quite
apart from the life-interest in Drumalig, beginning in 1711, he possessed
considerable property in Co. Monaghan (as is proved by his will), and the fact
that he built a handsome residence, before the end of the seventeenth century,
is enough to show that, even then, he was in easy circumstances.

[2] Francis himself left £100 sterling to be expended in educating the children
of a relative. It is quite possible that John Hutcheson may have considered
himself merely trustee for Francis, and that he paid him part or the whole of
the income. This conjecture is founded on the fact that Francis acknowledges
a sum of money from his father in 1726, at a time when he must have been in
affluent circumstances.

[3] *Munimenta Alme Universitatis Glasguensis*, Bk. III. p. 196. In a later entry
he is described as "Britanno-Hibernus," which may be accounted for by his
mother being of English extraction.

ecclesiastical associations has some claim to the title of the
St Andrews of Ireland. As early as 1574, it had been said,
"there is no place, in Europe, comparable to Glasgow for a
plentifull and gude chepe mercat of all kind of langages artes
and sciences[1]"; but two widely different causes had tended to
injure the efficiency of the University in the early years of the
eighteenth century. The re-establishment of Episcopacy after
the Restoration had deprived it of the greater part of its
revenues and in the year 1701 the College was in a pitiable
condition. The staff was reduced to the Principal, one Professor of Divinity and four Regents of Philosophy—"who taught
Philosophy and Greek by turns, one Professor of Mathematics,
but without any fund for a salary and no other Professor of any
sort whatsoever[2]." It must be remembered too that a second
cause for the decadence of the University lay in the want of
enlightenment in the West of Scotland. After the Revolution
"the new Professors were more remarkable for orthodoxy and
zeal than for literary accomplishments. From the parochial
clergy, professors in Colleges are usually taken. If tradition may
be trusted, which is, at best, a sorry guide in matters where party
has any share, some of the ministers of Glasgow at that period
would be regarded now-a-days as weak vulgar men. But as
they were much liked by their flocks, so it is hardly fair to
estimate the men and manners of simple times by those of a
more fastidious age, which judges of every thing by the polish
of elegance. If that were the case in great towns, it may be
presumed that the members of the university were little distinguished in those days[3]." This want of culture proved a much
greater disadvantage to the University than the want of funds.
Hutcheson was fortunate in arriving at a time when the sphere
of educational usefulness was widening; indeed, during the years
of his attendance no less than three Professorships were revived
or created. The low level of manners and culture, amongst the

---

[1] *Diary of James Melville*, p. 50.

[2] MS. "Memorial of the University of Glasgow as it was September 18th,
1701, and as it is now in 1717." *Wodrow Papers*, 41, No. 102.

[3] *Scotland and Scotsmen in the Eighteenth Century from MSS. of John
Ramsay of Ochtertyre.* Ed. Alex. Allardyce, 1888, vol. i. p. 271.

Professors themselves, was an evil that needed time to mend, and the final raising of the standard was almost wholly due to Hutcheson and his friends.   At his matriculation the teaching staff contained representatives of the old and new tendencies. Robert Simson, the eminent mathematician, had just been appointed, and like many other distinguished geometricians, he was a man whose nature had no place for the graces of life. He was a Dr Johnson in carelessness of externals, and in an eccentric habit of counting posts or steps—he was a Boswell in a childish curiosity[1].   From contemporary anecdotes it appears that, while cultivating some sides of traditional Cynicism, he neglected such precepts as related to the virtue of temperance —indeed it is significant of the social standard of the time that the gossips objected rather to his admitting "all and sundry to his symposia at a public-house" than to the "symposia" taking place[2].   Another original, though more polished teacher was the Professor of Medicine, John Johnston, "a free-liver and what was more in those days, a free-thinker."   Johnston is supposed to have been the prototype of "Crab" in *Roderick Random*, and, owing to his opinions, "his fund of wit and humour and even of profanity peculiar to himself," he was looked upon as a kind of heathen by the citizens[3].   Andrew Rosse, the Professor of Humanity, appears to have been undistinguished; his leanings seem to have been to the old school.   The other Professors were men of a different type.   Gershom Carmichael has left an honourable name as a thinker.   Alexander Dunlop, the Professor of Greek, was doing all that lay in his power to revive the study of his subject.   "He was universally beloved and respected for his worth and humanity as well as for his blameless, dignified manners, and what endeared him especially to his class was the pains he took to foster the blossoms of genius of which he was a good judge[4]."   John Simpson, the Professor of Divinity—"a man of more culture and erudition than most of

---

[1] There is an anecdote concerning R. Simson and Louden (afterwards Prof. of Logic) exemplifying this side of his character in *Scotland and Scotsmen*, i. pp. 278—9.

[2] Strang's *Glasgow Clubs*, pp. 20—21; MacGregor's *History of Glasgow*.

[3] *Scotland and Scotsmen, ut supra*, i. p. 277.

[4] *Ibid.*

his contemporaries "—was the leader of the attack upon the
prevailing provincialism, and his attitude brought him into
continual conflict with the Church, which eventually culminated in his trial upon the charge of heresy. In fact there
appear to have been two issues involved, the cause of secular
culture and the advocacy of a more liberal tone in theology;
and Simpson, by urging the claims of both, consolidated the
opposition to both.

It was under these teachers that Hutcheson studied. The
University, about this date, was described as "the chief ornament of the City, a magnificent and stately fabrick, consisting
of several courts; the first towards the city is of hewn stone
and excellent architecture, the precincts of it were lately
enlarged by some acres of ground, purchased for it by the King
and the State, and it is separated from the rest of the city by a
very high wall[1]." Hutcheson found little to attract him in the
conservative methods of some of the teachers, and one cannot
wonder at his sympathy with the new culture from the very
fact of the unattractive nature of the old methods. Fortunately these have been recorded, at first hand, by one of the
Regents in Philosophy, a John Low; and the document may be
dated about this time. Low seems to have considered that the
old way could not be improved upon; "it is," he says, "the same
old way y^t I was taught myself and has long been in use in this
College, by dited notes and disputs in all the parts of philosophy." In the Logic year the students were taught, two
months, from a text-book, to dispute three days a week "when
they were ready for it," also to read Greek and "to get lessons
by heart." He adds, enigmatically, "I have been in use to
teach something of Arithmetick and Geometry *in the way of
dictats*... sometime exegeses in the Class, but not every year,
nor yet always in every course finding y^r performances but very
weak sometimes[2]." It is little wonder that Hutcheson found
refuge from "Geometry by way of dictats," in the enthusiasm of
the Class-work done for Dunlop; and it is probable that to
this influence may be attributed his study of Greek Literature,

[1] *The Present State of Scotland*, 1715.
[2] *Lit. Memorials of the History of Glasgow*, pp. 124—5.

for which he was well known in later life. The Lectures in
Natural Philosophy were taken early in his course, though the
College records contain repeated rules between the years 1710–
28 that this class should not be taken before the third year[1].
He must also have given a considerable amount of time to
Mathematics, as he seems to have had a taste for the subject,
which even led him so far as to introduce mathematical
formulae, to express ethical facts, in the first edition of the
Inquiry concerning Beauty and Virtue. It has been customary
to assume that " the influence of Carmichael is manifest on the
whole cast of Hutcheson's thought[2]"; but Carmichael was
largely a Cartesian[3], and it is difficult to see how Cartesianism
could prompt the letter written a few years after to Clarke;
there are, besides, certain traces of Berkeleyanism[4] in his first
work that show his mental development was much more complex
than critics have hitherto believed. It will therefore be safer not
to dogmatize but rather trace out the indications that help us
to follow the growth of his thought. It would doubtless be
premature to attribute to him at this period the thoughts he
expressed three years later in a letter to Clarke, and yet the
mere fact of the criticism being written shows that, even as a
student, his attitude to Cartesianism cannot have been that of
an enthusiastic disciple. It is a fact, not without significance,
that in his Inaugural Lecture, delivered thirteen years after
leaving the University, he enlarges rather upon his recollections
of classical than of philosophical works[5]. Probably of all his

[1] *Munimenta Glas., ut supra, passim.* These lectures must have been
popular, for in Arbuckle's poem *Glotta* more space is given to this subject than
to all the rest put together.

[2] Veitch on "Philosophy in Scottish Universities" in *Mind*, ii. pp. 210—12;
and hence, because Dr McCosh finds Carmichael the teacher of Hutcheson, the
former is named "the true father of Scottish Philosophy"—in fact Scottish
Philosophy has had so many reputed fathers that one is reminded of the ancient
saw "'tis a wise child knows its own father."

[3] Cf.   "Or what more nearly touches human-kind,
             The powers and nature of Eternal mind,
             Which only conscious of its being knows
             Th' Eternal source from whence that being flows."
                              Glotta—a Poem. Glas., 1721.

[4] Cf. *infra*, p. 30.

[5] *De Naturali Hominum Socialitate*, Glasgoviae, 1730.

teachers, he was attracted most by Cicero, for whom he always professed the greatest admiration, and this influence is important as aiding the comprehension of his attitude towards Clarke.

After obtaining his M.A. Degree Hutcheson entered upon a new phase of College life by joining the Theological department in 1713[1], which exercised a greater influence upon his subsequent career. At this time Simpson was in the midst of his trials before the ecclesiastical courts upon charges of holding doctrines inconsistent with the "Confession of Faith." He was supposed to be doubtful about punishment for original sin and to have believed in Free-Will and the possibility of the salvation of the heathen. It is certain that Hutcheson was largely influenced by these views; for, when he himself became a preacher, some of his hearers objected to traces of these heresies in his sermons[2].

Midway in Hutcheson's theological course Glasgow passed through the throes of the Rebellion of 1715. During the month of August, the "masters" agreed to maintain a company not under 50 men, "engaging to make good and thankfull payment of 6d. per diem to each soldier[3]." Entrenchments were thrown up outside the city, volunteers were armed, barricades erected in the streets and armed with cannon, martial law proclaimed[4]. It is probable that Hutcheson did not return from Ireland till the time of panic was passed, but he must have been keenly interested in the struggle for which his father had raised men a few years before. It is strange, too, that Hutcheson, a member of a Whig family, became tutor, about this time, to the young Earl of Kilmarnock[5], who was executed after the second rising in 1745.

While studying under Simpson, Hutcheson seems to have been gradually forming philosophical and theological opinions, and in 1717 he sent a letter to Clarke criticizing the *a priori*

[1] *Munimenta, ut supra,* III. p. 253.
[2] *Vide infra,* p. 20.
[3] *Munimenta, ut supra,* II. p. 416.
[4] *Annals of Glasgow,* by W. Clelland; MacGregor's *Hist. of Glasgow,* p. 292; Rae's *History of the late Rebellion.*
[5] Wodrow's *Analecta,* IV. p. 99.

proof of the existence of God.   This letter was probably written
immediately after the close of his University career.

Though there is no record of the time at which he completed his theological course, there is sufficient evidence to fix
an approximate date.   Hutcheson is recorded to have expressed
the opinion that six years was the proper period for a student
to remain at the University and that this was the duration of
his own time of residence[1].   Now in 1717 this period of six
years would have just been completed.   During his last session,
Hutcheson seems to have turned his attention to philosophical
literature.   Clarke's works were much discussed, and, in their
relation to theology, seem to have made him enquire into the
validity of the proof employed.   Hutcheson, like Kames[2],
doubted whether an *a priori* proof was possible, and (like Kant
later) he urged the danger of applying demonstration in a
sphere in which it was inadmissible[3], thereby leading to doubt
both of the method and of the conclusion.   Clarke replied with
the same courtesy he had earlier shown to Butler and other
unknown critics, but his answer is not extant and its fate has
hitherto excited considerable curiosity amongst those interested
in the history of British Philosophy of this period.   Hutcheson
may have received Clarke's reply after his return to Ireland,
and, at that time, he was in the habit of discussing philosophical
questions with John Maxwell, a Presbyterian minister, who
eventually succeeded John Hutcheson at Armagh[4].   Many of
the letters written by the young men " were upon philosophical
and metaphysical subjects, and amongst these was a copy of
some objections which Dr Hutcheson had made to Dr Clarke's
a priori demonstration of the existence and attributes of the
Deity and had transmitted to its author.   Dr Clarke's reply

---

[1] *Belfast Monthly Magazine, ut supra.*

[2] *Memoirs of Life and Writings of Hon. Henry Home of Kames*, Edin., 1807,
vol. I. p. 27 and Appendix II.

[3] Leechman, *ut supra*, pp. iv, v.   Cf. Butler's first letter to Clarke, written
in 1713: "In your demonstration of the Being and Attributes of God...the
former part of the proof seems highly probable; but the latter part, *which seems
to aim at demonstration*, is not to me convincing."   Butler's *Sermons*, Oxford,
1874, p. 350.

[4] Stuart's *Armagh, ut supra*, p. 492.

was subjoined, an interesting unpublished document, now a desideratum in the literary world. Mr Maxwell died in 1763, and his papers, which were for some time in possession of his son, the late James Maxwell, Esq., have since been burned and these valuable letters are no more[1]." Stuart adds that he received this anecdote from a person who was well known in the district and who had read the letters, so that his narrative may be accepted as conclusively settling the question. No doubt the loss is exaggerated, for Butler objected to the same proposition and for similar reasons, and Clarke's reply to him[2] must have been similar to his later answer to the objections of Hutcheson. Besides, the letters between Hutcheson and Gilbert Burnet cover the same ground except that the former was then criticized instead of being the critic, and secondly it would be advantageous to make a comparison between the two expressions of opinion upon the same subject, separated by an interval of about nine years, during which Hutcheson passed through an interesting process of philosophical development.

[1] Stuart's *Armagh, ut supra.*
[2] Butler's *Sermons* (Oxford Edition), pp. 349—375.

CHAPTER II.

THE ACADEMY IN DUBLIN AND PUBLICATION OF THE INQUIRY 1717–1725.

FROM 1717 to 1719 information concerning Hutcheson is wanting. He appears to have held his tutorship to the Earl of Kilmarnock for a short time and to have returned to Ireland, where he sought to enter the ministry of the Presbyterian Church. At this period Irish Presbyterianism had entered upon a crisis in its history. The ministry embraced many divergent elements which had long threatened to break into revolt against the traditionary Calvinism that was the cherished dogma of the Ulster Congregations. Some of the clergy had been educated in Scotland; while others had returned from continental Universities and their wider ideas seem to have been far from satisfactory to some of the older clergy. The Belfast Society had been founded in 1705, and the views of the members, after fermenting for fifteen years, led to the schism of the Church which began with the conflict of the "Seven Synods." It was therefore a troubled arena that Hutcheson found himself entering, and there is little doubt that the interval between his return from Glasgow and his being licensed as a probationer[1] in 1719 was occasioned by the unsettled ecclesiastical outlook. Family discussions, too, may have led to the delay. John Hutcheson was a prominent supporter of the majority, while some of his relations (including M. Bruce of

---

[1] MS. Minutes of the Synod of Ulster, Library, Magee College, Londonderry. In July 1719 it was reported to the Synod by the Presbytery of "Ardmagh" that since last meeting of the Synod they had "licensed Mr Arch^d. Macclane jun^r and Mr Francis Hutcheson." The "Mr Macclane" was the uncle of the translator of Mosheim's *Eccl. History.*

Holywood) were upon the other side[1], and Hutcheson himself, as a pupil of Simpson, was altogether in favour of the "New Light," and so must have felt himself out of sympathy with his father. His delay in entering the ministry may therefore be attributed to the strained feeling of expectancy that preceded the actual conflict—a conflict that divided domestic ties amongst the Presbyterian clergy almost as much as the Civil War had embroiled families and neighbours in the century before.

When licensed as a probationer, in 1719, Hutcheson was in his twenty-fifth year. He must have brought a considerable reputation back from Glasgow, since a minister, named Wright, considered his opinions worth quoting in a letter to Wodrow as early as 1718[2]. He was an excellent Classical scholar and proficient in Mathematics. His philosophical views would be difficult to define except negatively. That he objected to Clarke's demonstrative method not only shows that he had not adopted the conclusions of the "rational moralists," but, also, the grounds of the objection—that an ontological demonstration was an impossibility—clearly prove that he had little sympathy with Cartesianism and therefore the teaching of Carmichael can have made but little impression, or it must have already given way to other ideas during the period of his theological course. On the other hand there is no evidence to show that he had, in any appreciable degree, fallen under the influence of Locke, so that, upon the whole, his philosophical attitude at this time seems to have been one of criticism; his mind was prepared to mould a system to his needs but there is no evidence to show that, prior to his arrival in Dublin, he had met with a mode of thought that proved attractive to him.

For the time, however, Hutcheson was more keenly interested in the exciting clerical differences of opinion than in Philosophy. He appears to have found a certain ecclesiastical pride and rigidity of thought amongst the older ministers of Ulster, and he writes to a friend, half in jest, complaining that

[1] *Christian Moderator*, London, 1828. Articles on "Non-Subscription to Creeds."

[2] Wodrow, MS. Letters, *ut supra*.

they were as ready as members of the Established Church to impose tests upon their congregations[1]. When it is remembered how much the Irish Presbyterians suffered from the "Test Act" and how bitterly they argued against it[2], it will be seen that the ironical comparison is not without its sting.

Hutcheson was eloquent, and it is recorded that in many places " his hearers were highly pleased with his discourses[3]"; while, in others, the New Light tendencies he could not suppress, grated sorely upon those who prided themselves upon the purity of their theological opinions. The following anecdote explains the grounds of his failure in the pulpit amongst the ultra-orthodox. " At Armagh, his father, who laboured under a slight rheumatic affection, deputed him to preach in his place upon a cold and rainy Sunday. About two hours after Francis had left Ballyrea (his father's residence) the rain abated—the sun shone forth—the day became serene and warm—and Mr Hutcheson, who found his spirits exhilarated by the change, felt anxious to collect the opinions of the congregation on the merits of his favourite son and proceeded directly to the city. But how was he astonished and chagrined, when he met almost the whole of his flock[4] coming from the Meeting-house with strong marks of disappointment and disgust visible in their countenances. One of the elders, a native of Scotland, addressed the surprised and deeply mortified father thus—'We a' feel muckle wae for your mishap, Reverend Sir, but it canna be concealed. Your silly loon, Frank, has fashed a' the congregation wi' his idle cackle; for he has been babbling this oor aboot a gude and benevolent God, and that the sauls o' the heathens themsels will gang to Heeven, if they follow the licht o' their ain consciences. Not a word does the daft boy ken, speer, nor

[1] Wodrow's MS. Letters, *ut supra*—quoted by Reid in the *History of the Irish Presbyterian Church*.

[2] Over one quarter of the Pamphlets, classed as controversial, in the Haliday Collection, R. I. A., for the period, deal with this question.

[3] Stuart's *Armagh*, p. 488. Reid in his *History, ut supra*, gives his reader the impression that Hutcheson was a failure as a preacher; but Stuart has recorded local tradition, and his opinion, being without bias, may be accepted.

[4] It appears that only the precentor and two other members of the congregation remained to hear the end of "the idle cackle."

say aboot the gude auld comfortable doctrines o' election, reprobation, original sin and faith. Hoot mon, awa' wi' sic a fellow[1].'" This forcible condemnation in the vernacular, worthy to rank with the best efforts of the sermon-taster of Drumtochty, is of considerable interest as an almost verbal reproduction of the heresies of Simpson[2]. The coincidence, not only of thought, but even of expressions, tends to prove that, at this period, Hutcheson was still a disciple of Simpson; and, if this be so, it follows that the theological belief in a benevolent God was prior to his subsequent maintenance of Benevolence as a philosophic principle. It is interesting, too, to notice that it was the theological heresies, learnt from Simpson, that, in all probability, prepared the way for the reception of the Philosophy of Shaftesbury, and further that even here, as elsewhere, with Hutcheson the didactic, practical and religious interests precede and dominate the speculative.

Despite his leanings to the heresies of Simpson, the "daft boy" soon received "a call" to the congregation of Magherally, the stipend of which was about £45 a year[3], not a princely income, but above the average for a country congregation. Just at this time the Presbyterian clergymen in Dublin sent Hutcheson an invitation asking him to open a private academy there, and probably guaranteeing him some support[4]. John Hutcheson had been minister of a congregation in Dublin from 1690 to 1692, and Francis had several friends settled there, who had been fellow-students at Glasgow. No doubt his reputation had, in this way, come from Scotland and Ulster, for the establishment of an "academy" in Dublin was the most ambitious educational movement hitherto made by the Irish Dissenters. It was obvious that the institution now to be started must be more carefully organized than those already tried at Antrim, Newtownards, Comber and Killyleagh, for it

[1] Stuart's *Armagh*, pp. 488—9.   [2] Cf. *supra*, p. 15.
[3] Reid's *History*, *ut supra*, vol. IV, Appendix.
[4] This would probably take the form of promises of a certain number of students. It is known, however, that the Church party in Parliament contended that the Presbyterians used the "Bounty fund" "to form seminaries to the poysoning of the principles of our youth and in opposition to the law"—*Address to the Queen by the Lords Spiritual and Temporal.* Dublin, 1711.

would, to a certain extent, be a rival of Trinity College, which was under the patronage of the Church. The enterprise needed scholarship; but, above all, tact, since the position of the teacher would be a difficult one. He must remain faithful to his own communion, without incurring the open enmity of the Established Church. These requirements were united in Hutcheson—there could be no doubt of his scholarship, and, as far as can be gathered now, all who came in contact with him were impressed by his pleasing manners and lovable disposition.

The Dublin dissenters traced their origin back to the Cromwellian occupation, when Winter had been Provost of Trinity College, and Presbyterian divines had preached in Christ Church and St Patrick's Cathedrals. At the Restoration, many of the leading Puritans had retained the estates they had gained by the famous "Settlement," so that the Dublin congregations numbered many persons of distinction and good social standing[1] which enabled them to press their political claims upon the government. This led to the repeal of the Acts which forced Protestant dissenters to attend the Established Church Services once every Sunday and which imposed a fine upon their ministers. Other circumstances contributed in making the time favourable for an educational venture. Many Presbyterian families had settled in Ireland after the Revolution and, as the leases fell in, their rents were raised, and this, added to the religious disabilities, caused many dissenters to leave the country. This was a difficult problem for the ecclesiastical administration of Archbishop King, which called for his "most serious consideration" and caused him to urge the clergy of his diocese to remove all causes of complaint as far as possible[2]. At such a time, it was hoped that an "academy" might be conducted successfully in Dublin, but it is difficult to determine the exact date of its foundation. Leechman gives very few

---

[1] E.g. *Funeral Sermon upon the death of the Countess of Granard*, a member of *Wood St. Congregation*, by Robert Craghead, Junr. Dublin, 1714. *Funeral Sermon on the death of Sir A. Langford, Collected Works of Rev. Joseph Boyce.* London, 1728. Cf. *Christian Moderator*, i. p. 36.

[2] MS. Letters of Archbishop King. Library, Trinity College, Dublin. King to Molesworth, April 16, 1720. King to Archbishop of Tuam, April 24, 1720.

dates, and the only indication in his *Account* is to be found in the assertion that Hutcheson conducted the "academy" for "eight or nine years." He left Dublin in the year 1730[1], so that this would give either 1721 or 1722 as the date of the opening of the Academy. Allowing for the time necessary for consultation, after the passing of the Toleration Act in 1719, Hutcheson may have reached Dublin in the year 1720, and, by the time a house was prepared and other arrangements made, it is probable that the Academy could not have been in full working order until the close of the year or early in 1721. This would make Hutcheson's residence in Dublin slightly longer than the period mentioned by Leechman, but if we accept 1721 or 1722 as the date it is difficult to account for the two or three years' interval from 1719, when Hutcheson is recorded to have received the invitation; and, besides, we find mention of a pupil of his entering Glasgow University as early as 1722[2].

Evidently Hutcheson and his friends determined to have a suitable site for the Academy. At this time Dublin was extending northwards and many handsome houses were being built on the rising ground overlooking the city. A Dr Dominick was building a new street[3], which still bears his name, and Hutcheson rented a corner house, at the intersection of this street and Dorset Street, which was then known as Drumcondra Lane[4]. Though the locality has since deteriorated, in Hutcheson's time the situation was healthful and pleasant, being high and surrounded by open country, except upon the city side.

During the first two or three years of his life in Dublin, Hutcheson must have been busily engaged in organization. At first he himself taught "all the branches[5]"; but later, when

---

[1] The election to the Professorship of Moral Philosophy at Glasgow took place on the 19th of December, 1729; and Hutcheson reached Glasgow late in the following year.

[2] *Christian Moderator*, II. p. 307.

[3] Dr Dominick built his own house (now 13, Lower Dominick St.) in 1727. *Irish Builder*, 1895, p. 37.

[4] *Belfast Monthly Magazine*, *ut supra*; *Christian Moderator*, II. p. 307.

[5] Leechman, *ut supra*.

success was assured, he was able to employ an assistant[1]. This assistant was Thomas Drennan (father of Wm. Drennan the poet), who became Hutcheson's life-long friend[2]. Drennan was two years younger than Hutcheson, being born in 1696; he had probably been a fellow-student at Glasgow, where he graduated in 1715. He was licensed at Belfast in 1726; and, after Hutcheson's departure from Ireland, he was called to the congregation of Holywood, Co. Down, in 1731, whence he moved to Belfast in 1736[3]. Hutcheson and Drennan corresponded, and it is owing to the care of the descendants of the latter, that Hutcheson's letters have been preserved.

During the early part of his residence in Dublin Hutcheson married; and fortunately the date can be determined. In a letter to a friend, dated February 20, 1740, he says that he has been married "now fifteen years[4]," and a memorial of a deed of " Fine and Recovery " dated Sept. 10, 1725, is executed jointly by Hutcheson and members of his wife's family[5]. Therefore the date of the marriage must have been prior to the end of September, 1725, and, most probably, either in the early part of the year or the close of 1724. Hutcheson's wife was a Miss Mary Wilson, the daughter of Francis Wilson of Tully, Co. Longford, " who had distinguished himself as a Captain in the service of William III." Now, as John Hutcheson had also married a Miss Wilson of the same family, it is probable that Hutcheson and his wife were cousins; and this fact of family history possesses some interest as explaining his position upon the question of " consanguineous marriages." " We see no dismal effects," he writes, " from the marriages of cousin-germans " whence " multitudes of families are beautifully interwoven with each other in affection and interest, and

---

[1] Wodrow's *Analecta*, iv. p. 99.

[2] MS. Sketches of the History of Presbyterianism in Ireland, by Wm. Campbell, D.D. For this reference and other important information, I am much indebted to the Rev. Alex. Gordon of the Memorial Hall, Manchester.

[3] *Christian Moderator*, i. p. 309.

[4] MS. Letter to Alexander Stewart, Library, Magee College, Londonderry, *infra*, p. 134.

[5] Registry of Deeds Office, Henrietta St., Dublin.

friendly ties are much further diffused[1]." The marriage proved
a very happy one; besides, it seems to have brought him a
considerable increase in fortune, which safeguarded him against
the precarious income of the Academy[2]. Another interesting
fact in connection with Hutcheson's marriage is that the latter
part of the *Inquiry* was composed during his courtship, and
hence we find something of a lover's transports in the section
on "the Beauty of Persons" and "Love between the Sexes."
"Love itself," he says, "gives a beauty to the Lover, in the
eyes of the person beloved... And this perhaps is the strongest
charm possible and that which will have the greatest power[3]."
"Beauty gives a favourable presumption of good moral dispositions, and acquaintance confirms this into a real love of Esteem
or begets it where there is little Beauty. This raises an expectation of the greatest moral pleasures along with the sensible,
and a thousand tender sentiments of humanity and generosity;
and makes us impatient for a society which we imagine big
with unspeakable moral pleasures; where nothing is indifferent, and every trifling service, being an evidence of this strong
love and esteem, is mutually received with the rapture and gratitude of the greatest benefit and most substantial obligation[4]."

Hutcheson's removal to Dublin was most advantageous to
the development of his philosophical enquiries. Hitherto,
though strongly impelled towards Philosophy, his interests
seem to have been practical and theological rather than speculative, and now, at about twenty-six years of age, he met a
number of men interested in philosophical enquiries, besides
coming in contact with a more modern type of thought than
the academic teaching of Carmichael at Glasgow. In Dublin,
at this time, there were many Presbyterians, who appear to
have been deeply interested in Philosophy. Leland, the author

---

[1] *System of Moral Philosophy*, ii. pp. 171—2.

[2] Hutcheson possessed considerable landed property in Co. Longford, which
came to him through his wife. These were probably "dower lands," since, to
carry out the intricate settlement of his real property, already mentioned, he
provides otherwise for his wife—mentioning that such provision is "in full bar
of all Joynture or Dower she may anyway claim."

[3] *Inquiry*, 4th Ed., p. 255.

[4] *Ibid.*, p. 257.

of the *English Deists,* frequently visited Dublin, though he did
not reside there permanently until 1730, having been driven
from his congregation after years of wrangling with the Synod.
Boyse possessed a considerable reputation amongst members
of his Church as a theologian. James Duchal, a man of win-
ning manners, considerable eloquence, and force of character,
has left little behind him, but he was very highly esteemed
by his contemporaries. A more intimate friend than any of
these was Hutcheson's own cousin William Bruce, the youngest
son of the minister of Killyleagh, but the date of his arrival in
Dublin is somewhat uncertain[1]. As early as 1728 his name
occurs on the title-pages of books, as a partner of John Smith,
a publisher; and it was by Bruce that the Irish editions of
Hutcheson's works were published subsequently. Bruce became
prominent amongst the Dublin Presbyterians and, at a later
date, he helped Abernethy in the composition of pamphlets
upon the "Test Act," which attracted considerable attention[2].
He is described by a contemporary as excelling in "the most
useful science of morals; deeply instructed in those foundations
on which it most securely rests, in these he showed profound
skill; and it was at all times quite easy to him to exhibit them
in the most convincing point of light. Indeed, no man better
understood Human Nature, the heart of man particularly with
its exquisite arrangements of instincts and affections[3]." While
the influence of these friends was doubtless stimulating to
Hutcheson, it proved indirect rather than direct; but a fresh
and decided impetus is due to his acquaintance with Lord
Molesworth, who had many Presbyterian friends. Molesworth
had been a wealthy merchant and had filled a diplomatic
appointment at the Danish Court, which occasioned his *Account*

---

[1] *An Essay on the Character of the late Mr Wm. Bruce, in a letter to a friend.*
Dublin. John Smith, at the Philosopher's Head on the Blind Quay, 1755.
Haliday Pamphlets, R. I. A.

[2] *Scarce and Valuable Pamphlets,* by the late Rev. John Abernethy. London,
1751, p. v.

[3] *Character of Wm. Bruce, ut supra,* p. 11. Lucidity of expression, joined
with heat in argument, seem to have been family characteristics. Both are
here attributed to Bruce, and Leechman makes the same remark about
Hutcheson.

of Denmark as it was in the year 1692.   This work introduced him to the notice of Locke and Shaftesbury.   He had corresponded with the latter as well as with Toland[1], and his letters show an appreciation of philosophic principles.   At this time he was a prominent figure in Dublin society, and, while still deeply interested in parliamentary affairs, he found his most congenial occupation in entertaining and conversing with persons of literary and philosophic tastes.   Even Swift, who was chary of praise, writes " I am no stranger to his Lordship ; and, excepting in what relates to the Church, there are few persons in whose opinions I am better disposed to agree[2]."

Molesworth has left no writings dealing with philosophy, but it is easy to gather the drift of his opinions.   Owing to his personal relations with many of the most prominent thinkers of the day, he was wholly on the side of what was then the most modern and advanced thought ; and he was most influenced by his friend Shaftesbury.   It is true that Shaftesbury's letters were written some years before Hutcheson and Molesworth had met ; but it can be shown that the latter adopted rather than diverged from Shaftesbury's opinions as time went on.   As late as 1722, three years before his death, he had written to Archbishop King, evidently defending Shaftesbury's view of moral obligation, which King criticizes in a letter, still extant[3] ; and, if further proof were needed, it would be found in the early essays of his followers, in the *Dublin Journal*.

It has sometimes been said that Shaftesbury had a few isolated adherents, but that there had been no Shaftesbury school ; yet, owing to Molesworth, his philosophy was perpetuated and became fruitful amongst a group of earnest young thinkers at Dublin.   Molesworth appears to have been a man of singular power in gaining conviction ; for, though he himself wrote nothing of a philosophical nature, his conversation left a deep impress upon the young men he gathered round him.   His

[1] *Biographia Britannica*.   There is an interesting letter in the King MSS. written in answer to one of Molesworth's in which he had defended Toland—it is needless to add that King is severe on the "Atheist."

[2] Swift's *Works*, Ed. Sir W. Scott, viii. p. 299.

[3] King's Letters, *ut supra*.   King to Molesworth, Jan. 2, 1722.

environment and circle of friends at Blanchardstown recall
some of the best traditions of what are often called the Greek
" Schools." There we find a man past the prime of life, who
had spent his youth in travel and in the service of the state,
who had come in contact with well-known thinkers of the day,
engaged in the discussion of abstract theories with younger
men—probably without any view of teaching as the word is now
understood.

It is very probable that Hutcheson made the acquaintance of
his friend Edward Synge at Lord Molesworth's. Synge came
of a family that had given many bishops to the Irish Church.
Educated at Trinity College, Dublin, he was elected Fellow
in 1710[1], and he became an intimate associate of Berkeley[2].
During the nine years he held his Fellowship he was in the
thick of the revolution of thought which had been brought
to a successful issue, partly by the efforts of Molyneux, and
partly by those of Berkeley. The long reign of academic
scholasticism was over and the " new philosophy" was now
accepted. By a curious coincidence both Synge and Hutcheson
were ordained in the same year, 1719[3]—the latter to the small
dissenting congregation of Magherally, and Synge to the
valuable College living of Cappagh in Co. Tyrone, whence he
was soon recalled to become Chancellor of St Patrick's Cathedral, Rector of St Werburgh's, Dublin, and later to find a place,
at an early age, on the episcopal bench. At this time he was
a young man of marked ability, of Hutcheson's age, or perhaps
a year or two older, and already in possession of a high reputation as scholar and divine. Like Hutcheson, he was a man of
great tact, for he enjoyed the confidence of both Archbishops, a
feat which involved no little diplomacy, in the strained relations
of the two Sees at the time. He and Hutcheson seem to have
been mutually attracted; and, from some opinions in his
Sermons, showing traces of the influence of Shaftesbury, it may
be concluded that he was a member of the coterie of Molesworth.

[1] *Dublin University Calendar*, 1877, vol. ii. p. 205.
[2] Fraser's *Life of Berkeley*, i. p. 21.
[3] MS. Notes to Ware's *Bishops*, by the late Dr Reeves, in Library, Trin.
Coll., Dublin.

It is unfortunate, however, that little more is known of his position towards the problems of thought of his day, for it cannot be doubted that he influenced Hutcheson largely, especially as Hutcheson frankly admits that Synge had "fallen into the same way of thinking before him"—an expression which, with regard to the context, should be understood in the sense of the systematizing of Shaftesbury's disconnected opinions and freeing them from direct opposition to Christianity[1]. While Synge's influence upon Hutcheson can only be conjectured, Hutcheson's influence upon Synge can be definitely traced, but in an unexpected direction. Hutcheson now began to occupy a somewhat peculiar position, for, while a Presbyterian, he was in frequent and friendly intercourse with Churchmen, and he seems to have been able to make this position respected. Thus the friendship of Synge and Hutcheson made the former one of the most tolerant and broad-minded ecclesiastics of the day. Indeed he was so impressed with the strength of the Dissenters' cause that he preached a sermon on "Toleration" before the Parliament, which received the thanks of the House[2]; and, owing to his attitude upon this question, he was attacked, upon several occasions, by a more orthodox Churchman, named Radcliffe[3].

To readers of the Philosophy of the time, Synge is best known as the friend of Berkeley[4], and the question naturally suggests itself, whether Hutcheson and Berkeley ever met. Berkeley had been absent from Ireland between 1713 and 1721, when he returned as Chaplain to the Duke of Grafton, then Lord-Lieutenant. He remained in Dublin engaged in College work until 1724, when he was nominated to the Deanery of Derry. For three years, therefore, Berkeley and Hutcheson were living in the same town and both had a common friend in Synge, so that it would appear probable that they knew each other, especially as there is direct evidence that Hutcheson was acquainted with almost everyone interested in philosophy in Dublin. Further

[1] *Inquiry*, Preface.
[2] Froude's *English in Ireland*, i. pp. 563—4.
[3] King's MSS., *ut supra*.
[4] Berkeley intrusted Synge with the winding-up of his affairs in Dublin. Berkeley's Letters to Prior in Fraser's *Life of Berkeley*, i. pp. 146—7.

than this it is impossible to go; there are no letters of either, extant for this period, in which such a meeting could find mention. The internal evidence of their works is very baffling. The two men were too much alike not to have made a great impression each upon the other. Both were men of large hearts and high aims, both were keenly alive to the importance of educational and social reform, and it seems reasonable to expect that such intercourse would have left perceptible traces in their works. It is true that there are traces of Berkeleyanism to be found in Hutcheson's earlier works[1], but these are of an incidental character and seem to be either survivals of a stage of thought in which Hutcheson had a leaning towards Berkeley's theory or else half-unconscious reproductions of conversational discussions—both of which would be sufficiently accounted for by the sensation caused by Berkeley's opinions, in Dublin, and by intercourse with Synge. On the other hand, Berkeley, in his later writings, adopts an exceedingly bitter tone in criticizing Shaftesbury, which would have been in very bad taste had he known Hutcheson, against whom the criticism is really directed; or, again, this indirect method of attack might be explained by supposing that Berkeley knew and liked Hutcheson, but disapproved of his opinions and adopted a mode of criticism which would keep Hutcheson's name out of the discussion. On the whole, therefore, it is impossible to form a decisive judgment on this problem of biography,—one, indeed, which is insoluble, failing documentary evidence.

The date of Hutcheson's introduction to Molesworth can only be determined approximately. Until the middle of the year 1722, Molesworth had been absent in London as a commissioner in the Enquiry concerning the South Sea Bubble[2]. From his letters to King, it appears that he had been pecuniarily interested in the scheme; and, when the investigation was finished, he retired to Dublin, resolved to devote the

---

[1] E.g. "Beauty, like other names of sensible Ideas, properly denotes the perception of some Mind." *Inquiry*, Ed. 4, p. 14.

[2] King MSS., *ut supra.* Correspondence between King and Molesworth, Feb. 6, 1720—July 17, 1722.

remainder of his life to study. It is possible that these facts are referred to in the original dedicatory lines which Hutcheson inscribed upon the MS. of the *Inquiry*, before giving it to him for correction—

> Si quid ego adjuvero, curamve levasso,
> Si quae te coquat, aut verset in pectore fixa,
> Jam pretium tulerim[1].

If this be so, it would fix the date of Hutcheson's meeting with Molesworth in the year 1722 or 1723, and it is evident that, in Shaftesbury as interpreted by Molesworth, he found a philosophic basis for much that he had learned from Simpson, at Glasgow. Acting under the impetus of this new stimulus, his first work was soon written (probably begun in the last months of 1723 and finished in the Spring or Summer of 1724), and then it was criticized and commented on by Molesworth[2], and afterwards by Synge, thus consuming the interval until the date of publication, in January or February 1725[3]. Internal evidence leads to a similar conclusion regarding the date of composition; there is an interval between the theory of the *Inquiry* and the two Articles "on Laughter" which Hutcheson contributed to the *Dublin Journal*, in June of the same year. In the former Hutcheson avows himself the disciple of Shaftesbury both in the Preface and also in the overburdened title-page—*An Inquiry into the Original of our Ideas of Beauty and Virtue; in two treatises, in which the principles of the late Earl of Shaftesbury are explained and defended, against the Author of the Table of the Bees; and the Ideas of Moral Good and Evil are established, according to the Sentiments of the Ancient Moralists: with an attempt to introduce a Mathematical Calculation in subjects of Morality*[4], which latter statements are

---

[1] *Inquiry*, Preface—in first edition.

[2] Hutcheson acknowledges his indebtedness to Molesworth for a modification of the argument connecting Final Causes and Beauty.

[3] In the notice of Hutcheson in the *Christian Moderator* Bruce mentions a letter of Charles Moore "giving an account of the publication of the *Inquiry*," which is dated February 13, 1725. The dedication of the second edition to Lord Carteret is dated June 19, 1725.

[4] In the fourth edition the mathematical formulae for ethical phenomena were withdrawn. The following is an instance taken from the first edition— "The moment of evil, produced by any agent, is, as the product of his Hatred

withdrawn in the subsequent editions. In the article, "on Laughter," on the contrary, instead of following Shaftesbury's analysis of Ridicule, he has already become more independent, assigning an ethical rather than an intellectual "use" for its exercise.

During the year 1724, Molesworth's followers in the philosophy of Shaftesbury gained a distinct accession of strength by the advent of James Arbuckle, who became an intimate of Hutcheson, and afterwards of Swift. The date of his birth is uncertain, but as he graduated at Glasgow in 1720, it is probable that he was born about 1700 to 1703[1]. He entered the faculty of Theology in 1721 and obtained the degree of M.D. in 1724[2]. As his father was pastor of Usher's Quay Congregation, it is probable he returned to Dublin as soon as his studies in Glasgow were finished[3]. He came to Dublin with a considerable literary reputation, having already published *Snuff, a Poem*; *An Epistle to Thomas Earl of Haddington, upon the death of Joseph Addison,* in 1719; and *Glotta, a Poem* in 1721. These are written in the metre that Pope had made so popular, and the only one that calls for remark is *Glotta*, which possesses considerable interest as a description of the University and the teaching of the time. The lines devoted to the philosophical department show[4] that, at this time, Arbuckle was under Cartesian influence, yet four years

into his ability or $\mu = H \times A$," p. 173. Other examples will be found in Mr Selby-Bigge's reprint in *British Moralists*, Oxford, 1897, I. pp. 110—11.

Sterne has rather an amusing parody of this side of Hutcheson's work. "Hutcheson, in his philosophic treatise on beauty, harmony and order, plus's and minus's you to heaven or hell, by algebraic equations—so that none but an expert mathematician can ever be able to settle his accounts with S. Peter—and perhaps S. Matthew, who had been an officer in the customs, must be called in to audit them"—*The Koran.* Sterne's *Works*, Edinburgh, 1799, vol. VIII. p. 161.

[1] There is an account of Arbuckle, in MS., prefixed to a copy of his poem *Glotta* in the Library of the British Museum, according to which his birth might be definitely assigned to the earlier of the two dates mentioned in the text (1700). There are reasons, however, which lead one to distrust the accuracy of this statement—cf. an article on Arbuckle in *Mind* (April, 1899), N. S. VIII. p. 195.

[2] *Munimenta Univ. Glas., ut supra,* III. pp. 53, 254, 305.

[3] *Sermons of John Abernethy*, London, 1748, I. p. xxxix.

[4] E.g. the lines quoted above, p. 14.

later, through the inspiration of Molesworth, we find him ex-
pounding the principles of Shaftesbury. In 1722 Arbuckle had
had a share in an agitation of the students, connected with their
right of choosing a Rector, which had been invaded by the
Principal; and the defence of Arbuckle, who was threatened
with expulsion, came oddly enough to be associated with the
case of another Dublin student, named John Smith, a son of
the publisher, expelled "for kindling a bonfire on intelligence
of Lord Molesworth's election as a Member of Parliament
reaching Glasgow[1]." Arbuckle also found himself in trouble
by composing the prologue for a representation of *Cato and
Tamburlaine* by the students, which was supposed to reflect
upon the College authorities.

Arbuckle had the misfortune to be a cripple from his boy-
hood, and hence Swift, who nicknamed all his friends, called
him "Wit-upon-Crutches[2]." He is described by a contemporary as well acquainted with other branches of literature besides those relating to his profession, and to have "thoroughly
understood the great principles of philosophy, both natural and
moral...His openness, frankness and warm honesty of heart
appeared in all his conversation and behaviour. No man could
be more distant from professing anything he did not believe, or
giving up anything he thought just and right, either from a
feeble complaisance to others or from design...The very man
appeared to you, at once, without disguise, and one had always
the same character to deal with...He had a heart truly honest
and a very liberal hand. His charity to the poor, in his attendance upon them, was conspicuous to all. And it is known
to such as were intimately acquainted with him that he was in-
dustrious in finding out ways of serving persons in concealed
distress of circumstances[3]. His sound understanding and good

---

[1] *Munimenta, ut supra*, ii. pp. 424—5. The defence is contained in a
pamphlet, *A short Account of the late Treatment of the Students of the University
of Glasgow*, Dublin, 1722. The copy in the University Library is endorsed—
"said to have been written by Mr Robertson, probably the same who was
expelled in 1725, but the sentence taken off by visitation 1727," and in another
hand, "*sometimes ascribed to James Arbuckle.*"

[2] Swift's *Works*, Faulkner's Edition, vol. xvii. p. iii.

[3] Leechman notices a similar trait in the character of Hutcheson—so true is
it that a man is known by his friends.

sense, joined with largeness of heart and warm affection, were excellent qualifications for the sacred offices of friendship, which he discharged with the utmost generosity, steadfastness, and fidelity[1]."

Arbuckle's arrival in Dublin gave a desire for literary expression to the little group of Molesworth's adherents. At this period the Essay was the favourite "literary vehicle," but it must not be supposed that Arbuckle's contributions were intended to be an Irish rival of the *Spectator*. Molesworth, in all probability, had sufficient influence with the proprietor of a paper, named the *Dublin Journal*, to induce him to publish all articles or "letters" sent him by Arbuckle, who acted as general editor. In the first article Arbuckle, after explaining his design (in terms almost identical with the preface of Hutcheson's *Inquiry*), adds "that several honest gentlemen have resolved to make the paper a canal for conveying to the public some little essays they have lying on their hands[2]." When the articles were collected and published in London in 1729 Arbuckle, in his dedication, mentions that many of his own contributions were composed under Lord Molesworth's roof[3], and this suggests the guess that the members of the Blanchardstown coterie were in the habit of writing papers and submitting them to the judgment of the others. It will be remembered that this happened in the case of the MS. of Hutcheson's *Inquiry*; this conjecture, too, would account for a certain want of coherency in the two treatises which compose the work, which have all the appearance of being compounded out of several different essays, dealing with cognate subjects, but each distinct and inartistically united in the work as published. If this be so the priority of the short essays would be explained by the exigencies of composition for the Molesworth-Shaftesbury Club.

The greater part of the Essays, which appeared in the *Dublin*

---

[1] *A Sermon from Ecc. vii. 4 on the death of Dr Arbuckle, a physician and member of Wood St. Congregation, preached Jan. 4, 1747.* Dublin, 1747.

[2] *Hibernicus's Letters,* a collection of Letters and Essays lately published in the *Dublin Journal,* London, 1729, i. p. 4.

[3] *Ibid.* p. v.

Journal from April 3rd, 1725, to March 25th, 1727, are philosophical and should be compared rather to Coleridge's *Friend* than to the *Spectator*. Many of these are written by Arbuckle, six by Hutcheson—three criticizing a writer in the *Spectator*, who follows Hobbes in his analysis of Laughter[1], and three others, Nos. 45–7, dated February 4th, 11th, 18th, in answer to Mandeville's *Fable of the Bees*, a second edition of which had appeared in 1723[2]. Samuel Boyse contributed two articles, and one paper is given up to some posthumous verses by Parnell; the remainder, with one exception, are by writers who were unknown to Arbuckle, and most of these are deficient both in thought and style; yet these are the only papers that profess to deal with those topics of general interest, that yielded such admirable results under the treatment of Addison and Steele. Those that emanate directly from the Molesworth coterie possess some interest in so far as they show how Hutcheson began gradually to distance his friends both in depth of thought and philosophic penetration. There is much that is the same in all, but Hutcheson and Arbuckle are gradually drawing away from each other in their respective expositions of Shaftesbury[3]. Synge seems to have remained stationary; and, if Hutcheson's account of his opinions be correct, one cannot help thinking that he deliberately avoided publication, lest his opinions should prejudice his career in the Church, which promised an exceedingly prosperous future. It is interesting, too, to notice how soon the death of Molesworth,

---

[1] Tenth, eleventh and twelfth articles in the *Dublin Journal* published June 5, 12, 19, 1725. The article criticized in the *Spectator* is No. 47. There is a careful analysis of these articles in Fowler's *Shaftesbury and Hutcheson*, pp. 173—7. Fowler, it may be noted, is in error in describing Hutcheson's articles "as contributed to *Hibernicus's Letters*, a periodical which appeared in Dublin 1725-7 (2nd ed. 1734)." In the first instance the "letters" were sent to the *Dublin Journal* by Arbuckle, who wrote under the name of "Hibernicus," and the articles were reprinted as *A Collection of Letters and Essays, &c.*, London, 1729. These when bound are generally found described as *Hibernicus's Letters*. A collection of the *Dublin Journal* from 1726 is preserved in the National Library of Ireland in Dublin.

[2] Hutcheson signed the first series "Philomeides" and the second by the initials P. M.

[3] *Vide* p. 183.

which took place on May 22nd, 1725, removed the incentive to philosophical enquiries amongst his young friends. Synge published nothing, and Arbuckle's contribution to philosophy ends with the completion of the series of his " Letters to the *Dublin Journal*," though he continued to contribute to the paper upon general subjects.

CHAPTER III.

THE VICE-REGAL COURT.

THOUGH Hutcheson appears all through his life to have been indifferent to personal advancement he was singularly favoured by fortune. At the very time when he was deprived of the friendship of Molesworth by the latter's death he was sought out by a more influential patron, almost against his will.

At this period the Lord-Lieutenant was Lord Carteret, afterwards Lord Granville, who reached Dublin in the last month of the year 1724 to find the country in a ferment, under the excitement of the "Drapier's Letters" against "Wood's Half-pence[1]." How he quelled the tumult by pacifying Swift— in public, by a Latin quotation, more privately by the gift of trifling appointments to his friends—falls outside the limits of the present narrative, except in so far as it gives an insight into the times and the man. What is more to the purpose is the fact that he endeavoured to act up to the *rôle* of a Maecenas[2], in what has sometimes been called the Augustan Age of English Literature. Unlike many self-constituted patrons, he was undoubtedly a man of cultured taste, and elegant, if not deep, scholarship. Swift says that he "carried away from Oxford, with a singularity scarce to be justified, more Greek, Latin and Philosophy, than properly became a person of his rank; indeed much more of each than most of those who are forced to live by their learning, will be at the unnecessary pains to load their

[1] Kippis, *Biog. Brit.*
[2] *A Poem to his Excellency the Ld. Carteret*, by Sir Michael Creagh—Thorpe Pamphlets, National Library of Ireland.

heads with[1]." "Greek and Latin books might be found every day in his Dressing-room, if it were carefully searched." Archbishop King in a letter dated October 3, 1725, describes him as "a person of very great parts, learning and experience[2]." The pamphlets of the time contain frequent eulogistic verses in his honour, one of which, entitled the *Birth of Manly Virtue* (Dublin, 1724), says:

> "Keep him in or turn him out,
> His learning none will call in doubt."

In a fable, *The Pheasant and the Lark* (1730), ascribed to Delany[3], Carteret's learning is magnified many times:

> "No Science was to him unknown,
> For all the Arts were all his own:
> In all the living learned read,
> Though more delighted with the dead."

Prose accounts are little less eulogistic. One of the few passable light essays in the *Dublin Journal* (No. 26) compares Carteret to Aristides. The writer says he can quite understand the desire of the Greeks to banish a man who was so universally praised, for, in Dublin, life had become unbearable since the name Carteret was in everyone's mouth. "I say then," he adds, "this C—rteret is a strange sort of a man, I think a thousand times worse than Aristides himself. For he has not only (to the prejudice of other his Majesty's good subjects of Ireland) got the appellation of C—rteret the handsome, C—rteret the polite, C—rteret the affable, C—rteret the sincere, C—rteret the learned, C—rteret the wise, C—rteret the just, but (what is most absurd in men of his fashion) C—rteret the religious and exemplary!" Delany expresses his gratitude in lines that betoken a lively sense of favours to come:

---

[1] A Vindication of his Excellency, John, Lord Carteret, from the charge of favouring none but Tories, High Churchmen, and Jacobites. Swift's *Works.*

[2] King MSS., *ut supra.*

[3] Delany was a contemporary of Berkeley at Trinity College, where he became a Fellow in 1709, and a Senior Fellow 1719. He was Chancellor of Christ Church Cathedral, Dublin, in 1727, Chancellor of St Patrick's 1736, and Dean of Down in 1744. He died in 1768.

"He drew dumb Merit from her cell,
Led with amazing art along
The bashful dame, and loos'd her tongue,
And, whilst he made her value known,
Yet more displayed and raised his own[1]."

This side of Carteret's character renders intelligible Leechman's account of his meeting with Hutcheson. "Such was the reputation of the work [i.e. the *Inquiry*] and the ideas it had raised of the author, that Lord Granville, who was then Lord-Lieutenant of Ireland, whose discernment and taste as to works of genius and literature is universally acknowledged, sent his private secretary to enquire at the bookseller's for the author; and, when he could not learn his name, he left a letter to be conveyed to him[2]." In consequence of this invitation Hutcheson came forward, and, in a few months, found a place amongst the scholar-guests at the Castle, to whom Carteret was in the habit of quoting "passages out of Plato and Pindar, at his own table, even when persons of great station were by[3]."

At this time the Court was exceptionally brilliant in wit, manners and costume. Upon its social side there was no order of rank but learning and a nimble wit, no unpardonable offence but dulness. The most commanding figure was undoubtedly Swift, familiarly known by his contemporaries as "The Dean," who by fits and starts cajoled, rated publicly, and lampooned anonymously the successive Viceroys. A contemporary writer gives a picture of the conversation[4]:

"When next your generous soul shall condescend
T'instruct or entertain your humble friend,
Whether, retiring from your weighty charge,
On some high theme you learnedly enlarge,
Of all the ways of wisdom reason well,
How Richelieu rose, and how Sejanus fell:
Or, when your brow less thoughtfully unbends,
Circled with Swift and some delightful friends,
When mixing mirth and wisdom with your wine,
Like that your wit shall flow, your genius shine."

[1] *A Libel on D[r] D[elany] and a certain great Lord*, 1730.
[2] Leechman, p. viii.
[3] Swift, *ut supra*.
[4] *An Epistle to his Excellency, John, Lord Carteret* [by Delany].

This society must have opened a new world to Hutcheson, and it would be strange if he did not meet the witty band of clerics, led by Swift, to make sport for the Lord-Lieutenant and to seek preferment for themselves. Hutcheson was a man of serious disposition and lacked the *esprit* that forms so large an ingredient of the Southern Irish character, and probably he would find it difficult to meet the scorn that Swift would vent upon a Presbyterian and a Whig[1]. From the fact that Hutcheson does not appear to have made friends amongst the frequenters of the Castle, it may be inferred that he occupied an isolated position, appreciated by Carteret, but regarded with jealousy by the "place-hunters" who thronged the Court. Carteret, indeed, treated him "all the time he remained in his government with the most distinguishing marks of familiarity and esteem[2]"; and overtures involving substantial promotion were made to Hutcheson, if he would conform to the Church. He himself uses the expression "a good living" as the inducement to conformity. Another circumstantial account alleges that Hutcheson was offered the Provostship of Trinity College, "with authority to make all such changes as were necessary for improving the institution[3]." This report is open to the greatest suspicion. Richard Baldwin was Provost from 1717 to 1758—that is from the date of Hutcheson's leaving Glasgow, until twelve years after his death; and, therefore, there was no vacancy during the time he was associated with Carteret. It is, of course, barely possible that there may have been rumours that Baldwin would follow the example of some of his predecessors and accept a bishopric; but, even in this case, there would have been no precedent for the appointment of Hutcheson. From the Revolution to the period of Hutcheson's residence at Dublin the five Provosts had been Fellows, and if the Cromwellian occupation and the time of the Revolution

[1] Swift at this date was greatly soured in temper, and he was moving towards the time when he speaks of himself as—

> "Deaf, giddy, helpless, left alone,
> To all my friends a burthen grown."

[2] Leechman, *ut supra*.

[3] MS. Sketches of the History of Presbyterianism, *ut supra*.

be excepted, in every case, since the foundation, the appointment was given to a member of Dublin, Oxford or Cambridge University. Besides this want of precedent, it is exceedingly improbable that Baldwin, who was wedded to the College would willingly leave it; or even if there had been a vacancy, that the Crown could have appointed a man who was a convert for the occasion.

Reports of this nature having reached John Hutcheson at Armagh he wrote to his son, no doubt a letter of admonition, and the following is Hutcheson's reply[1]:

"August 4th, 1726.

"HONOURED AND DEAR SIR,

I received your letter by Mr McConcky, with the money you mention. I would not by any means delay giving you all possible satisfaction upon the subject you mention, as giving you so much uneasiness, and that with the greatest freedom, as with the best friend I have in the world. I would sooner have wrote you on this subject, had I apprehended you were uneasy about it. I knew there was such a rumour, but reports of that kind are so common and so industriously spread, by those who are fond of converts, upon any Dissenter's meeting with any civility from persons of distinction, that I did not imagine they would make any impression upon my friends.

To have singular principles on some points, is incident, I believe, to the best of men; though the publishing of them without necessity is too often a sign of vanity. This latter I have endeavoured always to avoid; the former is either innocent in many cases or a pardonable weakness. As to the separation from the Church, I will own to you what I scarce ever owned to anybody else, that it seems to me only a point of prudence. I do not imagine, that either government or the externals of worship are so determined in the Gospel, as to oblige men to one particular way in either; [but rather think] that all societies may, according to their own prudence, choose such a form of government in the Church, and agree upon such external order of worship, as they think will do most good, to promote the true need of all real piety and virtue, but without any right of forcing others into it. Men may sin and act incautiously in rashly choosing an inconvenient form, such as I really look upon the established one to be. But when this is done by the majority, and yet neither argument nor request will procure any alteration, provided the essentials of religion are preserved entire, it seems then, as to every particular person, a question of prudence, whether he will comply or not. That is to say, if in his circumstances he can propose to

[1] *Christian Moderator,* II. pp. 350—3.

do more good by separation than by conformity, the former is his duty ; if not, the latter. To apply this closer to the present case, I think the Scotch Church had alwise a right to insist on their old way, and to resist episcopacy ; since it was never regularly introduced, but in a tyrannical manner, contrary to the consent of the people, and illegally and cruelly enforced by the most unjustifiable methods, and was a less prudent institution or form than their own. But in King Charles the First's reign, in England, had I lived then, I would only have enquired, whether an actual separation would probably have done more good than the contrary, and accordingly practised. Before there was any considerable body of Dissenters, and while the opposite party was high, it would not seem to me to have been any person's duty to have openly separated, or to have encouraged others to do it, to their ruin. I cannot say, that in such a case, there was any sin in conformity to all parts of the worship established, at least for laymen. After the separation was made, and great numbers agreed in different forms from what was established (and I am convinced more prudent ones) and yet, upon the Restoration, the Episcopal form [was] turned into law, and most unjustifiably enforced upon those, who thought it absolutely sinful, with the most cruel treat-ment of many of the best subjects in the nation, it was honourable and good and the duty of every man, who was convinced of the goodness of their cause, to continue their dissent, and not to submit to these religious penal laws, which, it seems to me, no magistrate can ever have a right to make. I think the same reason for dissent continues still : that there is no obligation from the command of a magistrate in a matter beyond his province ; but the same reasons justify dissent, which would justify refusing Ship-money, or anything commanded by the King, in points not belonging to his prerogative. The Dissenters have a right to continue as they are ; and I firmly believe their cause, in most of the disputed points with the Church, is the better, and their methods more expedient and conducive to the ends of religion than that which is established. I should look upon it as my duty continually, as far as my influence could go, to promote the interest of that cause. But as one, who liked a republic or limited monarchy better than an absolute monarchy, might justify swearing allegiance to an absolute monarch when there were no hopes of altering the constitution ; so, I think, much more, might one receive from such a monarch the largest powers, with a view to prevent worse coming into the place, or to be more capable of recovering the liberties of the country from a tyrant. So I would not blame any man of my own principles, who, for very important purposes, did conform, if these ends proposed were such as would overbalance the damage which the more just cause would sustain by his leaving it, particularly if he had any prospect of getting an unjust establishment altered. This prospect I see not the least possibility of, and assure you as little purpose have I of ever acting with other intentions. After the concern you have expressed on this head, I assure you I know not any worldly consideration which I could propose or expect by conformity, that I would not reject rather than give you the uneasiness I should apprehend from it.

I cannot, however, think you would have reason to be so much concerned in this affair, were my resolutions different from what they really are. I am sensible of great corruption, not so much in the constitution of the Established Church (though it is not free from it) but in the general practice of its members. Yet, it is certain, they have some of the most valuable in this age among them; and it is not every corruption in a Church, which makes communion with it sinful. Nay, it is sometimes the more men's duty to continue to endeavour, while there is any hope, to make matters better. I often imagine, that were it not for the offence, which would be given on all sides, by any person, who had not obtained already a most undisputed character, it would be advisable to hold communion, with all Protestants, frequently, to show not only our good will and charity, but to show our dislike of these little divisions, occasioned sometimes by too much keenness upon both sides about trifles; such things as are not determined by any command of God, which no man, perhaps, has a right to constrain those to practise who dislike them, and which yet the bare doing of is not at all sinful.

The reason why I imagine so much left in religious matters to human providence is this, that I see no such particular distinct orders about the government or worship of the Christian Church in the New Testament as some allege. I am sure any of the founders or law-givers of human societies are much more particular in all the orders of their commonwealths, and the several powers of their magistrates, and the manner of proceeding in their several offices. From this I imagine no imperfection of the Holy Scriptures, but that much of these external things were left to human prudence. I wish you saw Sir James Harrington's *Treatise on Ordination* against Hammond's *Episcopal Form*, and, he seems to me, to prove the same of the Presbyterian, that both models were, in different places, practised by the Apostles, and consequently neither necessary nor lawful. When the whole body of the people agree in any of these forms, which are undetermined, in Scripture, unless the corruption be very great, separation is needless. Where a body is already separated upon a more convenient form, if they behave charitably to others, their separation is no sin, but rather laudable; and they are under no obligation to return[1]. Things may be left to human prudence to guide, where men agree without the power to compel.

I have wrote with more freedom in this letter than I have used before with anybody. The only reason of the rumour was my Lord Carteret's talking publicly of his resolution to have me brought over to the Church,

---

[1] This sentence gains weight in view of the schism in the Irish Presbyterian Church at the time. The action of the Non-Subscribers—many of whom were Hutcheson's friends—was, to him, "no sin, but rather laudable."

to a good living, and the Bishop of Elphin professing the same intention. They have both talked to me upon the subject of the scruples of the Dissenters, and of my sentiments of the constitution of the Church. I generally evaded the debate, and spoke of the Church more charitably than they expected, from whence they have concluded more than I ever intended. I had the like discourse with the Bishop of Down, where I was a little pinched with argument. He, however, I know, spoke more positively than he had any ground for. If it were proper to tell you a jest upon such a subject, it would perhaps make you laugh to hear his opinion of all these debates with Dissenters, summed up thus—"We," says he, "would not sweep the house clean, and you stumbled at straws." I own I look upon the matter of debate as of more consequence.

The ecclesiastic power, in any body associated, seems to me founded in the same manner with the civil ; and, to oblige all who have consented to it once, to obedience, unless where the abuse of power is so great as to overbalance all the advantages of the government, and to compensate all the disorders arising from an alteration of it. I imagine both to be in the same manner from God, who requires of us to do whatever may tend to the general good, and particularly to submit the ordinary debated points, either about civil or ecclesiastical matters, to the cognizance of arbitrators, chosen by ourselves, and limited according to our prudence[1]. If in these matters I am mistaken, I am sure, I do no harm to others, since I have kept my mind pretty much to myself in these matters, and resolve to do so   I assure you, if I should ever take contrary resolutions, of which I have no present presumption, I will let you know it, and consult you on everything, which appears difficult to me ; and pray, if you have leisure, let me know what you think faulty in what I write to you.

I am, with duty to my mother, your most dutiful son,

FRAS. HUTCHESON.

Pray write me farther on this subject, and assure yourself that there is no ground for your uneasiness. Were I disposed in that way, there is nothing to be got worth acceptance, without some vile compliance to which I would not submit.

To Rev. Jno. Hutcheson
    at Ballyrea near Armagh."

This lengthy letter is of theological rather than biographical interest, but it deserves a place in an account of Hutcheson's

---

[1] It is interesting to note that the argument contained in the concluding portion of this letter (which had been written after the publication of the first two editions of the *Inquiry*) was afterwards expanded and added to sections dealing with "Rights" in the fourth edition published 1738, pp. 293—9.

life as showing his attitude to the principles of Church government, and the points upon which the stress of argument fell in his day—arguments that may have had weight with Butler prior to his ordination in the Established Church of England.

At first sight it would appear that Hutcheson's action is contrary to all the rest of his life. Leechman enthusiastically describes him as a man " whose integrity was strict and inviolable : he abhorred the least appearance of deceit in word or action : he contemned those little artifices, which too frequently pass in the world for laudable arts of address and proofs of superior prudence : his nature was frank and open and warmly disposed to speak what he took to be true : you saw, at first sight, his sincere and upright soul, and in all further intercourse you found him always the same[1]." Yet, in his letter, he characterizes separation from the Church as a point of prudence —a prudence, which, in later life, it was his practice to condemn in no measured terms !

The letter, however, is too carefully thought out to be dismissed in this summary manner—indeed it is more an essay than a private letter, in which Hutcheson's character for moral honesty depends upon the peculiar sense in which he uses the word " prudence," not as mere " worldly prudence," but as the course of conduct that will produce most good ; or in other words he applies his principle of Benevolence, in fact judges as a modern Utilitarian would. He then mentions in a somewhat academic manner various historical instances in which conformity and dissent, respectively, were productive of most good, explicitly affirming, it is to be noted, that " the Dissenters' cause, in most disputed points, is the better." Farther on he adds, that in his own case, he could see no counterbalancing advantages that would atone for the damage to the more just cause by his desertion of it. Therefore, leaving theological questions aside, Hutcheson emphatically asserts his adherence to the Presbyterian Church on the grounds of religious liberty. He afterwards gives two additional or supplementary reasons, first that no possible advantage could outweigh the uneasiness and distress his secession would occasion to his father ; and secondly

[1] Leechman, *ut supra*, p. xxiv.

that, even if his opinions were different, he could not stoop to the " vile compliance," he believed to be a necessary step to gain anything worthy of acceptance.   These reasons are characterized by the historian of the Irish Presbyterian Church, as " exceedingly frivolous, and the whole answer is written in a strain which indicates how far his mind was now perverted by the speculations of a false philosophy[1]"—a statement which leads to the interesting conclusion that zeal for civil and religious liberty, filial affection and sturdy independence are to be found in a mind " perverted by the speculations of a false philosophy" —for it must be remembered that Hutcheson refused the preferment and that he never conformed to the Church !

At the same time there is something wanting in the tone of the letter.   If his father was anxious lest he should go over to the Established Church, one would imagine that a sufficient answer could have been given in a sentence ; and that the disquisition on Church History, Controversial Literature, and the relation of Civil to Canon Law was wholly unnecessary. To Hutcheson's honour, it should be remarked that he does not discuss the bribery implied in the offer of a " good living," but takes higher ground throughout—in fact, such an offer would present small temptation to a man of his temperament, circumstances and expectations.   Nevertheless, he seems almost to protest too much, though it may well be—especially when one remembers his scrupulous honesty as a child in refusing praise he knew he did not wholly deserve,—that, knowing his father would approve his decision, he did not wish to gain a good opinion of his conduct without stating the motives from which it resulted, which he felt would not be praised so unreservedly.

The spirit of the whole letter is liable to misinterpretation, without that of John Hutcheson's to which it is an answer. Probably the father first mentioned Hutcheson's philosophical opinions, and to this he replies by upholding the innocency of singular opinions upon some subjects.   Then John Hutcheson may have mentioned the reports of his conforming to the Church, possibly alluding to some case of a person who had sacrificed religious principle to temporal advancement.   This

[1] *Hist. Irish Pres. Church,* IV. p. 295.

clue explains much of the complexity of Hutcheson's reply.
While he states that he himself had no intention of conforming,
he is careful to add that he would not condemn another who
acted differently. Moreover one can well believe, that altogether apart from the difference of opinion on the New Light
controversy, the points of view of father and son were necessarily divergent. The latter had experienced all the clemency
and none of the rigours of the Established Church. He was in
touch with both sides of the question; and, meeting religious
opponents in friendly intercourse, he saw many of the points of
difficulty were little more than vain trifles, exaggerated by heat
of temper[1]; and therefore he considered himself justified in
accepting the favour shown him as a scholar, as long as he
refused any material advantage that would bind him to the
sacrifice of his freedom of thought[2].

At the time, this plan of action was a dangerous one and
liable to be misunderstood. Once it was known that the Court
party had approached him with offers of advancement, his
wisest course would have been to put his position beyond all
doubt. Instead of declaring his own opinions, he admits that
he "kept his mind very much to himself," "generally evaded
the debate" or discussed the position in the abstract. Perhaps,
even if so disposed, he found it difficult to give a direct refusal—
indeed Carteret was too much of a diplomatist to make a
definite offer until he was sure of Hutcheson's attitude to the
Establishment. This he contrived to conceal, for he was proud
of his social success and of the fact that he was on a friendly
footing where few of his birth and religion had been received
before, and he doubtless feared to risk the favour he enjoyed.
In his letter he feels that this temporizing had been injudicious,
and hence the prolix nature of his answer. He was prepared
to refuse preferment; but, at first, he could not bring himself
to be sufficiently decisive in his reply to silence rumour.
Doubtless he was wrong, but he was a young man, dazzled by

[1] *Inquiry*, p. 211.

[2] It is not without bearing upon this question that such influence as was
used afterwards during the election to the Professorship at Glasgow came from
Hutcheson's own family.

an unexpected success and the change from dissenting society
to that in a brilliant Court. His own opinions too made his
position more difficult. From his leaning to the " New Light,"
he could not approve unreservedly of everything Presbyterian ;
and, when the Thirty-nine Articles and the Westminster
Confession were used as the respective cries of political parties,
it is little wonder that a man who found fault with some of the
views held by adherents of both might be misunderstood,
especially by those who were anxious that he should conform
to the Church. This error is one of the very few in a singularly
perfect life, and against it is to be set the actual refusal of the
overtures and still more the higher virtue by which Hutcheson
showed he was incapable of treating matters of belief in the
mercenary manner too common amongst his contemporaries[1].

Hutcheson's refusal of Carteret's good offices did not injure
him with his would-be benefactor, indeed it rather advanced
him in favour. Carteret had found his Court crowded with
place-hunters—as he explained to Swift,

"My very good Dean, none ever comes here
But has something to hope, or something to fear,"

and the society of a man who neither hoped nor feared anything
from him must have been an agreeable change. This contrast
between self-seeking ecclesiastics and the independent Dissenter may have cooperated with weightier reasons in making
him more favourably disposed to the Presbyterians than the
majority of his predecessors. In the discourses upon religious
questions, Hutcheson had at least defended his own faith in the
abstract ; and he solemnly declared to his father " that he held
it his duty continually, as far as his influence could go, to
promote its interests." That such advocacy weighed with the
Viceroy is confirmed by the fact, that when Hutcheson returned
to Ireland after a year's residence in Glasgow, he was pained to
find Carteret less favourably disposed to the Presbyterians than

---

[1] About the same date Clarke writes that he would not accept "any see
unless it were the highest which would make him independent of his brethren
on the bench...the expectation of which might incline him to use more caution
not to make himself incapable of it." Letters to Emlyn, quoted in *Christian
Moderator*, i. p. 128.

he had been a few years before[1]. This change of front coinciding with Hutcheson's departure from Dublin may be merely fortuitous, but the coincidence gains additional weight from the fact that the most tolerant Churchmen of the day—Primate Boulter and Edward Synge—were also his friends; and if this be so, if Hutcheson endeavoured to use his influence in favour of the Dissenters, such action is the most complete answer to the doubts thrown upon his disinterestedness and honesty.

The favour which Hutcheson received at Court was only a portion of his social success in Dublin. Upon the publication of the *Inquiry* one of his friends, Charles Moore, had given him the following letter of introduction to Archbishop King[2]:

"The author of this book, which you will receive along with this, thought it proper to conceal himself, till he saw how it would be received by the world. This reason prevented him from presenting it to your Grace sooner; but, since he finds it has pleased some very great names, he humbly presumes it will not be disagreeable to your Grace, and that he shall make some small return in kind, for the great pleasure he has lately received by reading your Grace's book upon a subject, which has oft perplexed his thoughts, *De Origine Mali*[3]."

This introduction stood Hutcheson in good stead, since "two several attempts were made to prosecute him in the Archbishop's Court, for daring to take upon himself the education of youth, without having qualified himself by subscribing the ecclesiastical canons and obtaining a licence from the Bishop. Both these attempts were effectually discouraged by his Grace, with expressions of hearty displeasure against the persons who were so forward as to commence them[4]." The fact that these prosecutions were started between 1725 and King's death in the beginning of 1729, rather than at an earlier date, may be traced to jealousy, and not to an effort to enforce canon law; indeed it is by no means improbable that the first charge was brought forward immediately after Carteret's offer of the "good living"—it would have been an amusing eighteenth century *cause célèbre* to find the Court Philosopher and a possible Dean charged in the police-court of the Church.

[1] Wodrow's *Analecta*, IV. p. 298.
[2] *Christian Moderator*, II. pp. 349—350.
[3] Published 1702. [4] Leechman, *ut supra*, p. viii.

King was no doubt favourably disposed towards Hutcheson, being engaged in similar studies, which he continued up to the end of his life. In addition, it must however be remembered, that he was deeply impressed with the inexpediency of putting the law in force against Dissenters. The argument derived from the emigration of Presbyterians had considerable weight with the Government, and, as the depression in trade continued, the same reasons for inactivity would hold with even greater force. As late as 1726 he says that " Ireland is in a more poor and miserable condition than I .ever knew it to be since the Revolution[1]," and, soon after the passing of the "Toleration Act," he had stated in his " Charge " that the " Clergy should remember the late Act of Parliament, by which a full liberty is given to all sects to set up their meetings, and to propagate what doctrines they please, by this neither the Civil nor Ecclesiastical Courts have any power over them[2]." From this it would appear that the projected prosecutions were wholly malicious, and King's letters contain no reference to them[3]; but the fact of such attempts may have made Hutcheson more anxious to be successful in his application for the Professorship at Glasgow, which became vacant after he had lost the protection of King.

Meanwhile Hutcheson had been building up a considerable reputation as an author. No doubt the Lord-Lieutenant's interest in the *Inquiry* may have helped; but the backbone of his popularity was the public demand for the book in England, which was quite independent of Carteret's favour, since a second edition was published, within six months after the appearance of the first. As in the case of other works of the period, it is difficult to collect the opinions of contemporary thinkers, many of which were expressed in letters, and a few in

---

[1] Letter to Molineux, April 5, 1726; King's MSS., *ut supra*.

[2] To Archbishop of Tuam, April 24, 1720.

[3] King, writing to the Rev. Mr Radcliffe on June 25, 1725, says—"I looked over your discourse against Dr Hutchinson and gave Dr Travers my sense of it " —which "sense" appears from a subsequent letter to have prevented the publication of it. This "Dr Hutchinsoh" (whose Christian name was also Francis) was a Churchman who afterwards became Bishop of Down.

conversation, all of which are now irrecoverable[1]. John Clarke of Hull had objected to the Moral Sense theory from the standpoint of the Selfish Moralists, in a criticism of the *Inquiry* contained in his *Foundation of Morality in Theory and Practice,* deducing all affections from Self-Love ; and, as the result of a subsequent conversation, Hutcheson admits that his deduction "seemed more ingenious than any which he ever saw in print[2]." The first part of Balguy's *Foundation of Moral Goodness* appeared in 1728, simultaneously with Hutcheson's next work, the *Essay on the Passions.* Of other criticisms Hutcheson says generally, that " the gentlemen, who have opposed some other sentiments of the author of the *Inquiry,* seem convinced of a Moral Sense "—a statement which is interesting owing to the fact that, later, the Moral Sense bore the brunt of criticism. Almost the only touch of bitterness occurs in Hutcheson's answer to Le Clerc's comments on the *Inquiry,* which, he contends, show such a want of appreciation that " either I don't understand his French, or he my English, or that he has never read more than the titles of some of the sections ; and if any one of the three be the case, we are not fit for a controversy[3]."

The longest investigation of Hutcheson's work appeared in a series of " letters " written to the *London Journal* during the summer of 1728. These letters were signed " Philaretus," and were written by Gilbert Burnet—a son of Bishop Burnet. He examined the Moral Sense, from the standpoint of Clarke, alleging that it gave no sufficiently certain foundation for Moral Philosophy. This criticism applied more especially to the editions Burnet had before him, which contained the mathematical formulae. Hutcheson replied to each letter, and the discussion continued more amicably than most of its kind, until Hutcheson found that he could not give sufficient time to the preparation of his replies, when he wrote to Burnet privately, saying that he was prepared to continue the discussion later when he hoped to have more leisure[4]. The death of

---

[1] *Essay on the Passions,* Preface.

[2] *Ibid.,* p. xii ; *infra,* p. 109.

[3] *Essay on the Passions, ut supra,* p. xxii.

[4] *Ibid.,* p. xx.

Burnet ended the correspondence, and the letters and replies, with an additional note by Burnet, were published in 1735. This controversy was helpful to Hutcheson by bringing him into direct contact with an opposing theory, and the probable explanation of his withdrawal from the discussion was that he felt the need of strengthening the statement of his own opinions, and this again led to the composition of the con- cluding " treatise on the Moral Sense " in his work published in the same year (1728) and entitled an *Essay on the Passions*. Though Burnet's letters occasioned the publication of this work, it owed much to Butler and Wollaston—the *Sermons* of the one and the *Religion of Nature Delineated*[1] of the other having both been published in 1726. To each of these Hutcheson was much indebted, but in different ways. While criticizing Wollaston[2], he learnt from his work to supplement some of his own defects of terminology. His relation to Butler is very much closer. With the power of rapid assimilation of ideas he undoubtedly possessed, Hutcheson soon made the principles of the *Sermons* his own, and hence one finds the *Essay on the Passions* full of echoes of Butler.

Quite apart from competent criticism Hutcheson had to face the strictures of persons who honestly believed that his speculations ran counter to some popular or favourite theological dogma. At this time it was a bold act to have placed Shaftes- bury's name upon the title-page of the *Inquiry*—in fact Shaftesbury was then the *bête noire* of the combative theologian. Leland classed him amongst the English Deists, and by many he was thought to be a dangerous opponent of religion, an opinion which Hutcheson had endeavoured to counteract in the preface of his first work. A satirical writer ironically suggests the foundation of a University for the encouragement of " Free- thinking," and he proposes Shaftesbury's *Characteristics* as one of the text-books to be mastered before a student can rise from the first class, " Risor," to the second, that of the

---

[1] An edition of the *Relig. Nat. Del.* had been printed in 1722, "four or five copies" of which were given away and some others sold privately, unknown to the author.

[2] *Essay on the Passions*, Treatise II. § 3.

Irrisors[1]. While popular opinion was in this condition, Hutcheson must have suffered several attacks. A pamphlet, published in Dublin with the quaint title *St Paul against Shaftesbury* in 1734[2], may have been intended to confute the writer's conception of Hutcheson's teaching of Shaftesbury's heresies; and Dr Calamy, an English Non-Conformist, when he heard of the election to the Chair of Moral Philosophy at Glasgow, said "that he was not for Scotland as he thought from his book; that he would be reckoned as unorthodox as Mr Simpson[3]." Such criticism, joined with the dissatisfaction which must have been occasioned by the favour Hutcheson enjoyed at Court, no doubt raised detractors if not enemies, and one would expect that some of these would have expended their venom outside the ecclesiastical courts, in anonymous pamphlets, after the fashion of the time; but, if such attacks were made, they cannot now be traced. The following lines may indeed possibly refer to Hutcheson, though it is more probable they were directed against Thomas Sheridan, a friend of Swift, a teacher who was frequently ridiculed under the name of Punsibi:

> "The linsey-woolsey poor objections
> Of his illiterate reflections
> Have fully proved how ill the Fool
> Hath read the authors of his school.
>   Ye hapless youths who pay him sterling
> For puddling through unclassic learning,
> Who hear him oft torment Apollo,
> His sad example doomed to follow[4], etc."

The years 1728 and 1729 were full of incident for Hutcheson. Besides his letters published in the *London Journal* and the *Essay on the Passions*, the same year saw an Irish edition of the latter work published by his friends Smith and Wm. Bruce, "with the errors of the London Edition emended[5]." In

---

[1] *Essay for the Better Improvement of Free-thinking—in a letter to a Friend.* London, 1732.

[2] Haliday Pamphlets, R. I. A.

[3] Wodrow's *Analecta*, iv. p. 227.

[4] *A Libel upon the Dublin Dunces*—Printed in the year 1734.

[5] Advertisement in the *Dublin Intelligencer*, March 23, 1727-8. The London edition was sold for 5s. 5d. and the Dublin one is announced at "two British Shillings."

the next year a third edition of the *Inquiry* was published in London, and his letters to the *Dublin Journal* were reprinted in the collected edition by Arbuckle, and attributed to "the learned and ingenious author of the *Inquiry into the Original of our Ideas of Beauty and Virtue*'."

These literary successes were unfortunately more than counterbalanced by domestic trials. His father—"the best friend he had in the world"—died in February, 1729[2], and he lost a child about the same time, a double affliction which preyed upon his spirits for a considerable period[3]. Hutcheson now succeeded to the income of one-half of the Co. Down property, under the will of his grandfather Alexander Hutcheson; and his father devised to him his books and manuscripts, though it is probable that he transferred such of the latter as concerned Presbyterian affairs to the editor who prepared John Hutcheson's *Narrative of the Seven Synods* for the press[4]. During Hutcheson's visits to his father at Armagh, and, subsequently, when winding up his affairs[5], he became acquainted with Primate Boulter, who had just arrived from England to become head of the Irish Church. He was, therefore, able to approach Irish religious controversies without local prejudice, and Hutcheson seems to have influenced him in favour of the Presbyterians[6]. It was through Hutcheson that Boulter gave a sum of money to the University of Glasgow at a later date.

The mention of Hutcheson's connection with Glasgow leads up to his appointment as Professor of Moral Philosophy. In 1729 his old teacher, Gershom Carmichael, had died, and three candidates were thought of for the vacant chair—a Mr Warner, Frederick Carmichael, son of the deceased Professor, and Hutcheson. The election soon resolved itself into a struggle between the adherents of the old spirit and those of the new in

---

[1] *Hibernicus's Letters, ut supra*, II. p. 429.

[2] Reid's *History, ut supra*; Witherow's *Memorials*.

[3] Wodrow's *Analecta*, IV. p. 191.

[4] Will of John Hutcheson. Public Record Office, Dublin.

[5] The will of John Hutcheson is endorsed—"sworn to by Francis Hutcheson, one of the executors, April 6, 1729," at the Archbishop's Court, Armagh.

[6] Cf. Stuart's *Armagh*, p. 482.

the University. The Principal and others of the old school supported Carmichael; while Alexander Dunlop, the Professor of Greek, and the younger men were in favour of Hutcheson. He was eventually elected, on December 19, 1729, by a majority of one vote. According to Wodrow, this result was due to influence exerted by Dunlop, who was keenly interested in the contest, partly from opposition to the Principal, partly through family reasons, having recently married "Hutcheson's aunt's daughter[1]." The following is the official account of the meeting and election:

"At the College of Glasgow 19th December, 1729, Sederunt Mr Neil Campbell Principal, Mr Will. Wishart, D.F., Mr J°. Simpson, S.T.P., et alii—

This being the day appointed for the election of a person to supply the vacancy caused by Mr Carmichael's death, the Principal produced a letter from the Rector, dated Edinburgh, 16th inst., signifying he was sorry it was not possible he could be present at the election upon this day, and wishing a happy choice for the good of the University. Then, after several of the members had discoursed about a fit person, the question was put, who shall be elected to the vacant profession of Philosophy. And, the Clerk having called the roll, it was carried by a majority, that Mr Francis Hutcheson, of Dublin, should be elected. And, therefore the faculty, in consideration of the known merit, learning and good repute of the said Mr Hutcheson and of his other good qualities, elect him in the aforesaid terms to succeed to the vacant profession of Philosophy in this University[2]."

On February 20, 1730, "the Faculty appointed the following subjects to be given to Mr Hutcheson, in order to his making discourses upon them, to be delivered in presence of the Faculty, viz.:

In Logick—'De Scientia, Fide et Opinione inter se collatis.'
In Ethicks—'An sit una tantum morum lex fundamentalis, vel, si sint plures, quaenam sint.'
In Physicks—'De Gravitatione Corporum versus se mutuo (sic).'"

Hutcheson does not appear to have moved finally to Glasgow until the latter part of the year 1730. After his election he seems to have remained in Dublin and to have continued the

---

[1] *Analecta*, IV. p. 99.
[2] *Munimenta Univ. Glas.*, ut supra, III. p. 402.

work of the Academy, and then to have transferred the majority
of his pupils to Glasgow in time for the beginning of the next
academic year[1].   He arrived in Glasgow in October, signed the
Confession of Faith upon the 29th of the month, and was
co-opted "in numerum magistrorum" on November 3rd[2].   On
the 30th of the month he was publicly admitted, when he gave
his inaugural lecture *De Naturali Hominum Socialitate*, defending his principle of Benevolence; but owing to his "deliver-
ing it very fast and low, being a modest man, it was not well
understood[3]."

[1] Wodrow, *ut supra*.
[2] MS. Records, University of Glasgow.
[3] Wodrow, IV. p. 167.

CHAPTER IV.

HUTCHESON'S INFLUENCE AS A PROFESSOR.

HUTCHESON, upon his arrival at Glasgow, doubtless found the University greatly changed. During the thirteen years of his absence, difficulties, that had not yet come to the surface while he was a student, had plunged the academic body into strife and dissension. The old contest between mediaevalism and modernism still continued, but this was necessarily confined to the Professors and their relations with the Church. Naturally the Professor of Divinity suffered most, and the suspension of Simpson marks a temporary triumph of the devotees of conservatism in knowledge and of the opponents of a liberalizing culture. It reasserted the claim of the established Church that the University should be an appendage of the Presbytery, that the teaching staff should be recruited from the West-country ministry, and above all that the orthodoxy of the University should be under the control of the General Assembly. Such claims are common to the histories of different universities during the first half of last century, and, even at the present day, though they are little known in higher education, they still revive spasmodically in the working of secondary schools. A peculiar interest centres round the insistence upon them by the clergy in the neighbourhood of Glasgow, since, though all testimony is in favour of their religious zeal, there can be little doubt that they were far from being intellectually distinguished[1]. With them the ideal of a university was a severe rigid orthodoxy, and some of them looked upon all culture and style with a certain amount of suspicion. In

---

[1] *Scotland and Scotsmen*, I. p. 271.

the language of Matthew Arnold they aimed at making the
university religiously provincial, and, had they eventually
triumphed, it would probably have become the seminary of a
sect, not an important educational establishment representing
a national Church.

If one pictures Hutcheson, the disciple of Shaftesbury, fresh
from the traditions of a somewhat brilliant Court, a young man
valuing the showy culture of the society of his day, all the
more, perhaps, because he was scarcely to the manner born, but
had won it by his merits, according to his friends, or by chance,
as no doubt his detractors said; if one adds, too, a tolerance
partly constitutional and partly a result of his fashionable
training, it is easy to understand that he must, inevitably, have
taken sides with the more modern and progressive party.

Besides, there was a personal element that converted him
from a passive sympathizer into an active partizan. However
the Scottish Presbyterian might differ from the colony of the
same Church in the north of Ireland, there was more than a
superficial resemblance between the more conservative clergy
in both countries. The Ulster Presbyterian in the earlier part
of the eighteenth century had emerged from a time of struggle,
and, remembering the "massacres" of 1641, and Cromwell's
demand for "an eye for an eye and a tooth for a tooth," and
their ancestors' sacrifices during the siege of Derry, it is little
wonder that they looked upon themselves as God's garrison in
a conquered country, holding the outposts of the true faith
against the Anglo-Irish Episcopalian and the Celtic Roman
Catholic. Such historical facts naturally led to a rigour and
sternness that left little room for the graces of culture. The
religious life was intensely serious, having involved, in the past,
enormous sacrifices and, arguing from the past, as their descendants do at the present day, likely to involve further sacrifices in
the future; for it is always to be remembered that Ireland is
the home of Churches militant, and, then as now, each religious
body stood at arms, dreading the aggression of its neighbours.
Such an attitude had made the Presbyterian Church intolerable
to the group of younger men known as the "Belfast Society,"
who later became the "Non-Subscribers." Nearly all of

these were Hutcheson's friends, and he could hardly fail to
condemn what he no doubt considered the shortsightedness of
a Church that had deprived itself of such a vigorous offshoot.
Upon his arrival in Scotland he identified the more conservative West-country ministers with the non-progressive Irish
party ; and therefore he was not only opposed to them from
his whole cast of thought, but also on account of the mis-
fortunes of his friends.   Such is the complex interweaving of
historical events that the schism in the Ulster Presbyterian
Church had a considerable influence in the liberalizing of the
University of Glasgow !

Quite apart from the clerical aspect of the question, there
were numerous elements leading to a great change in the
University.   During Hutcheson's absence in Ireland, the academic body had been trying to readjust itself after the confusion of the Rebellion.   The Principal, John Sterling, who had
been appointed in 1701, seems to have been a better pilot in
stormy than in calm waters.   In his old age he endeavoured to
enforce the severe disciplinary measures that had been necessary during the troubles.   About the year 1720 the students
were in a ferment, owing to their being deprived of the privilege
of electing a Rector, the decision having been usurped by the
Principal and Regents.   Sterling, too, was charged with forming
a party and transacting important business during vacations,
when only his own supporters were present in the Senatus.   It
was alleged that, being the sole custodian of all documents, the
minutes were "frequently scored, interlined and margined,"
with his consent[1].   With such complaints in the air there
was insubordination amongst the students ; some were expelled,
with the result of a Visitation and appeals to the Courts.   The
Principal's supporters adopted an overbearing tone to the
students, as for instance, when one of the students, who had
been expelled for lighting a bonfire and drinking (amongst
other healths) the liberties of the Students of Glasgow, returned
with a suspension of his expulsion, Simson told him " he might
light his pipe " with the document.   On the other side some of

[1] *A Short Account of the late Treatment of the Students of the University of
Glasgow*, Dublin, 1722.

the Regents who opposed the Principal were charged with inciting the students to riot[1], so that, on the whole, discipline for a time seemed to be in abeyance.

One of the results of this state of affairs was that a Commission was appointed, which, by a Statute and Act of 1727, revolutionized the whole system of teaching, by changing the mediaeval system of Regents into the modern professorial one. The Regents represented a tutorial system, by which each student entered under a certain Regent or "master," who taught him throughout his course, and they were also responsible for the conduct of their own pupils, much like college tutors elsewhere. As Glasgow College last century had chambers for a number of students, this system was possessed of obvious advantages, and, in fact, the method of teaching, by "Regents," died hard in some of the other Scottish Universities. At Glasgow, the new method was accepted with little difficulty considering the magnitude of the change, but it is obvious that the fact of Hutcheson's coming at such a time led to his being more and more identified with the progressive party. In so far as the change affected the Philosophical Classes, the language of the Act of 1727 is sufficiently precise. "The Commission having recommended to the Masters of the saids three Philosophical Classes, to make their election, which of the classes they were severally to take, and they having agreed amongst themselves, and Mr G. Carmichael (Hutcheson's predecessor) having made choice of the Ethick Class, Mr John Loudoun of the Logick Class, and the teaching of the Physick Class falling to Mr Dick, the Commissioners statute and ordain that the saids persons, respective, shall, in time coming, have the teaching of the said severall classes, by them chosen, and Mr R. Dick teach the class falling to him, and that they remain so fixed to the said classes, and that all other and subsequent Professors of Philosophy, coming in to the said university, shall be still fixed to one class, and the teaching of the forsaid parts of philosophy allotted to the class in which he shall be fixed." Further, since it had been customary for the Regents to delay

---

[1] Wodrow MSS. 41, Nos. 95—99.

the opening of the Classes until December or even January[1], the Act further determines "that the Professors above specified shall either continue their Colleges from the first day of November to the last day of May yearly, or, if their classes be sooner finished, that they shall weekly thereafter give public prelections to the last day of May," a course which Hutcheson seems to have always followed, though he complained that it prevented his visiting friends in Ireland, besides depriving him of leisure for literary work.

It is, therefore, easy to guess that Hutcheson, entering upon a new field of work at Glasgow, with a reputation little likely to recommend him to old-fashioned people, found himself in a troubled atmosphere that needed all his tact. Towards the middle of the century academic differences between the "gown" and "other" professors had degenerated into petty squabbles, but, from 1728 to 1750, the University was divided upon lines of a broad policy, as to whether its whole tendency should be progressive or stationary—if not retrogressive.

Hutcheson's arrival gave him a foretaste of the reactionary ideas of some of his new colleagues. William Anderson, who had been appointed Professor of Ecclesiastical History in 1721, had been selected to teach the Moral Philosophy Class after Carmichael's death[2]; but, at the beginning of the session in 1730, Loudon, Hutcheson's old teacher in Logic, and now Professor of the same subject, claimed that he had "a right to make choice of the Ethick Class under the late Commission of Visitation." However, some twenty English students, who had come for the session, upon the express understanding that Hutcheson was "to teach morality," sent in a petition stating that, unless Hutcheson lectured in Moral Philosophy, they would go to Edinburgh, and, though such dictation from the class must have been galling, Loudon had to yield. He managed at least to retreat with decency as he represented that, "in regard his state of health was not so firm as to allow him to venture upon a change now, he resolved to keep the semi-class[3]"—

---

[1] *Literary Memorials of Glasgow*, p. 122.
[2] MS. Records of Glasgow Univ.
[3] *Ibid.*

evidently the eighteenth century Professor knew the value of the "diplomatic cold"! The extraordinary feature of the whole affair is that, while Hutcheson had been elected to the Chair of Moral Philosophy, and the Act of 1727 expressly states that Carmichael, Loudon and Dick should remain "fixed" to the respective classes they had chosen, the Senatus records that Loudon "had the right" of choice, plainly showing that University statutes were at the mercy of the majority of the dominant party.

About the middle of October Hutcheson arrived from Dublin, bringing eighteen or twenty of his old pupils with him[1]. Upon October 29th he subscribed the Confession of Faith, and upon the 3rd of November was admitted "in numerum magistrorum[2]," being publicly admitted on the 30th. Wodrow, whose sympathies were rather with the old school, says he was "well spoken of"; and, writing later in December, adds that "he was much commended," especially as he did not frequent taverns, like Simson. "That he carried himself gravely" was in part due to grief for the loss of his father and one of his children. His chief friends were the William Anderson already mentioned and John McLaurin, a minister, whose name is remembered as brother of a celebrated Edinburgh professor, a prominent Glasgow minister, writer of tracts, and as an unsuccessful candidate for the Chair of Divinity. "In party matters," Wodrow adds, "and some politicks, as to smaller matters, it's like he will be on the side with Mr Dunlop[3]," who was Professor of Greek, and, though far from a young man, was wholly on the side of reform and progress.

Hutcheson's first step was to discipline his class, "by keeping the students to rules, catalogues, exact hours &c. wherein there is certainly a very great decay[4]," and then to organize the class work. This was altogether a new departure, as, under the Regent system, much time was spent in elementary work. Hutcheson, instead of confining himself to an oral commentary

---

[1] Wodrow's *Analecta*, iv. p. 185.
[2] Glasgow Univ. Records.
[3] Wodrow's *Analecta*, iv. pp. 190—1.
[4] *Ibid.*

in Latin upon some scholastic text-book, inaugurated a new method of lecturing in English, and he covered the whole field of " Natural Religion, Morals, Jurisprudence and Government," in the five daily lectures he gave each week[1]. At first, he taught Pufendorf and the "*Compend*" of his predecessor Carmichael[2], but later, he delivered written lectures with many digressions and additions, which were substantially the same as the *System of Moral Philosophy*, edited after his death by Leechman, and which varied little from year to year[3]. On three days each week he co-operated with his friend Dunlop by lecturing upon ancient ethics, thereby fostering the renaissance of the study of Greek which both had at heart, besides following the Shaftesbury precept of inculcating the excellence of the moral systems of the ancients. Though these lectures were useful to the students, they were far from gaining the approval of Hutcheson's opponents, and it is probably this side of his work that called forth the elephantine satire of Witherspoon— " Recommending virtue from the authority and examples of the heathen is not only highly proper, because they were highly virtuous, but has this manifest advantage attending it, that it is a proper way of reasoning to two quite opposite kinds of persons.... It is well known there are multitudes in our islands who reckon Socrates and Plato to have been greater men than the Apostles.... Therefore let religion be constantly and uniformly called virtue, and let the heathen philosophers be set up as the great patterns and promoters of it[4]."

Hutcheson also held private classes, like most of the other professors, which were largely attended by " tradesmen and youths from the town"; and, on Sundays, he gave lectures on the evidences of Christianity, and, either upon Sunday night or Monday morning, he examined his class very closely on the Sermon as well as his own lecture[5]. These Sunday lectures followed Grotius *De Veritate Religionis Christianae*, but the

1 Leechman's *Life of Hutcheson*, p. xxxvi.
2 Wodrow's *Analecta*, IV. p. 185.
3 Leechman's *Life*, p. xxxiv.
4 Witherspoon's *Works*, 2nd Edition, p. 17.
5 Wodrow's *Analecta*, IV. p. 185.

subject was treated both popularly and with eloquence, so that, as no fee was charged, there was always a very large outside audience[1].

Not only was the lecturing in English a new departure, but Hutcheson's whole manner was a revelation to the students. He was in the habit of walking up and down " the arena of the room" as he spoke. "Since his elocution was good and his voice and manner pleasing, he raised the attention of his hearers at all times, and, when the subject led him to enforce his moral duties and virtues, he displayed a fervent and persuasive eloquence which was irresistible[2]." Leechman, who was later his colleague and biographer, mentions that " his happy talent of speaking with ease, with propriety and spirit, rendered him one of the most masterly and engaging teachers that has appeared in our age[3]." He did not confine himself to the mere teaching of Philosophy, but aimed at making his students moral men, in other words his work included more of the art than the science of Ethics. Here he proved himself the disciple of Shaftesbury in his enthusiasm for virtue, which led him into frequent bursts of eloquence, in praise of all that was noble and beautiful in a rightly ordered life. Thus he dealt diffusively " upon such moral considerations as are suitable to touch the heart and raise a relish for virtue," for he regarded the " culture of the heart as a main end of all moral instruction[4]." Such lectures constituted a revolution in academic teaching. In his popular mode of exposition and comprehension of other theories, Hutcheson was admittedly the superior of his predecessors, but to this he added the rare gift of eloquent expression, brightening his argument with the graces of oratory, and joining to the knowledge of the Professor the fervour of a preacher. The freshness of his thought, its departure from the usual academic spirit, his eloquence and earnestness all tend to justify the wonderful hold he had upon the minds of young men. But it needed something more to explain his remarkable personal influence, and here the key-note will be found in the fact that he was a Professor-preacher, intertwining, in a double expression,

[1] Carlyle's *Autobiography*, p. 70.   [2] *Ibid.*
[3] Leechman's *Life of Hutcheson*, pp. xxx, xxxi.   [4] *Ibid.*

two different gospels, one the claim for the modern spirit, for light and culture, the enthusiasm for Benevolence and Beauty; and the other, of an artistic nature, in so far as he endeavoured to mould the plastic young minds around him into so many living realisations of his ethical ideal. Further, in his lectures on the State (which gave Adam Smith an interest in Political Economy), he always insisted "with the greatest strength of argument and earnestness of persuasion" upon the then burning questions of civil and religious liberty; and as most young men are Idealists, if not Radicals, in politics, one can readily credit Leechman's statement that "few, if any, of his pupils, ever left him without favourable notions of that side of the question which he espoused and defended[1]."

It will have been seen that Hutcheson's influence as an author was felt to a large degree outside the university, and that this influence was but a faint reflex of his own personal magnetism inside the class-room. He felt that his life-work lay in the moulding of young men's characters, and mere academic teaching was always secondary to this. "What he thought, he loved; and what he taught, he was"—indeed, one might add, what he loved, he tried not merely to teach but to *make* his students[2].

This side of Hutcheson's life-work suggests the reflection of the diversity of the world's monuments to great men—for, without doubt, Hutcheson was a great teacher, and that in the most important and difficult sphere, the university. Possibly it would have been almost better had " he scorned the untruth of leaving books behind " him, for his works give little clue to the force of speech that gave a new horizon to the Glasgow students of his day. Such notice as he had received depends upon his positive contributions to philosophy, drawn from these very works, and yet with him theory was always secondary to prac-tice. He was in no sense a system-builder, but rather a teacher who *preached* Philosophy, to whom a positive system was little more than a text, and, it will be seen, these texts were drawn from different sources and not always quite

---

[1] Leechman's *Life of Hutcheson*, p. xxxvi.
[2] Martineau, *Types of Ethical Theory*, II. p. 524.

consistently.   And while those who have come after him have
given him false honour for the discovery of a "moral sense"
which was not his but Shaftesbury's, or for the foundation of
a "school" which involves a historical anachronism—his life,
wherein lay his power, has been overlooked, and one is inclined
to charge his contemporaries with lack of taste when they
speak, as one man, of his personal charm, his earnest power of
conviction, and remarkable or "irresistible" oratory.   Still
even here, on looking deeper, there is found a strange historical
compensation; and that too the stranger, because it has worked
unconsciously or automatically.   While posterity has neglected
Hutcheson's true claim to fame, and left him without a real
monument, all the time, history, tradition, or chance has given
him the monument he himself would have chosen, for the
didactic element in his teaching has become and remained a
characteristic of the Chairs of Moral Philosophy in the Scottish
universities—a feature found nowhere else—and continues a
dominant influence down to the present day.   In all other
universities, where Philosophy is taught as an Arts subject (as
apart from Theology) Mental and Moral Philosophy are on an
exact footing of equality; in Scotland, on the other hand, there
is a tradition, now, perhaps, half obliterated by time and
progress, yet still very prevalent, especially outside the universities, that there should be a difference between the teaching
of the two Chairs.   Mental Philosophy is more precise and
scientific, while Moral Philosophy is wider in its scope, more
didactic, and supposed to exert an actual ethical influence—the
force of this belief is still to be noticed in the preference
of Theological students for Moral Philosophy.   It is a little
curious to think that in the long range of Scottish Professors
of Moral Philosophy, after Hutcheson, however far many of
them may have diverged from his system and beliefs, all have
been, more or less, according to their characters and surround-
ings, influenced, in the form of teaching, by the lost lectures
delivered over a hundred and fifty years ago at Glasgow[1].

[1] A recent instance of Hutcheson's enduring influence in Scotland may be
noted in the tribute to his memory by Prof. James Seth in his Inaugural
Lecture, Oct. 21, 1898, *The Scottish Contribution to Moral Philosophy*, pp. 7—17.

The permanence of such an ideal is a most remarkable testimony to Hutcheson's influence, which would, possibly, only have endured in the conservative atmosphere of a university—one could scarcely mention a single maxim in state-craft of the same date that remains a motive force in modern politics. This may in part be explained by the fact that, at this time, politics were governed, in a large degree, by the two Stuart rebellions (these nearly coinciding with Hutcheson's whole connection with Glasgow), which were unsuccessful; whereas Hutcheson's teaching was one element in a change—almost an academic revolution—which was so successful that antecedent conditions are of merely historical interest.

The power of this tradition of Hutcheson's methods naturally raises the question of the value of his educational aspirations; for it would appear that the Scottish universities are beginning to emerge from the influence of this ideal of last century. Owing to the empiricism of universities even yet, it is exceedingly difficult to give any definite answer. Is the ideal of a university to turn out morally good men, or intellectually strong men or is one a consequence of the other? Hutcheson's whole life was an eloquent defence of the first alternative, and, if modern higher education is to contain any didactic elements, these find a place most readily in the teaching of Moral Philosophy. Upon the other hand, it must be remembered, that since Hutcheson's day Modern Philosophy has been practically reborn, and that the limited time at the Professor's disposal, as well as the more minute analysis and greater technicality of the more important systems, practically force the teacher to recognize, that entering upon didactic details is liable to involve a certain superficiality of treatment, and that, if "the heart is cultivated," the head is likely to suffer. It will be seen, too, in the sequel that Hutcheson had certain ecclesiastical ends in view, and this throws some light upon the difficulty. In that complete university of the future, which, as yet, remains for the contemplation of the wise, in the heavens, teaching such as Hutcheson's would find its fittest place as an adjunct to the Theological School or College, where its eloquence and earnestness would be both of moral and educational value, while the

more scientific exposition of the subject would be the proper
care of the Arts Chair. At the same time, whatever may be
the opinion formed upon methods of teaching Moral Philosophy,
there can be little doubt that it is to Hutcheson's, and the
general acceptance of it, under different modifications, as
applied to different subjects, that Scotland owes the peculiar
clearness and finish of the generality of the university lectures,
which distinguish them from the professorial or tutorial teaching of other universities; and it was thus peculiarly appropriate
that Hutcheson's arrival at Glasgow almost coincided with the
conversion of the "regents" into professors, for it was the
standard he set as a lecturer, that made the paper change a
really effective one.

Quite apart from Hutcheson's activity in the class-room
was another and even more important side of his work in the
university or rather in the College. Complaints had often
been made of the aloofness of the Professors[1]. Hutcheson
immediately set himself to remedy this. "He did not confine
himself to the pupils immediately under his care, but laid
himself out to be useful to the students of all the different
faculties, whenever any opportunity offered: and he was especially solicitous to be serviceable to the students of Divinity,
endeavouring, among other important instructions, to give them
just notions of the main design of preaching[2]." Not only did
he take an active interest in the students, but he met them
outside the class-room in a friendly spirit. His kindness of
heart and freedom from false pride is shown by an anecdote of
Carlyle, who was a student of Divinity in 1743–4. "Not long
afterwards," he writes, "I had certain proof of the candour and
gentleness of this eminent Professor; for, when I had delivered
a discourse in the Divinity Hall, it happened to please the
Professor (Leechman) so much that Hutcheson wished to see it.
When he read it he returned it with unqualified applause,
though it contained some things which a jealous mind might
have interpreted as an attack upon his favourite doctrine of a

---

[1] A Short Account of the late Treatment of the Students of the University of
Glasgow, Dublin, 1722.

[2] Leechman's Life of Hutcheson, p. xxxviii.

moral sense[1]." It was not only by advice and conversation that
he aided students, but also, having since his father's death a
considerable private income, by more material help; to some
students who needed it, he gave money delicately, and admitted many others to his classes without requiring the usual
fees[2].

One can readily understand that he had a warm corner in
his heart for students who had come like himself from Ireland,
especially as some of these were relatives of his friends.   These
Irish students, so far from home—as far in time, then, as the
American student in Europe is now—were subject to many
temptations. A moderator of the Synod of Ulster and graduate
of Glasgow University sums up their position as follows : "They
are left with little check or controul over them; they seldom
brought letters of introduction; they had no acquaintance, and
they kept almost entirely to themselves; even, in the Divinity
Hall, they generally sat, in a back place, by themselves, and
formed little acquaintance with the other students. Besides
what they did there was unknown to their parents and guar-
dians here; and, from what I have heard, I have no doubt that
many of them fall into practices very dangerous to them[3]."
Many of the Professors used to dread the high spirits of the
Irish students, who, less under restraint than the rest, seemed
to have endeavoured to shock the sober people of Glasgow.
Reid always spoke of them as "the wild Irish teagues." Hutcheson himself complains that "our countrymen very generally
have such an affectation of being men and gentlemen immediately and of despising everything in Scotland, that they
neglect a great deal of good, wise instruction they might have
here. I am truly mortified with a vanity and foppery prevailing among our countrymen, beyond what I see in others; and a
sauntering forsooth which makes them incapable of any hearty
drudgery at books. We have five or six young gentlemen,
from Edinburgh, men of fortune and fine genius, at my class,
and studying law. Our Irishmen thought them poor book-

[1] Carlyle's *Autobiography*, p. 101.
[2] Leechman's *Life of Hutcheson*, p. xxvi.
[3] *Christian Moderator*, II. p. 264.

worms; and indeed they dreaded contracting acquaintance with Blackwood[1] and Haliday[2] in particular."

Hutcheson acted as banker, friend and guardian to all these youths, encouraging one or admonishing another. His letters to his former colleague, Thomas Drennan, who was now settled in Belfast as assistant to the Rev. S. Haliday, show his earnest care of the young men, besides throwing interesting side-lights upon the student-life of the time. The following may be taken as an instance of his difficulties as the students' banker.

"GLASGOW,
January 31, 1737.

"DEAR THOM,

Yours of the 20th instant surprised me much. Mr Arbucle sent over in December a letter to John Stark giving credit to Mr Williamson for £40. The boy brought it to me, I went with him to John Stark, and having to pay masters for the whole Session, a gown, books, a quarter's lodging, he took the value of £20 Irish, viz. £17. 18s. 9d. This he employed me to pay out for him and give him as he needed, and, before me, drew a bill for £20 Irish on Mr Arbucle, which he gave to John Stark. The boy received no more money from any mortal but from me and has drawn for no more than the said £20 Irish. Stark died about eight days after this payment, his executors showed me his letter-book ; and besides, in consequence of Mr Arbucle's letter, Mr Hartson should pay Mr Arbucle only for what Mr Williamson draws and not any draughts on John Stark . . . . I fancy you need not let Mr Hartson be in any trouble, in this matter, I will advance Mr Williamson what he shall further need and draw on Mr Hartson in favour of Brother Robin at as low exchange as anyone here. I happen to want to remit, which is very seldom the case with me.

Pray let Mr Duchal know that I am concerned that Mr Shane has not returned this Session, that I lent him, in May last, two guineas and have not heard anything about him since."

There is a touch of unconscious humour in the last sentence, which shows that even the eighteenth century Professor had made acquaintance with the proverbial shyness of the debtor.

---

[1] Sir John Blackwood of Ballyleady, Co. Down.
[2] A son of Haliday, a non-subscribing minister in Belfast, who had been senior colleague of Drennan, Hutcheson's assistant in Dublin, to whom this letter is written.

Sometimes students, specially recommended, ill repaid Hutcheson's care of them. A little later he writes:

"You recommended to me, one James Stuart, from Dublin College. I wish he had continued there. I am cautious of hurting a lad's character, but I much fear, he has had some bad influence, to lead some people you wish very well to, into idleness and drinking.

We almost constantly suffer by such as come from Dublin College. I never desire to see one of them. He is straitened for money, has not paid his lodging yet, and I am sure 'tis not from any high payments made to masters.

I wish their friends would employ some merchant in town to pay honest fair amounts for them and give them what they are allowed for pocket-money.

There is such suspicion of his conduct here, that I believe it will be insisted upon by severals of the Professours that he bring certificates of his regular deportment in Dublin College, attested to be genuine by some hand we know. If you are concerned about him you can get me a certificate from one or two of the Fellows of his good behaviour. Jack Smith[1] meets them often and his attesting the genuineness of the certificate will do. Without this I cannot agree to his getting a degree. We have been hurt by such steps formerly.

I would not have you divulge my bad impression of him but to such friends as could either influence him to better conduct here and pay his debts or remove him in time."

From a subsequent letter it appears that the student's friends employed Hutcheson to find out his debts and pay them.

Soon after the death of Haliday (Drennan's colleague) his son Robert Haliday, who was a student at Glasgow, gave Hutcheson considerable anxiety. Owing to Drennan's connection with the family Hutcheson's letters to him record in detail his struggle with an impetuous young man, and the final success that rewarded his tactful labours. As this was in all probability only one of many similar missionary efforts, the account of it is worth recording as a hidden side of his character.

"GLASGOW,
                                                    June 1, 1741.

"DEAR THOM,
            ... I must next write you about an affair that gives me a great deal of trouble. Bob Haliday is not in a right way as to his conduct.

[1] Hutcheson's publisher in Dublin.

I gave him several of the strongest admonitions I could, I had many fine promises, I confined him in his expenses, he seemed to take all well and to promise diligence.   All seemed to me tolerable, till of late, that I find he has run in debt with comerads, and for some trifles in shops ; and is quite idling away his time.   Nay, what is worse, I fear, he is hurting others.

The boy has a good genius, but that is the poorest satisfaction, to me, about anyone I wish well to.   He is conceity, thinks himself a wit and scorns advice from Gabriel Cornwall or Mr McMeehan, and trifles away money and time for nothing.

I know not how to write to Mrs Haliday, but, as matters appear to me, at present, there is little hope of his succeeding in any learned Profession, and, consequently, he can have no business here.   Cornwall and Mr McMeehan dread him about their pupils, and both set upon me to send him home as soon as possible.   I am distressed about Mrs Haliday, whom I used to encourage with the best accounts of things.   I would not send him home suddenly, till she were in some way prepared for it, and must beg it of you to begin the matter, and prepare her to receive him.

If any friends were for giving him a further trial, as to study, they should send him, without my knowledge, about £10 to pay off concealed debts. . . .

I have mortified Haliday very heartily last night.   His spirits will perhaps be up today or tomorrow. . . .

You must not show this to Mrs Haliday, but let her know that I wrote you, that I cannot get him to be tolerably diligent, or cautious in his expenses.

Pray write Bob Haliday as soon as you receive this, and don't fail to write me, upon chatting with Mrs Haliday.   Bob wants a companion.

I have said a great deal against the army, as the last [of] all good shifts, to men who have not interest in Shires or votes in Parliament.   But I fear nothing else will suit his turn of temper, unless he alters a good deal.   I shall be impatient to hear from you.

I am, dear Thom,

Your most obedient Friend and Comerad,

FRAN. HUTCHESON."

"GLASGOW,

June 15, 1741.

"DEAR THOM,

My last which was a most necessary step, would give you and poor Mrs Haliday so much pain that I am again impatient to write you. I find my discourse and some other engines I have employed about Bob Haliday have had such effects, as begin to give me better hopes, and some discreet folks, particularly McMeehan, who were most earnest for my sending him home are now encouraging me to let him stay.

I find he is heartily mortified, and has continued so, this fortnight, retired and studious and owning his faults.

The boy has a good genius and worth the taking care of, provided I could fall on the way to do it to purpose. You can scarce imagine how desolate we are in Glasgow, and how safe during the Summer. Pray let Mrs Haliday know this. I don't profess reconciliation yet, to him, but I cannot conceal my agreeable hopes from her. Pray write to Bob, now and then, in a very grave strain, exhorting him to caution and spiriting him to a generous ambition.

The wretched turn their minds take is to the silly manliness of taverns. Jack Blackwood was a bad sight this way to lads of smaller fortunes, tho' otherways of a fine temper. But this expense always leads to disingenuous shifts and to some other mischiefs. Satisfy poor Mrs Haliday. I hope all will go well."

"Glasgow,

April 12, 1742.

"Dear Thom,

     . . . My present occasion of writing is that you should deliver the enclosed to Mrs Haliday yourself and give her what advice you can about her son.

He has not yet got habits of vice in the sense of the world. But I fear he is conceited, pert and self-willed. I have often told him my mind very freely. He was in haste to be a man, and thought company in taverns mighty genteel and could rally the folly of bookish studious lads and saw too much of the vanity of the sciences. I write freely his faults that you may the better direct your conversation with him.

I am at a loss how he explains his accounts to Mrs Haliday, she allowed him £10 or £9. 5s. British, for any secret accounts. But I gave him, in the beginning of November, £3. 12s. to pay Anatomy lectures and some books, and two guineas, for the surgeon, whose shop he attended for the *Materia Medica*. But I found he applied the money to other purposes, as he had done two guineas I had given him the former year to pay for a class, and I had this to charge in the account again. This discouraged me about him : otherways I had entrusted him with his money this year. He has spent £120 these two Sessions, and there is not twenty of this for cloathes or books.

There's another point you must manage and discreetly as you can. About this time two years, I had given him four guineas, to give, as a compensation to a very worthy lad, one Whitley, who had assisted him all the preceding winter. He had offered it, as I hear, but at the same time made such intreaties and representations of his distress, how to clear some little debts, that Mr Whitley returned it to him, for that purpose. Whitley is a very worthy lad and indigent, 'tis quite wrong he should want it.

I cannot give Mrs Haliday the pain of writing this to her now, but you can take a proper season for it.

I have had a great deal of pain by Bob Haliday, and to little purpose. I believe he is at present confounded ; good company and advice may perhaps do him more good, now, than at another time. We all ow this to his worthy father, and all is not lost, that's in danger. My wife's and my most hearty respects to Mrs Drennan.

I am, dear Thom,
Yours most heartily,
FRAN. HUTCHESON."

It is satisfactory to learn from a letter dated Feb. 20, 1744, that Hutcheson at length believed that his anxiety in this case was lessened. He writes, " Pray tell Mrs Haliday her son is doing very well, that she should hear from me often did I not trust to Mr Brown's informing her."

It will have been seen from Hutcheson's efforts in this single instance that he was not merely a brilliant, enthusiastic lecturer, but the earnest and far-seeing friend of the student outside the class-room. Either side of his character would have won him the respect, which the Scotch student always yields unsparingly to his Professor, but both together made him venerated by the young men throughout the University. The ideal of life he showed them was such that " they panted to be what they beheld[1]." " He spread such an ardour of knowledge," Leechman says, " and such a spirit of enquiry everywhere around him, that the conversation of the students at their social walks and visits turned upon subjects of learning and taste, and contributed greatly to carry them forward in the most valuable pursuits[2]." When the impression he made was so powerful, it is little wonder that " students, advanced in years and knowledge," paid him the remarkable tribute of attending his lectures four, five or even six sessions[3]. Adam Smith, who attended his class in 1740, spoke of him as "the never to be forgotten Hutcheson." Dugald Stewart sums up the impression of his work in the following passage : " Those

---

[1] Leechman, *Life of Hutcheson*, p. xxxiii.

[2] *Ibid.*, p. xxxvii.

[3] *Ibid.*, p. xxxiii.

who have derived their knowledge of Dr Hutcheson solely from his publications may perhaps be inclined to dispute the propriety of the epithet 'eloquent,' when applied to any of his compositions; more particularly when applied to the *System of Moral Philosophy*, which was published after his death, as the substance of his lectures in the University of Glasgow. His talents, however, as a public speaker must have been of a far higher order than what he has displayed as a writer; all his pupils whom I have happened to meet with (some of them, certainly, very competent judges) having agreed exactly with each other in their accounts of the extraordinary impression which they made on the minds of his hearers. I have mentioned, in the text, Mr Smith as one of his warmest admirers; and to *his* name I shall take this opportunity of adding those of the late Earl of Selkirk, the late Lord President Miller, the late Dr Archibald Maclaine, the very learned and judicious trans-lator of *Mosheim's Ecclesiastical History*. My father[1], too, who had attended Dr Hutcheson's Lectures, never spoke of them without much sensibility ... His great and deserved fame in this country rests now chiefly on the traditionary history of his academical lectures, which appear to have contributed very powerfully to diffuse in Scotland that taste for analytical discussion and that spirit of liberal enquiry, to which the world is indebted for some of the most valuable productions of the eighteenth century[2]." Ramsay of Ochtertyre says that "long after his death I have heard orthodox useful ministers, who spoke of their old Professor with enthusiastic veneration[3]." A more powerful testimony than any of these occurs in a tract, written as late as 1772—thirty-six years after Hutcheson's death—expressly to discredit the methods of teach-ing at Glasgow. Amidst universal censure the writer is constrained to speak in high terms of "this illustrious teacher of morality, himself a perfect and ready master of Greek and Latin. He introduced or revived a high taste for Classical learning in this place, and, while he lived, he kept it alive. If

[1] Dr Matthew Stewart, Professor of Mathematics at Edinburgh.
[2] Smith's *Works*, Ed. Stewart, v. pp. 523—5, Note B.
[3] *Scotland and Scotsmen*, I. p. 276.

ever a Professor had the art of communicating knowledge and
of raising an esteem and desire of it in the minds of his
scholars; if ever one had the magical power to inspire the
noblest sentiments and to warm the hearts of youth with an
admiration and love of virtue; if ever one had the art to create
an esteem for Liberty and a contempt for tyranny and tyrants,
he was the man! What a pity was it, that, for three or four
months a year, such superior talents should have been thrown
away on metaphysical and fruitless disputations! When these
were got over, how delightful and edifying it was to hear
him[1]!"

Knowing that Hutcheson himself refused offers of Church
patronage it is a curious instance of the irony of history to find
an appreciation of his works exacted from candidates for
preferment. The circumstances are thus related in Burdy's
Life of the Rev. Philip Skelton. In 1749 Skelton paid a visit
"to a distant northern Bishop of great consequence, whose wife
was what you may call a learned woman, and had such influence
over her husband as often to dispose of the livings to her own
favourites; so that, as Mr Skelton remarked, the lady was a
sort of bishop herself. She was on this account courted by the
clergy, who humoured her in all her notions. She professed
herself an admirer of Hutcheson's system of Moral Philosophy
and the clergy consequently approved her taste . . . Having
lately got a new book by one of Hutcheson's disciples, she
ordered it to be put in the room where he (Skelton) slept . . .
In the morning an Archdeacon, by the lady's directions, came
to Skelton's room to sound him on the book . . . Skelton said
he would lay him a wager, that opening the book at any page
he pleased, he would show him nonsense in it. The Archdeacon
agreed, and, while he was reading the page, Skelton stopped
him now and then and said, ' That's nonsense.' ' Yes, it is,' he
owned, and thus he was forced to admit there was nonsense in
every page . . . The Bishop's lady, when she knew how con-
temptibly he spoke of the book . . . could hardly keep her
temper . . . Accordingly after dinner, before the Bishop and a
large company of clergy and others, she said to him, ' Mr

[1] *The Defects of an University Education,* London, 1772, p. 9.

Skelton, I heard you preached in St James's Chapel when you were in London.'—'Yes, Madam, I did.'—'Well, Sir, a lady friend of mine, who heard you, told me you preached very absurdly, talking of Hell's fire and such coarse subjects, as one never introduced in so polite a place.'"

CHAPTER V.

NEW LIGHT IN THE UNIVERSITY.

THOUGH some of the older or the reactionary Professors were suspicious of Hutcheson's methods, one or two of the more envious a little jealous of his influence over the students, yet the academic body, as a whole, was prepared to trust to his experience of the world and knowledge of business. Even amongst the students it was well known that Hutcheson had much to do with the finance of the College. Carlyle says that Dunlop, " with the aid of Hutcheson, directed and managed all the affairs of the University (for it is a wealthy corporation, and has much business), besides the charge of presiding over literature, and maintaining the discipline of the College[1]."

Evidently the Senatus did not believe in specialisation in matters of business, since Hutcheson, soon after his arrival, was a member of every Committee, upon all kinds of different affairs. Academic bodies at this time—not unlike other public boards, of much later date—seem to have found a Committee the universal panacea for all their ills, and hence they appointed one upon the most trivial occasions. Thus, in 1731, Hutcheson was delegated, with others, " to view Mr Rosse's[2] class-room, and to order the placing of the seats, in the most convenient order[3]." About the same time, it is of some interest to note, the Senatus " enacted and ordained that, after the ending of the present Session of the College, the least payment to be made to any of the Professors of Philosophy, Mathematics, Greek and Latin shall not be less than 30s. sterling: but it is

[1] *Autobiography*, p. 71.
[2] Andrew Rosse, Professor of Humanity (1706–1735).
[3] MS. Records of University of Glasgow.

hereby declared that this act shall not extend to any of the private Colleges given by the said Professors[1]."

At different times, Hutcheson was a member of the Library Committee, the Committee appointed to draw up a Library Catalogue, the Committee to inspect the College property and another to inspect the College lands. He was regularly included in any Committee to wait on Presbyteries, generally in reference to the appointment of a minister to a Professorship, when a Committee from the University prayed the Presbytery "to loose him from his charge." In 1740 he was one of a Committee to write to Lord Panmure to ask for a copy of the Chartulary of Glasgow Cathedral, and we find him later again on a Committee to consider the terms of Snell's Will, and here there is rather an interesting example of individuality, as, having enquired into the matter, and having learnt that an action was pending, he proposed that the case should not be prosecuted beyond one hearing in Chancery. He also was one of the keepers of the Charter Chest, and on all occasions when Simson, the regular clerk of the Senatus, was absent, he was appointed clerk *pro tempore.* As Quaestor from June 26, 1732 to 1734, he had the control of the small sum given in aid of the Library and also of some other funds. As there was no regular librarian at this date, the superintendence of the Library being divided between the Quaestor and one of the Bursars, this office must have made considerable inroads upon his scanty leisure during the Session. It was unfortunate that Loudon, the previous Quaestor, had ordered so many books at the auction of Le Clerc's Library at Amsterdam, that Hutcheson had no funds at his disposal during the first year he held the office. In the second Session he received Loudon's accounts calculated down to the fraction of a penny—one wonders how the item of "two pennies and three-fourths" arose—and it is rather surprising to notice that his additions include no modern works, though ancient Philosophy is fairly well represented[2].

Upon matters more in his own hands he expended most time, and left traces of his individuality. Archbishop Boulter of Armagh had given the University a sum of money through

---

[1] MS. Records of University of Glasgow.   [2] *Ibid.*

Hutcheson, which was received in April, 1733, and this was invested in lands at Provanside, which fact accounts for the exceedingly satisfactory return upon the capital yielded, at present, to the Armagh Bursars, this being the title under which the benefaction is now known. Hutcheson himself left £100 sterling in his will to be added to the fund[1].

In 1737 he was added to Dunlop and Morthland to deal with the Professors' houses, the "Glasgow Professors' Manses" as Mr Rae calls them. Dunlop and Morthland appear to have acted as contractors for the University and to have built six new houses. The project had been started in 1724 but it was not until 1737 that their accounts were ready to be audited. Hutcheson reported favourably and both Professors were thanked by the Senatus. Still the matter was far from being ended. In the first place there were two "old houses" which were not considered as desirable as the new ones. Then, as there were not enough houses to go round, a complicated scheme was devised whereby each Professor who had a "College house" made an annual payment to those who had not. Such payments were difficult to assess, owing to the fact that a debt had been incurred, upon which all the Professors, who had College houses, paid interest. Evidently here were numerous elements calculated to cause a considerable amount of friction. In 1739 Hutcheson proposed a plan to the Committee, which was calculated to make matters simpler. The debt was to be extinguished, and an annual value put upon the old and new houses respectively. This having been accepted by the Professors, it was a mere matter of arithmetic to calculate how much each Professor, who occupied a new house, owed to one who was content with an old one, and finally how much each class should pay to those who were too junior to have a residence of either kind. This decision seems to have given satisfaction; but the University householders, having agreed amongst themselves, had next to deal with the town authorities who promptly taxed the new houses at £10 per annum. The occupiers refused to pay, and the town adopted the very effectual old-fashioned method of "distress," by quartering soldiers upon

[1] Will of Francis Hutcheson.   Public Record Office, Dublin.

them. Then the University grew indignant and declared that "the imposing any stent or burden by the town of Glasgow on any of the members of the University, or houses possessed by them, is directly contrary to the privileges of the University" ... and they "do, therefore, order the agent to raise a process of declarator ... for the reduction of the said stent[1]."

It is little wonder, amongst these multifarious College duties, Hutcheson complains to his friend Drennan that he is "much hurried by many letters of business." Yet he found time to assist any deserving project that came under his notice. It is thus we find him giving advice and assistance towards the foundation of the publishing house of the brothers Foulis. Robert Foulis had attended Hutcheson's lectures and attracted his notice. Under the Professor's patronage he started business as a printer and bookseller in 1741, and, as a publisher, the following year[2]. Hutcheson watched the progress of the young firm with attention, and never tired of recommending its work. Thus we find him writing to Drennan:

"A worthy lad of this town, one Rob[t] Foulis, out of a true public spirit, undertook to reprint, for the populace, an old excellent book, *A Persuasive to Mutual Love and Charity*, wrote by White, Oliver Cromwell's Chaplain, it is a divine, old fashioned thing. Some are cast off, in better paper and sold at 9*d.*, in marble paper, the coarse ones are sold at 5*d.* in blue paper and at 4*d.* to booksellers. I wish your bookseller would commission a parcel of both sorts....The *Persuasive* is, in the old edition, an half-crown book."

Again, under date May 31st, 1742, he writes:

"The bearer Mr Hay takes over some copies of a new translation of Antoninus, the greater[3] half of which, and more, was my amusement last summer, for the sake of a singular worthy soul, one Foulis, but I don't let my name appear in it, nor indeed have I told it to any here, but the man concerned. I hope you'll like it, the rest was done by a very ingenious lad, one Moore[4]. Pray try your critical faculty, in finding out what parts I did

[1] MS. Records, Univ. Glasgow. In the next generation the same point arose in reference to the town dues demanded from Students upon the meal brought from home for their food during the session. *Life of Adam Smith*, by John Rae. London, 1895, p. 67.

[2] *Memorials of Literary History of Glasgow*, p. 12.

[3] The word "first" erased and "greater" written over it. From a note in Foulis's catalogue of books, it appears that Moore translated the first two books and Hutcheson the remainder, *infra*, p. 144.

[4] Moore succeeded Dunlop as Professor of Greek, *infra*, p. 95.

and what he did. I did not translate books in a suite, but, I, one or two, and, he, one or two. I hope if you like it, it may sell pretty well, with you, about Belfast. I am sure it is doing a public good to diffuse the sentiments, and, if you knew Foulis, you would think he well deserved all encouragement."

It was probably owing to Hutcheson's influence that Foulis was appointed University Printer in March 1743, the following being the minute of appointment :—

"Robert Foulis, having this day given in a petition to the University that he had provided himself with fine types, both Greek and Latin, and desiring that he may be made University Printer, the Meeting, having seen specimens of his printing, and found it such as he deserves very well to be encouraged, did choose the said Robert Foulis into the office of University Printer and grant unto him all the privileges belonging thereto, upon this condition, viz. that he shall not use the designation of University Printer, without allowance from the University Meeting, in any books, excepting those of ancient authors[1]."

The subsequent history of this celebrated firm "whose Homers and Horaces more than rivalled the Elzevirs and Etiennes of the past," falls outside the limits of Hutcheson's life; but one can see that the two brothers never forgot their early benefactor, to whom they owed the first impulse that had started them on the road to fame. As long as the business continued, they printed all Hutcheson's works, and even collected his occasional papers, and earlier books of which frequent editions were issued.

Besides these public engagements, there was a distinct and very different undercurrent in Hutcheson's relation to the University and his colleagues. Like most reformers, he was in a minority; though unlike many, it was not a minority of one, for he had the support of Dunlop—"old Dunlop," as he affectionately calls him, "the greatest hero I have known, who, under two most formidable growing distempers, keeps his heart and teaches with great reputation and spirit[2]"; Simson, whom with equal enthusiasm he calls "the best geometer in the world[3]," and he could occasionally count upon the support of Hamilton the eccentric Professor of Anatomy, and Rosse, who

---

[1] MS. Records, Univ. of Glasgow.

[2] Letter to Drennan. Undated owing to a money order having been written at the top and cut off—but from the context evidently written Sept.—Nov., 1744.

[3] Ibid., Aug. 5, 1743.

held the Chair of Humanity. Almost all the others belonged to the Principal's party—Neil Campbell having succeeded John Sterling in 1728. This was the party of reaction. Hutcheson's first open rupture occurred in 1736 over a matter of favouritism. In 1724 Clothworthy O'Neil[1], a member of a distinguished Antrim family, had matriculated, but, being "too gay and expensive," left the University without taking a degree. Later on, when he had learnt the value of an academic title, he adopted a graceful and polished method of obtaining the missing distinction by purchase, through a donation of £20 to the University Library. The Senatus gravely carried out its part of the farce in the following terms:—"Clothworthy O'Neil, Esquire, at present High Sheriff of the County of Antrim, in the Kingdom of Ireland, having applied for the degree of M.A., the Faculty, considering that he had formerly studied Philosophy in this University, and that the Masters, whose scholar he was, give him a good testimony, and that he is one of the best families in Ireland, resolved to give him the Degree of Master of Arts and appoint a diploma to be expeded to him.

Mr Hutcheson desired it to be marked that he dissented[2]."

The grounds of Hutcheson's protest are to be found in a letter to Drennan showing the principle for which he contended. "I must now tell you a shamefull story of our College. My letter I wrote from Dublin stopped Clothworthy O'Neil's getting his degree upon his first application. He got some folks, in this country, who are tools of the Court, to recommend the matter to our Principal. He made a compliment of 20 guineas to the College Library, and the Principal watched an opportunity, when there was a thin meeting, but his tools all present, and carrying to give him a Degree in [Arts] and that, too, only an honorary one, and declared so in the Diploma, without any certifying to his learning or manners. My dissent is entered in the books and four more masters declined signing it."

Such a state of tension was doubtless considerably aggravated by the prosecution of Hutcheson, by the Presbytery of

---

[1] Amongst the Students who entered under Loudon in 1724 was Clothworthius O'Neil, filius natu secundus Joannis O'Neil de Shanes Castle in Comitatu de Antrim Hibernus. *Mun. Univ. Glas.*, III. p. 227.

[2] MS. Records, Univ. of Glasgow.

Glasgow, for "teaching to his students in contravention to the Westminster Confession the following two false and dangerous doctrines, first that the standard of moral goodness was the promotion of the happiness of others; and second that we could have a knowledge of good and evil, without, and prior to a knowledge of God." This trial of course excited the profoundest feeling among the students, and they actually made a formal appearance before the Presbytery and defended their hero both by word and writing[1]. Though Hutcheson spoke of this to Drennan as the "whimsical buffonery about his heresy," it taught him that there was war to the knife between the old and the new spirit; and from this time onwards he, in conjunction with Dunlop, prepared a counter plan of campaign, which was designed to give his party a majority, in course of time, upon the Senatus. A further element in the scheme was the carrying the war into the enemy's country by influencing the teaching of Theology. Whatever may have been the tactical merits of such aggressive operations, it must be admitted that Hutcheson was going beyond his own sphere of duties in interfering in the teaching of Theology. He claimed that the ministers had no right to influence his own work, and yet he himself adopts precisely the same attitude through his interference with the teaching of Divinity. "He laid himself out," his biographer says, "to be especially useful to students of Divinity," and even went so far as to give them hints on the preparation of sermons. This was a distinct and scarcely legitimate addition to the methodology of Moral Philosophy. Yet at the same time one can hardly judge these envenomed disputes by the canons of the present day. We may not be better—nor even more decorous—in wrangles over public affairs, but our *fin-de-siècle* egoism tells us that the matters of contention are more important, and better worth the fighting for—but will this be the judgment of history?

At least there is this excuse for Hutcheson, that he was thoroughly sincere, in his belief, that he was fighting for the future of the University—a contest which had two sides, the one of a public nature in the championing of the modern spirit

---

[1] *Life of Adam Smith*, by John Rae, p. 13.

of " unmuzzled Philosophy " and of culture generally—the other, of a personal nature, since, if his schemes ended in failure, it might have led to his own suspension. Whatever may be one's opinion as to the justice of Hutcheson's position, there can be little doubt of the consummate ability with which he and the veteran Dunlop took the field against their opponents. Nothing was hurried and every step was made sure before the next was attempted. Thus, the first election of a Professor after Hutcheson's arrival at Glasgow, though it happened to be the crucical one of Divinity which was vacant in 1740, passed without a sign, Hutcheson and Dunlop voting with the majority for Michael Potter as against McLaurin, the Glasgow minister already mentioned. Hutcheson in fact was one of the Committee who waited on the Presbytery of Dunblane and laid before it the fact of Potter's election[1]. Probably he and Dunlop had no candidate ready, though they had one in view in William Leechman, whom Dunlop " had always wished to get into the College[2]."

Leechman's connection with Hutcheson is of considerable interest, as throwing light upon the characters of both and showing how careful had been Hutcheson's proving of the man he supported afterwards as a colleague. Leechman was born in 1706, being twelve years younger than Hutcheson, and educated at the University of Edinburgh. In 1727 he became tutor to Mure of Caldwell, who afterwards became the friend of Hume and a Baron of the Exchequer in Scotland. Through the influence of the Caldwell family he was made minister of Beith in Ayrshire in 1736; and notwithstanding that the temperateness of his views was little likely to recommend him in the stormy days of the Secession, he was elected moderator of the Provincial Synod at Irvine in 1740[3] and preached the Synod Sermon on " the Temper, Character and Duty of a minister of the Gospel." The following undated letter may refer to the composition of this very sermon.

[1] MS. Records, Univ. of Glasgow.

[2] *Sermons by William Leechman*, edited by James Wodrow, London, 1789, p. 18, and Hutcheson's letter quoted below, p. 88, where he says Leechman "was the man I wished to be, in the first place, our Professor of Divinity."

[3] Leechman's *Sermons, ut supra*, pp. 1—16.

[? end of 1740 or beginning of 1741.]

"DEAR THOM,

The enclosed you're not obliged to me for. I was intreated by an old friend, who was to preach a synod sermon, to suggest him some materials, which I undertook, and, thinking of you, cast them into form, with some enlargements, but really, in great haste, while I was in a gentleman's house[1] in the country, and interrupted every half hour. They're not in method, have repetitions and things proper to this country only. My friend here used a good deal of it, in a better method and a diction more suited to this country, and made an admirable sermon ; but, tho' it were printed, few would ever dream he had seen the inclosed, tho' they read both, and you are only the third person who knows anything of the matter. If it proves of little use to you, I have got it franked for you, otherways it would have cost you too dear."

If the materials mentioned were used by Leechman, Hutcheson would probably have supplied the general headings and several remarks. The following passage in the sermon, for instance, whether actually written from Hutcheson's material or not, certainly recalls his general mode of thought and style ; it agrees too with what Leechman himself says of Hutcheson's teaching with regard to the composition of sermons, and is besides of interest as giving evidence of the tendency for which he was reproved by Witherspoon and others of the old school.

"After having studied the great principles of natural religion and morality, and learning the important truths of Christianity from an honest enquiry into divine revelation, it must be our next care to store our minds with a large treasure of the best moral and divine sentiments: these are the choice furniture of our souls ; and, from a plentiful store of them, we shall find we are both qualified and disposed to teach others in the most instructive and effective manner. The Holy Scriptures will furnish us with a rich variety of the purest and sublimest sentiments, moral and divine: and in other writers, ancient and modern, we shall find a great number more, or, at least the same greatly diversified and set in a thousand beautiful and striking lights. That our minds may be replenished with an abundant store and

[1] If the Sermon was intended for Leechman the gentleman's house may have been Mure of Caldwell, with whom Hutcheson was intimate.

delightful variety of such thoughts, sentiments and impressions
as the best of mankind have felt and described, concerning God,
Providence and Virtue, and everything relating to the great
interest of mankind, we must gather from all quarters: whether
the writers be Christian or Pagan, let us think it our duty to
borrow whatever is good and true, whatever bears the marks of
a heart smitten with the love of truth and virtue[1]." The
following sentences too seem to have a ring of Hutcheson.
"The heart is the seat of all the virtues[2]." "What appears
fair and beautiful to men in the theory, they are inclined to
believe must have possession of their hearts and a mighty
influence on their lives[3]." "The heart really and justly moved,
never fails to dictate a language plain and easy, full of natural
and continued vigour, which has in it nothing soft, nothing
languishing. All is nervous and strong, and does not so much
please the ear as still and ravish the soul. Further let it be
taken notice of, as a thing of the utmost importance, that
sincerity alone, and a real desire to interest and persuade, will
banish all affectation, either of sentiment or language[4]."

Leechman's next publication was a sermon "on Prayer,"
which Hutcheson calls "a noble one, by one of my Scotch
intimates who sees all as I do[5]." The first edition was sent to
Hume, who was then a young man, by Mure of Caldwell; and
it is interesting, though somewhat incongruous, when one
remembers Hume's later reputation for scepticism, to imagine
him gravely commenting upon this subject, at some length.
"'Tis a natural infirmity of men," he concludes, "to imagine that
their prayers have a direct influence; and this infirmity must
be extremely fostered and encouraged by the constant use of
prayer. Thus all wise men have excluded the use of images
and pictures in prayer, though they certainly enliven devotion;
because 'tis found by experience that with the vulgar these
visible representations draw too much towards them, and
become the only objects of devotion[6]."

[1] Leechman's *Sermons*, I. pp. 111—12.
[2] *Ibid.*, p. 115. [3] *Ibid.*, p. 145.
[4] *Ibid.*, p. 160. [5] Drennan Letters—June 15, 1741.
[6] *Life and Correspondence of David Hume* by John Hill Burton. Edinburgh,
1846, I. p. 164.

Soon after Leechman's marriage, which took place in 1743, he received a call from an important Belfast congregation—the vacancy having arisen through the death of Hutcheson's friend Dr Kilpatrick—which would have yielded him a better stipend[1]. The negotiations were conducted through Hutcheson, and his interest in the matter may be gathered from the following letters.

" GLASGOW,
August 5, 1743.

" DEAR THOM,

    I have had two letters of late from Mr Mussenden, one about five weeks ago, with an invitation to Mr Leechman to succeed Dr Kilpatrick. Leechman was then just upon his marriage. I concluded the matter quite impracticable and returned an answer to that purpose, and, upon conversing with Leechman, found I was not then mistaken.

He was lately very ill-treated by our judges, in a discretionary augmentation he applied for, which they could have given with full consent of parties. His wife [is] not so averse to removal as formerly.

Indeed, you never knew a better, sweeter man ; of excellent literature, and, except his air, and a little roughness of voice, the best preacher imaginable. You could not get a greater blessing among you of that kind.

As I have heard nothing from other hands, I want fuller information. Are the people hearty for Leechman, upon the character they hear ? Is there no other worthy man in the field ? Unless these points be cleared, he will take no steps. I remember one Millar, an assistant, pray is he to be continued, and no way afronted or neglected in this design ?

Leechman is well as he is and happy, tho' preaching to a pack of horse copers and smugglers of the rudest sort. He would do nothing hard or disagreeable to any worthy man and has no desire of change. But, if the field be clear, it would be *peccare in publica commoda*, not to force him out of that obscure hole, where he is so much lost[2]. Pray don't fail to write me fully next post.

He was the man I wished to be, in the first place, our Professor of Theology."

" GLASGOW,
September 20, 1743.

" REV. AND DEAR SIR,

    I had the favour of yours by Mr Blow, but could not return an answer by him, being much employed in promoting the affair you wrote

---

[1] Leechman's *Sermons*, p. 18.
[2] Beith, *supra*, p. 85.

about. I had also very urgent letters from Messrs Mains and Duchal to the same purpose. 'Tis very difficult to persuade a modest worthy man, who is tolerably settled, to adventure upon a new scene of affairs among strangers. I shall use my utmost endeavours to prevail upon him, as I have been doing for some time past. I am sorry I cannot give you great hopes of success ; but, I don't yet so despair as to quit solicitation, as he is exceedingly moved by the affection and generosity of that people.

My most humble and hearty respects to your brethren of your Presbytery, whom I shall always remember with the greatest esteem and affection.

I am, Sir,

Your most obedient and humble Servant,

FRANCIS HUTCHESON.

To the Rev. Mr John Henderson or Mr Thomas Drennan in Belfast."

" GLASGOW,

October 29, 1743.

"DEAR THOM[1],

I am very sorry to tell you [that] my utmost importunities had no effect [upon Mr] Leechman. His wife's[2] friends seemed to [incline to it, but it was] with such views as Mr Leechman [would have] never come into ; that is to make Belfast [a mere step], till they tryed for some time what [interest they] could make to remove him thence to Edinburgh. In that view Mr Leechman abhorred to go to such a kind generous people ; and his wife's friends, as well as his own, urged much, that he should not go with a view to setle in Belfast for life. For my own part, I would prefer Belfast to either Edinburgh or Glasgow, unless one had many sons, disposed to be scholars.

I am heartily sorry you're disappointed."

The *arrière pensée,* in the minds of Leechman's friends may have been an expected vacancy in the Chair of Divinity. At all events Potter died on Nov. 23, and Hutcheson writes, in the last week of the month—between four and five weeks later than the foregoing letter—saying,

" I have been these ten days in great hurry and perplexity, as I have for that time foreseen the death of our Professor, who died last Wednesday, and some of my colleagues join me in labouring for Leechman to succeed. We cannot be certain of the event, but have good hopes. If he succeeds, it will put a new face upon Theology in Scotland."

[1] The MS. of this letter is very imperfect. The words in brackets are supplied to give the general sense.

[2] His wife was "Mrs Bridget Balfour of the family Pilrig near Edinburgh." Leechman's *Sermons,* p. 17.

Here at last Hutcheson declares himself, and confesses to his friend the true object of the campaign—to liberalize theology or in his own forcible words "put a new face upon Theology in Scotland." Some idea of the keenness of the contest may be gathered from the following letter, written to Mure of Caldwell, which is unsigned but evidently Hutcheson's, from the style.

"GLASGOW,

November 23, 1743.

"DEAR SIR,

Our Professor died this morning. Beside the letters from Messrs Rosse to George (who I believe is fixed our friend already) could you not obtain a letter from the Duke [of Montrose], our Chancellor, to Charles Morthland [Professor of Oriental Languages]. You may represent Leechman as acceptable to the best of this society of his friends viz. Messrs Dunlop [Professor of Greek], Simson [Professor of Mathematics], Hamilton [Professor of Anatomy], Rosse [Professor of Humanity] and myself : nay Morthland pretends to be for him too : only Loudon [Professor of Logic] and Anderson [Professor of Church History], our standard of orthodoxy, oppose him ; but that, his Grace's letter to Morthland would not only fix him but perhaps Loudon and Forbes [Professor of Civil Law].

You may represent, what is abundantly known, that he is universally approved of for literature and eloquence[1], and, that Anderson, who is his chief opposer, made himself ridiculous to all men of sense by dangling after Whitefield and McCullogh. I want this to be known to Andrew Mitchel [Private Secretary to Marquis of Tweeddale] and Tweedale [Secretary of State for Scotland]; that, we are not without hope of carrying him, by some of the other side, which might be thought a disagreeable obligation, and [we] would far rather have him attached by this favour of his Grace. He can scarce scruple to write a letter to his old friend Morthland, to be communicated to Loudon and others, representing his good impressions of Mr Leechman, and zeal to oblige some friends of Mr Leechman's, who applied on his behalf, for his Grace's recommendation, that, so he may be carried by his Grace's friends. If you get Chs Rosse or other members to join with you, in this respect, so much the better.

I am perhaps too sanguine, but even Mr Dick is declaring for him, but you know his instability.

I am

Yours,

You know my hand.

[1] *Ante*, p. 88.

You might show this letter, if my name could do any thing, or tell the contents, only my name must not be mentioned in his Grace's letter to his friends here[1]."

The late Dr McCosh speaks of Hutcheson's "bringing influence of a very unscrupulous character (as I reckon it) to carry his point," and adds, that "it seems that the advocates of liberality could not tolerate that a man should be favourable to a revival of religion[2]." In this he altogether misapprehends Hutcheson's argument. If the right of a professor bringing influence of any kind to bear upon the election to a Professorship be admitted, Hutcheson's letter is forcible as an unanswerable *argumentum ad hominem.* Anderson posed as ultra-orthodox, and yet a little before he had taken a prominent part in such heterodoxy as "revival meetings"—plainly the cry of orthodoxy merely veiled the antagonism of the old spirit to the new.

Besides Leechman there were at first two other candidates, Craig and McLaurin, who had been defeated by Potter. The latter appears to have been a man of sterling character, of the old school, and though a contemporary compared his tracts to Butler's Sermons[3], he was, by his own admission, far from being a stylist, as he writes that the roughness of his "style is not so polite as to please the palates of some[4]."

Leechman's biographer thus relates the course of the contest. "The election was in the hands of the Faculty; that is, the Court of ordinary Professors, who, in some former important questions, had been accustomed to divide into two nearly equal parties. In the one party Mr Craig, then a minister in the city, had some who preferred him to all others, but he from modesty, friendship, and a regard to the interests of religion, refused to interfere at all; so that this party soon united in favour of Mr Leechman. The other party pitched upon Mr John Maclaurin, one of the ministers of Glasgow; a candidate, highly respectable for his learning and piety, and well qualified for the station, had he had *the same aptness to*

---

[1] *Caldwell Papers*, Part II. vol. I. p. 53.
[2] *Scottish Philosophy*, p. 65.
[3] Gillies, *Historical Collections*, Edinburgh, 1796.
[4] *Scotland and Scotsmen*, I. p. 272.

teach with his rival. The people of the city and neighbourhood interested themselves warmly in the fate of this election ; as it was indeed an event of no small consequence to the future education of their clergy. They befriended one or the other candidate according to their acquaintance with him, and their opinion of the conformity of his religious sentiments to their own. Mr Leechman had the good wishes of all the hearers of his friend Craig, who considered themselves as the people of taste and education ; and Mr Maclaurin the good wishes of a much larger body, even all the rest of the town[1]."

The election was held upon December 13th, less than three weeks after Potter's death, thus presenting a startling contrast to the leisurely proceedings in vogue at present. It is interesting to notice that Hutcheson's machinations against Morthland appear to have been successful as he did not vote for McLaurin. Even after this secession the reactionary party was strong, as Loudon, Anderson and Forbes followed the course Hutcheson had outlined in his letter, and they were supported by the "instable" Dick, Principal Campbell and Johnston (Professor of Medicine). This left the votes of the two parties exactly equal, and one needs little imagination to picture the excitement when Bogle, the Rector, gave his casting vote in favour of Leechman, who was accordingly declared duly elected, whereupon Anderson protested against the appointment being determined by the casting vote of the Rector, and Dunlop "counter protested[2]."

This was far from being the end of the matter, for when Hutcheson and Hamilton made a formal appearance before the Presbytery of Irvine and laid the appointment before it, Anderson also appeared on behalf of the minority and endeavoured to prove a controverted election. This plea broke down, and Leechman got as far as Glasgow, where the Presbytery refused to allow him to take the necessary formal steps prior to the commencement of his teaching. This forced him to appeal to the Synod against the action of the Presbytery and after some delay he was enabled to lecture by the end of the Session.

[1] Leechman's *Sermons, ut supra,* i. pp. 18—19.
[2] MS. Records, Glasgow University.

Even yet his troubles were far from being ended, as he had next to face a "process of heresy" founded upon certain expressions in his Sermon on Prayer[1]. All these proceedings Hutcheson seems to have viewed with a chastened joy—he had won a hard-fought battle, and the futile efforts of his adversaries to avoid the confession of defeat were not altogether displeasing. Thus he writes to Drennan, complaining of his being a bad correspondent, and to pique him into writing remarks as it were incidentally under date of Feb. 20, 1744: "I could tell you a good deal of news upon the unexpected election of a Professor of Divinity and the furious indignation of our zealots[2], but you deserve no news from anybody." Towards the end of the year he writes: "We have at last got a right Professor of Theology, the only thoroughly right one in Scotland. The numbers of young Divines are not half what they used to be, all over Scotland, and yet we have already more than I ever remember here." This testimony of Leechman's popularity is confirmed from other sources. Wodrow his biographer says that "the Divinity Hall at Glasgow was crowded in his time with a greater number of Scholars than any other in Scotland[3]." Carlyle, who attended the class during the Session 1743–4, mentions that "his judicious choice and arrangement of his matter formed the most instructive set of lectures on Theology that had, it was thought, ever been delivered in Scotland. It was, no doubt, owing to him and his friend and colleague, Mr Hutcheson, that a better taste and greater liberality of sentiment were introduced among the clergy in the western provinces of Scotland[4]." This led to the formation "of a new school in place of the former narrow and bigoted clergy[5] who had never ventured to range in their mind

---

[1] Leechman's *Sermons, ut supra*, p. 22.

[2] A term borrowed from Shaftesbury—it occurs frequently in *A Letter concerning Enthusiasm and the Essay on the Freedom of Wit and Humour.*

[3] Leechman's *Sermons*, i. p. 70.

[4] *Autobiography*, p. 68.

[5] The following anecdote shows there was some need for Hutcheson's campaign in favour of more culture amongst the clergy. "In a parish near Glasgow a candidate preached who had a very severe cold. Having forgot his handkerchief, he was obliged often, while breathing, to wipe his nose with his hand. The people fixed on him as a homely lad, that blew his nose on his *loof*." *Scotland and Scotsmen*, ii. p. 554.

beyond the bounds of strict orthodoxy. For though neither of these Professors taught any heresy, yet they opened and enlarged the minds of the students, which soon gave them a turn for free enquiry, the result of which was candour and liberality of sentiment[1]." It will thus be seen that the "putting of a new face upon Theology in Scotland" was soon started, and the effort was now made to send from the University "a polite and pious, a philosophical and useful clergy, who, without neglecting the common people, should strain every nerve to make the higher classes of men devout and exemplary ... It is allowed that the clergy under Leechman's auspices were inferior to none in the kingdom in elegant accomplishments. A number of them would have done credit to any church in the present times. If others of them who had shining talents took a worse turn and were little useful, the fault did not lie in their professor[2]." Such is the contemporary judgment upon the revolution in favour of culture amongst the clergy and a resulting liberality in the universities; and so far Hutcheson's campaign had been highly successful.

Evidently the feeling aroused by Leechman's "unexpected" election had greatly enraged the other party, which Hutcheson speaks of as the "zealots." It left the two parties exactly equal, since at the last trial of strength, Morthland had, to use a vulgarism, been "squared" by titled influence. Therefore so far there was no decisive victory, and the two factions gathered their forces for the final trial of strength, which took place eighteen months later in the summer of 1746. This contest must have been epoch-making in the history of the University, but, following so soon upon the other, contemporary comments upon it are few. It arose through Dunlop's resignation of the Chair of Greek, and one gains a faint idea of the sturdy old diplomat's tactics from the fact that his resignation was some time in doubt owing to certain curious stipulations he endeavoured to enforce about continuing to occupy his Professor's house[3]; probably this was a ruse to bring on the election at

[1] Carlyle's *Autobiography*, pp. 84—5.
[2] *Scotland and Scotsmen*, I. p. 283.
[3] *Lit. Memorials of Glasgow*, p. 128.

a favourable opportunity, at all events he no doubt timed his retirement to suit his friends. The Culture or New Light Party had a strong candidate in James Moor, who had joined with Hutcheson in the translation already mentioned, and who was now University Librarian.

Hutcheson fully realized the importance of the contest and writes to Drennan with considerable anxiety about this "most intricate business, upon which the very soul of this College depends, and all may be ruined by the want of one vote." The election took place upon June 27th, and, after an exceedingly close contest, Moor was elected. From this event may be dated the triumph of the new party, which culminated in Leechman's election as Principal in 1761, but it must have been a victory marred by sorrow, for Hutcheson only survived it by just six weeks, and his name must be added to the long list of those who have died in the hour of success. For him, as for others, after a long sojourn in a wilderness of strife, there remained only a Pisgah glimpse of the "Promised Land," for which he had toiled, but which he was doomed not to enjoy.

CHAPTER VI.

In the midst of the campaign in favour of freedom in the University, Hutcheson bore his part in the literary movements of the time. Although his works, written in Dublin, had appeared anonymously, he was well known as the author, and their success had shown that the "virtuosoship" of Shaftesbury had now to be reckoned with as a serious philosophical development; for under no other hypothesis can the fresh attention given to Shaftesbury's theories after the publication of Hutcheson's *Inquiry* be explained. It is impossible to decide how much of this movement is due to the vitality of Shaftesbury's work and how much to Hutcheson's restatement and systematisation of the theory—just as the resultant of two forces follows the direction of neither of them, or as one of two confluent rivers appears to absorb the other, so here, opponents and supporters, alike, find a point of contact with Shaftesbury, and single out his name either for criticism or praise. That this should be so, follows naturally from Hutcheson's identification of his own work with Shaftesbury's, even to the printing of the name of the latter upon the title-page of the early editions, which were the only ones, at this time, before the public. Yet, while there are no data for determining the respective spheres of influence, it is certain that a definite one belongs to Hutcheson, even though he is not mentioned by name. It is, therefore, not surprising that the two leading thinkers of the day—Butler and Berkeley both—not only mention Shaftesbury's theory, but, by a curious coincidence, return to it, by adding to works already published. It will be remembered that Hutcheson in his *Essay on the Passions* (which appeared in 1728) seemed inclined to count Butler as an adherent of the "Benevolent system of morals[1]," and it is probably to correct this misapprehension that Butler endeavours to show, in the Preface to the second Edition of his *Sermons*, published in 1729, that Benevolence (which he admits) is not a sufficient moral criterion, without enforcing upon ourselves the authority of "Conscience[2]," his argument being reducible to the contention that Shaftesbury postulates Optimism, and therefore "a sceptic not convinced of the happy tendency of virtue" would be under no moral obligation; whereas such Pessimism would, on his own system, "still leave men under the strictest moral obligations." In the second "Dissertation," published with the *Analogy* in 1737, he probably had Hutcheson before his mind, when he wrote that "some of great and distinguished merit have, I think, expressed themselves in a manner, which may occasion some danger, to careless readers, of imagining the whole of Virtue to consist in singly aiming, according to the best of their judgment, at promoting the happiness of mankind in the present state[3]"—against which he contends that the "extension" of the term virtue should be widened to contain the two remaining members of his trinity of human obligations, Justice and Veracity. For reasons that will appear, in their proper place, Hutcheson did not reply to this criticism.

With regard to Berkeley, it must be remembered that, during the five years of Hutcheson's popularity in Dublin, he had been absent in Derry and afterwards in America, suffering the sickness of hope deferred, in his missionary schemes. In 1732 *Alciphron or the Minute Philosopher* appeared, and the third Dialogue is an open attack upon Shaftesbury. Speaking of the Moral Sense, he writes, "Seized and rapt with this sublime idea, our Philosophers do infinitely despise and pity, whoever shall propose or accept any other motive to virtue."... Cri.: "The love, therefore, that you bear to Moral Beauty, and your passion for abstracted truth, will not suffer you to think with patience of those fraudulent impositions upon mankind,

---

[1] p. xix.   [2] pp. xvi, xvii.   [3] *Analogy*, (Oxford Edition) p. 325.

Providence, the Immortality of the Soul, and a future retri-
bution of rewards and punishments[1]." Later on, one finds that
Berkeley limits the perception of Beauty to the mere usefulness
of the beautiful object, and to this criticism, alone, Hutcheson
replied in the fourth edition of his *Inquiry*, published in 1738.
It is a curious effect of the exigencies of controversy upon
natural tastes, that Berkeley, in his anxiety for religion, de-
preciates Beauty, though his letters from Italy show an appreciation of Art, far beyond anything contained in Hutcheson's
writings, who rarely ventures beyond vague generalities, in
speaking of Music, Painting or Sculpture[2]. Upon Berkeley's
return from America, he found the Shaftesbury Philosophy
making progress rather than losing ground, and, in the *Theory
of Vision, Vindicated and Explained*, published in 1733, he uses
" a harshness equally unwonted and unwarranted[3]." There is
certainly a greater acerbity in the later remarks, which may
possibly be attributed to the importance given to Shaftesbury's
theory by Hutcheson's two early works. " There seems to be
a certain way of writing," he says, " whether good or bad, tinsel
or stirling, sense or nonsense, which, being suited to that size
of understanding, that qualifies its owners for the minute
Philosophy, both marvellously strike and dazzle these ingeneous
men, who are by this means conducted they know not how, and
they know not whither...All that is said of a vital principle of
order, harmony and proportion, all that is said of the natural
decorum and fitness of things, all that is said of taste and
enthusiasm may very well consist and be supported without a
grain even of natural religion, without any notion of Law or
Duty, any belief of a Lord or Judge or any religious sense of a
God—the contemplation of the mind upon the Ideas of Beauty
and Virtue, and order and fitness, being one thing, and a sense
of religion another. So long as we admit no principle of good
actions but natural affections...so long as we apprehend no
judgment, harbour no fears and cherish no hopes of a future
state, but laugh at all these with the author of the *Character-*

---

[1] § 3.   [2] *Vide infra*, Chapter IX.
[3] *Dissertation on the Progress of Ethical Philosophy*, by Sir James Mackintosh.
Edinburgh, 1836, p. 158.

istics, and those whom he esteems the liberal and polished part of mankind, how can we be said to be religious in any sense[1]? "

These attacks upon the Shaftesbury point of view called forth a counterblast, the author of which is true to Shaftesbury's application of ridicule, by affecting to defend Berkeley from the "scandalous imputation" of being the writer of *Alciphron,* and he points out Butler's indebtedness to the much maligned *Characteristics*[2].

The general tone of Berkeley's remarks, as well as the possible slighting reference to Hutcheson, in the phrase "ideas of Beauty and Virtue," which appears in the title of Hutcheson's first work, gives some slight negative evidence towards the solution of the biographical problem as to whether the two men had met at Dublin.   On the one hand it might be argued that both having a common friend in Synge, with whom they each corresponded, both having the *entrée* of the Vice-regal Court, and a common circle of friends and being the best known philosophical writers in Ireland, they would, in all probability, have met; and to all this must be added certain half unconscious traces of Berkeleyanism in Hutcheson's earlier works.   Yet on the other hand, had they met, it is difficult to see how two men of such high and similar ideals could have failed to appreciate each other: and the caustic criticism of some of Hutcheson's favourite philosophical beliefs by Berkeley is quite inconsistent with any such theory.   In the beginning of last century to impugn an opponent's religious beliefs was as unforgiveable as to accuse the modern member of Parliament of peculation of public moneys.   Therefore it may be concluded that the two had never been intimates, and the few echoes of Berkeley in Hutcheson may be explained as having filtered through Synge, or some other of Berkeley's friends amongst the Molesworth coterie.   In this unsatisfactory state the difficulty must rest, failing additional evidence, for the further

---

[1] Fraser's *Berkeley,* I. p. 373.
[2] *A Vindication of the Rev. D—— B——y from the scandalous imputation of being author of a late Book entitled Alciphron or the Minute Philosopher,* 1734.

question whether the two may have exchanged greetings at a *levée* is quite unimportant.

Another event of quite a different nature that added very much more to the popularity of Shaftesbury's ideas than the support of sympathizers, or the envenomed criticisms of opponents, was the publication of Pope's *Essay on Man* in 1733–4. Here may be noticed an example of a rule, of general application, in Modern Philosophy, that a system, to exercise a vital influence, is always aided by the picturesqueness and popularity of literary expression as such. It has indeed been said, and with considerable reason, that, when a philosophy has been popularized, it ceased to be strictly philosophy; but, at the same time, the literary expression of a philosophy is far from being a popular philosophy, in any bad sense,—rather, such literary expression is the natural complement of any system worthy of the name. For, if it is to be an intellectual power, it must, in the first place, have had its origin in a great national need, and in such cases the philosophical solution of necessity finds its expression in Literature, which crystallizes conclusions, quite apart from the systematic nexus of logical proof from which these conclusions have been logically deduced. Every man may be potentially a philosopher, but the point of view is different. Given the national need or the intellectual need, the professed thinker concentrates his attention on the process of proof; he requires some kind of "Dialectic moment"; whereas the plain man of Butler (whether "honest" or not) demands a picture of the system, brought into focus with his requirements, knowledge and other beliefs. This is not a matter of profundity, but rather of artistic insight; Pope himself, curiously enough, expresses this idea in a letter he wrote to Warburton thanking him for his defence of the *Essay on Man*, against Crousaz—"It is indeed the same system as mine, but illustrated with a ray of your own, as they say our natural body is the same still when it is glorified...You understand me as well as I do myself, but you express me better than I could express myself[1]."

It may perhaps be said that the *Essay on Man* is to be

[1] Pope's *Works*. Dublin, 1764, x. p. 283.

traced directly to the influence of Bolingbroke, who gave Pope the skeleton outlines, and who is eulogized as the poet's "guide, philosopher and friend." While there does not appear any reason to doubt that while Bolingbroke supplied the "first principles," his ideas were slightly modified to make them palatable to Pope, and this led at once to the suppression of some of Bolingbroke's naturalistic views and to a closer approximation to Shaftesbury[1]. Amongst others, Voltaire was quick to recognize how much Pope was indebted to the ideas of the *Characteristics*. He says "*L'Essay sur l'Homme* de Pope me paraît le plus beau poëme dedactique, le plus utile, le plus sublime qu'on ait jamais fait dans aucune langue. Il est vrai que le fond s'en trouve tout entier dans les *Caractéristiques* du lord Shaftesbury ; et je ne sais pourquoi M. Pope en fait uniquement honneur à M. de Bolingbroke sans dire un mot du célèbre Shaftesbury, élève de Locke[2]." Pope is especially close to Shaftesbury in his optimism, the idea of a system of the universe, of harmony and proportion, as he expresses it :

> "All nature is but Art, unknown to thee,
> All chance, direction, which thou canst not see ;
> All discord, harmony not understood ;
> All partial evil, universal good.
> And, spite of pride, in erring reason's spite,
> One truth is clear, Whatever is, is right."

At the same time, he faithfully follows Bolingbroke, and diverges from Shaftesbury (and still more from Hutcheson) in making Self-Love that

> "master passion in the breast,
> Like Aaron's serpent, swallow all the rest."

Plainly, here, there is no room left for Benevolence, which, absorbed in Self-Love, becomes merely

> "The scale to measure others' wants by thine."

Doubtless Hutcheson had such a train of thought before his mind, when he speaks of those who "plead that our most

---

[1] Cf. Johnson's *Life of Pope—Lives of the Poets*, II. p. 350. *Works of William Warburton.* London, 1811, vol. XII. p. 335.

[2] *Œuvres Complètes de Voltaire.* Paris, 1879, XXII. p. 178. He adds epigrammatically, in comparing Plato and Pope, that the former wrote as a poet in prose, the latter as a philosopher in verse.

generous affections are subordinate to private interest, by
means of *sympathy*, which makes the pleasures and pains, the
happiness or misery of others, the constant causes of pleasure
or pain in ourselves[1] "—a view which, of course, he criticizes.

Besides these important names that are landmarks in the
history of Philosophy, there are very many minor writers, whose
activity makes the interval between the publication of the
Essay on the Passions and Hutcheson's next work—that
is from 1728-1734-5—one of varied if not very profound
criticism. It would be difficult to select any other six or seven
years, during which so many works of a philosophical period
appeared, and there is probably no other instance of such a
rapid production of books being so speedily forgotten. Tindal's
Christianity as old as the Creation (1732) may be remembered
as having caused Butler's *Analogy*; Bishop Peter Browne, once
Provost of Trinity College, Dublin, as an ardent Jacobite,
who wrote pamphlets showing the folly of Irish Orangemen
"drinking to the memory of the dead" King William; as well
as the acute criticism of Locke in the *Procedure and Limits of
the Human Understanding* (1728, and 2nd edition, 1729) and
*Things Divine and Supernatural conceived by Analogy with
things Natural and Human* (1733). It may be mentioned, too,
that Dr Watts, the writer of certain well-known hymns, was
also a controversialist, having written *Philosophical Essays on
Various Subjects* (1733, 2nd edition, 1734) as well as his *Treatise
on Logic*. Besides these there were many, even less known
works, some arising out of the dregs of the Lockian controversy,
such as Samuel Colliber's *Free Thoughts concerning Souls* (1734),
Conyers Place's *Essay towards Vindication of the Visible
Creation* (1729) and Zachary Mayne's *Two Dissertations concerning Sense and the Imagination, with an Essay on Consciousness* (1727). Others continued the metaphysical side of the
controversy over Clarke's system, which somewhat resembles a
family feud, owing to the fact of so many of the combatants, on
both sides, bearing the same name. Edmund Law of St John's
College, Cambridge, afterwards Bishop of Carlisle, started the
dispute in his translation of Archbishop King's *De Origine*

---

[1] *System of Moral Philosophy*, I. p. 47.

Mali in 1731, which he afterwards followed by the *Inquiry into Space, Time, Immensity and Eternity* &c. (1734). Then a brother of Samuel Clarke—John Clarke, Dean of Sarum—replied, also strange to say, another John Clarke of Corpus Christi College, Cambridge. These defences were attacked by a Joseph Clarke, Fellow of Magdalene College, Cambridge, in one of those comprehensively named treatises, the title-page of which was also a table of contents—*Dr Clarke's Notions of Space Examined in Vindication of the Translator of Archbishop King's Origin of Evil—Being an Answer to two late Pamphlets, entitled, the one, " A Defence of Dr Clarke's Demonstration of the Being and Attributes of God," etc. Lond.* 1733, *and the other A Second Defence.* A further pamphlet was equally explicit, *A Farther Examination of Dr Clarke's notions of Space ; with some considerations on the possibility of eternal Creation, in reply to Mr John Clarke's Third Defence of Dr Samuel Clarke's Demonstrations....*London, 1734. It will be seen presently that the followers of Clarke were simultaneously defending themselves against Hutcheson's exposition of Shaftesbury, and this eventually became the more important discussion of the two.

To rightly understand the criticism of the period which is somewhat involved it is necessary to remember that it really resolves itself into a complicated " triangular duel." There were at least three distinct tendencies—the Shaftesbury-Hutcheson, Moral Sense and Benevolent theory, various theories of " egoistic hedonism," and finally the " rational moralists," and each of these was subject to the attacks of the other two—for instance Hutcheson's theory of a Moral Sense, approving of Benevolence, was attacked by the Rational Moralists as sensuous, and by the egoistic hedonists, because of its universalistic tendencies—for after all, with Hutcheson, Benevolence is sometimes not distinguishable from universalistic Hedonism. Mr Selby-Bigge says that " for the sentimentalist, therefore, it was ' a war with two fronts,' and, when he faces one enemy, he generally exposes his flank to the other[1],"—and, to continue the metaphor, one might add that every

---

[1] *British Moralists, being selections from Writers principally of the Eighteenth Century,* by L. A. Selby-Bigge. Oxford, 1897, i. p. xli.

advance must be made under a cross-fire. It is not altogether
uninteresting to notice Hutcheson entering upon this dangerous
"zone," where the first criticisms against him, in point of time,
and perhaps of importance, were made by John Balguy,
Vicar of Northallerton, who published a number of Treatises
between 1726[1] and 1733, in which latter year they were
collected. In his *Foundation of Moral Goodness*, the first
part being published in 1728, and the second the following
year, Balguy speaks as a follower of Clarke, and his criticisms
partly derive force from the general position of the "Rational-
ists," partly from the view he took of Hutcheson's exposition
of Shaftesbury. The following are his chief objections in the
First Part of the *Foundation of Moral Goodness*; (*a*) Virtue, as
founded upon "Instincts," is arbitrary[2], (*b*) If men had had no
natural affections towards Benevolence, and "notwithstanding
Intelligence, Reason and Liberty," there would have been no
such thing as Virtue. (*c*) Balguy's third criticism raises a more
interesting point, namely that Hutcheson's system would allow
some "degree of Morality" to the animal creation—this corollary,
though drawn by an opponent, is a partial anticipation or rather
a mention of the present-day sub-human morality[3]. These
criticisms will serve as a specimen of Balguy's work—they are
chiefly interesting historically, as showing the Pseudo-Platonism
of Shaftesbury and Hutcheson attacked by Platonic arguments.

The Second Part of the *Foundation of Moral Goodness* is
more important both to Balguy and Hutcheson. A defender of
Hutcheson is supposed to have sent Balguy objections to his
first part which he answers one by one. The question, as to
how moral distinctions are apprehended, having arisen, Balguy
explains his term "Moral Perception," which, he claims, can
give absolute "relations" (not merely relative ones, like a
sense), but he admits that Moral Perception is immediate and
passive[4]. This concession is of considerable importance in the

---

[1] *Letter to a Deist*—directed against Shaftesbury.

[2] *The Foundation of Moral Goodness or A Further Inquiry into the Original
of our Idea of Virtue.* Edition 4, 1734, pp. 46, 47. *British Moralists*, II. p. 61.

[3] Cf. Hutcheson's formula for his Benevolent Principle—"The greatest
Happiness of the *sensitive* system," *infra*, Ch. XIV.

[4] Balguy's *Tracts*, 151—157.

growth of Hutcheson's system, and in his next work he will be found speaking of Moral Perception as an alternative to the Moral Sense with which he started.

In the *Second Letter to a Deist* (1731) perhaps the most striking part relating to Hutcheson, is the defence of the Sublimity of Christianity[1].

The tract *Divine Rectitude* performs the same function of criticism towards Hutcheson's Æsthetics, that the *Foundation of Moral Goodness* did to his Ethics. Balguy here contends that Hutcheson's "Uniformity amidst Variety" consists of "real relations," and that relations can only be perceived by the Understanding; therefore he concludes "there is an intellectual perception of Beauty as well as the sensation of pleasure[2]." This, like many other doctrines of the time, has a suggestion of Hamilton's Perception proper and Sensation proper. The rational point of view in this pamphlet found an answer in another, entitled *Divine Benevolence*, and there was also a third, published in 1734, under the title *Wisdom the First Spring of Action in the Deity,* both of which show traces of Shaftesbury's influence, and the second of which was answered by Balguy, in his *Supplement to the Law of Truth* (1734).

The slight approximation between the Rational Moralists (as represented by Balguy) and Hutcheson, has already been noticed. This was further accentuated in Balguy's *Sermons,* published at a later date, where he claims for the "supreme faculty" of Reason or Intelligence, "the apprehension of moral relations, the discernment of Right and Wrong, Good and Evil. Again, hence it is that we can turn our thoughts back upon themselves, and clearly perceive the powers and operations of our own minds[3]," that is, "intellectual perception" becomes the equivalent of Locke's reflection, and this again is Hutcheson's later Internal Sense, and the sole question that remains in dispute is its "subjectivity."

While Hutcheson drops some of the Hedonism with which he had started in his *rapprochement* to the followers of Clarke,

[1] Balguy's *Tracts*, p. 293.

[2] *Ibid.*, pp. 226—232. Cf. passages cited from Hutcheson, *infra*, pp. 216—7, 222.   [3] Balguy's *Sermons*, I. 361.

he is the more exposed to the criticisms of his other opponents, for his "benevolence" has now become less hedonistic, and he is gradually feeling his way to an approach to Butler's supremacy of Conscience, in so far as he has an uncertain tendency to give the highest place in the mental hierarchy to something other than feeling: this tendency was accentuated by the attacks of his hedonistic critics.

One of the first hedonistic criticisms appeared under the title of Ἀρετὴ Λογία early in 1728[1]. The authorship of this work, which is of considerable length, is of some interest. It was really written by Archibald Campbell, Professor of Ecclesiastical History at St Andrews, but the first edition of 1728 appeared under the name of Alexander Innes, who had only contributed the prefatory Introduction (in which he says Hutcheson is all soul and Mandeville all body[2]) and some marginal notes, which Campbell described as blunders showing a "shameful ignorance of the meaning of the text[3]." The second edition almost rivals Cudworth's work, in its wealth of classical quotation, and it contains a considerable number of additions. In it, Campbell complains somewhat bitterly of the reception given to his work, after he had owned it, by some who boldly affirmed that it was "that hellish system of immorality, which the fallen angels and ungodly men are governed by[4]." Such forcible expressions lead the reader to expect some pungent writing, and he is not disappointed. Campbell complains that Hutcheson was "so much out of temper," as to brand hedonists as followers of Epicurus. "I do not indeed complain," he says, "of scurrilous treatment or any personal reflections against those whom he makes to differ from him... But to what purpose does this learned gentleman go about to

---

[1] Ἀρετὴ Λογία or an Enquiry into the Original of Moral Virtue &c., by Alexander Innes. Westminster, 1728.

[2] Ibid., p. xxxix.

[3] An Enquiry into the Original of Moral Virtue, wherein it is shewn (against the author of the Fable of the Bees, &c.) that Virtue is found in the Nature of things. ...With some reflections on a late book, intitled, an Enquiry into the Original of our Ideas of Beauty and Virtue, by Archibald Campbell. Edinburgh, 1733, p. xxxii.

[4] Ibid., p. vi.

brand us with this odious character? I am only sorry he would have the world to think of us, that we are no better than the disciples of Epicurus[1]." To which censure of Hutcheson's, he provides an *argumentum ad hominem* by virtually accusing him of " snobishness," with a considerable amount of sarcasm about " polite Virtue" and its relation to the "*beau monde* and the fashionable part of the world[2]." After several similar personalities, there is a certain humorous naïveté in his remark, " I would fain think I have said nothing in the course of my argument that does not sute [sic] with justice and honour... But if any one will be pleased to point me out any thing I have said any where unhandsom and ungentlemanny [sic], I do here promise, if my book comes to another impression, to take care to have it rectify'd[3]." After these preliminary skirmishes, he comes to the direct attack and endeavours to show that Hutcheson's Benevolence is merely Self-Love disguised, and that the Moral Sense is a mere instinct. Lest the pleasures which form the basis of Self-Love should be held to be similar irrational quantities, he is careful to show a means of estimating their values, and this is worthy of note as one of the earliest, if not-the first explicit attempts at a " hedonistic calculus." First of all, pleasures are to be reckoned in respect of value, as positive, pains as negative quantities. There are three elements to be considered: Degree, Duration and Consequents, i.e. " the degrees of pleasure or pain in the consequent perceptions." From these data, we reach the formula of the calculus—to multiply Degrees into Duration and add (or subtract) the Consequents[4].

---

[1] *Ibid.*, p. xiii.

[2] *Ibid.*, p. 325, Ed. 1, p. 231.   [3] *Ibid.*, p. xviii.

[4] *Ibid.*, p. 275, Ed. 1, p. 197.

The following is an example of the Calculus in operation: A and B are two possible pleasures—

A has degrees	15 pleasure
,, duration	20 hrs.
B ,, degrees	12 pleasure
,, duration	60 hrs.
consequent	20 hrs.
	6 degrees *pain*,

therefore $A : B :: (20 \times 15) = 300 : [(12 \times 60) = 720 - (6 \times 20) = 120] = 600$

or $A : B :: 300 : 600.$

At the risk of a brief digression it may be worth mentioning, that a work written less than twenty years afterwards, named *An Enquiry into the Origin of the Human Appetites and Affections, showing how each arises from Association, with an Account of the Entrance of Moral Evil into the World : Written for the use of the Young Gentlemen at the Universities* [of Oxford and Cambridge], Lincoln, 1747[1], has a somewhat similar calculus, rejecting however the "consequents" of Campbell. "All pleasure is relative to the faculty perceiving it and is in compound ratio of its intenseness and duration. Hence, in equal degrees of intenseness, the pleasure is as the duration; and in equal durations as the intenseness. Consequently, when the intenseness of one pleasure is to the intenseness of another, as the duration of *this* is to the duration of that, the pleasures, strictly speaking, are equal, and it is perfectly indifferent whether of them be chosen, provided man's existence is commensurate to each, and the enjoyment of neither of them incompatible with the enjoyment of others. Whence we see that an infinitely small pleasure may be preferable to an infinitely great one, provided the duration of the former surpasses the duration of the latter in a greater ratio than the intenseness of the one exceeds the intenseness of the other[2]." The author of this important work has not been discovered, but it seems probable that the tract may be attributed to John Gay of Sidney Sussex College, Cambridge, whose *Dissertation concerning the Fundamental Principle of Virtue or Morality*, had been published in 1731 as a prefix to Edmund Law's Translation of King's *De Origine Mali*. In the *Dissertation* Gay accuses Hutcheson of "rather cutting the knot of difficulty (connected with the approval of Virtue) than untying it," by a Moral Sense that verges closely on the heresies of occult qualities, Innate Ideas and instincts[3]. Further he argues that a Moral Sense is unnecessary since "our approbation of Morality and all affections whatsoever, are finally resolved

[1] *Metaphysical Tracts by English Philosophers of the Eighteenth Century.* Prepared for the Press by the late Rev. Samuel Parr, D.D.   London, 1847.
[2] *Ibid.*, p. 168.
[3] *Dissertation—British Moralists, ut supra,* II. 270.

into reason pointing out private happiness...and that, whenever this end is not perceived, they are to be accounted for by Association of Ideas[1]." This sentence is the text for the later work which, long before Hartley wrote, lays down the main principles of Associationalist Psychology; and it may be noted in passing that the author, whether Gay or some unknown writer, is in advance of similar British work, done towards the end of the century, in explicitly laying down the principle of "indissoluble associations," which he speaks of as an "inseparable union" of ideas, and also in anticipating, in almost identical terms, Hamilton's theory of latent mental modifications, which he calls "dormant latent impressions[2]." Hutcheson's works, as will be seen, were written too early to enable him to make any use either of Hume's *custom* or the theory of Association of the Author of the *Enquiry into the Origin of the Human Appetites and Affections*, &c., but it may have been Gay's early work that he had in his mind, when he admitted somewhat inconsistently the influence of Association "to represent certain actions as good, others as evil[3]."

Besides the critics already mentioned, the same fruitful period produced Thomas Johnston's *Essay on Moral Obligation*, 1731, Philip Glover's *Discourse Concerning Virtue*, &c., 1732, and Joseph Foster's *Two Essays: The one on the Origin of Evil; the other on the Foundation of Morality*, 1734. More important than these is the work of yet another John Clarke, who was Master of the Grammar School at Hull, and who had already published several works dealing with Latin texts, and in 1725, *An Examination of the Notion of Moral Good and Evil, advanced in a late book entitled The Religion of Nature Delineated.* Between 1725 and 1728[4], he published *The Foundation of*

[1] *Ibid.*

[2] Dr Parr's *Tracts, ut supra*; *Enquiry, &c.*, pp. 68, 73.

[3] Hutcheson's *System, ut supra*, I. p. 30.

[4] This book was published at York without any date on the title-page. Mr Selby-Bigge consequently dates it 1730 (*British Moralists*, II. 387), but Hutcheson in the *Essay on the Passions* (1728), in defending his system against egoistic criticism, gives as his reference "see Mr Clarke of Hull, his remarks on Treatise 2," i.e. Second Treatise in the *Inquiry* (*Essay on Passions*, p. 14), therefore Clarke's book must have appeared before the *Essay on the Passions*, and after the *Inquiry*, i.e. between 1725 and 1728.

Morality in Theory and Practice considered in an Examination of Dr Samuel Clarke's opinion concerning the Original of Moral Obligation: as also the notion of Virtue advanced in a late book entitled an Enquiry concerning our Ideas of Beauty and Virtue, in which he criticizes Hutcheson's views on Benevolence, from the stand-point of the "Selfish School." "The love of a Benefactor," he writes, "does as certainly arise from Self-Love as the Love of Oysters[1]." Clarke's criticism has at least one point of individuality, namely his admission of Hutcheson's Moral Sense, for purposes of Egoistic Hedonism. He endeavours to show that it cannot approve of Benevolence to the exclusion of other affections, since Benevolence is at bottom "Self-Love," but yet after depriving the Moral Sense of the function Hutcheson had given it, he does not dismiss it as a useless mental supernumerary; on the contrary, "the main use of the Moral Sense and the principal Intention of Nature therein seems to be to put the mind of man upon the hunt, to see if such actions as appear at first sight beautiful, may not be attended with greater pleasures than the first view presents[2]." Another writer, John Brown, whose *Essays on the Characteristics* appeared later[3], may be mentioned here as evidencing the same general line of criticism as Clarke. He is rather original in twitting Hutcheson with speaking metaphorically of the beauty of Virtue, as if he had been describing the charms of some "sovereign fair," of whom he was enamoured, and therefore accusing his opponents of "either wanting eyes or common discernment, in not at first sight falling in love with this matchless lady[4]."

Contemporaneously with these various attacks, the Shaftesbury-Hutcheson Philosophy received a considerable amount of support. Besides Pope, whose *Essay on Man* has been mentioned above, the polite world gave its adhesion, but this was not productive of literary expression. The great contributors to Philosophy at the time, Bishops, Deans and other clergymen,

---

[1] *British Moralists, ut supra,* II. p. 233.
[2] *Ibid.,* p. 242.
[3] The Second Edition appeared in 1751.
[4] p. 162.

for conscientious or professional reasons, were opposed to it, and
so its supporters are to be found amongst the free-lances of
controversy, men like Thomas Chubb, the glover of Sarum,
who were free to write as they pleased.   It is curious that
of all the writers of the day, Chubb is perhaps the most modern
in his terminology, but, at the same time, he is far from being
one of the most consistent of the group.   The following are his
chief ethical tracts : *A Discourse concerning Reason*, &c., 1731 ;
The Sufficiency of Reason farther considered, 1731 ; *Some
Reflections upon the Comparative Excellence of Moral and
Positive Duties*, 1731; *A Vindication of God's Moral Character*[1] ;
in the last of which one notes the influence of Hutcheson in
the prominent position he gives to the Beauty of the Divine
Character[2].   In 1730 he published two volumes containing
thirty-five tracts or pamphlets ; the most important of which
are *Some Short Reflections on Virtue and Happiness, wherein
it is shewn...that Virtue is solely founded on Benevolence*, &c.,
and *Further Short Reflections...wherein it is shewn what kind
of Virtue is in Reason rewardable*, &c.[3]   Though it was not till
1745, that *The Ground and Foundation of Morality considered :
wherein it is shewn that disinterested Benevolence is a proper and
a worthy Principle for Intelligent Beings*, &c. &c.[4], was published,
this tract also may be mentioned for the sake of completeness.
Another work, published a little later, should be noted here,
which, though written under the influence of Clarke[5], also
shows traces of the influence of Shaftesbury and Hutcheson.
This is the *Moral Philosopher* (1737), by Thomas Morgan, to
which Warburton replied in his *Divine Legation of Moses*.   The
following passage is one of several, showing his indebtedness to
Shaftesbury.   "Let our Moralist now look without him and
contemplate the vast stupendous fabrick of the Heavens and
Earth...He will see an innumerable family of creatures raised
and provided for by an unseen hand, and contrived and placed

---

[1] Contained in Chubb's *Collected Works*, vol. IV.

[2] *Ibid.*, p. 51.

[3] Chubb's *Works*, vol. II.

[4] *Ibid.*, vol. III.

[5] The author says that "by moral Truth, Reason and the fitness of things
he means the same as Dr Clarke." *Letter to Eusebius.*

in a mutual dependence and necessary relation to each other, by an invisible unsearchable Wisdom. And when he carries his sight farther, he will still discover more and more wonders *in infinitum*, and be more and more charmed and delighted with new Beauty, Order and Proportion[1]."

To all these numerous works may be added two others, which, though they occupy an isolated position, influenced Hutcheson. The first of these was Cudworth's *Treatise concerning Eternal and Immutable Morality*, which, though written long before, was first published in 1731[2], and the second, " Immateriality " Baxter's *Inquiry into the nature of the Human Soul*, which appeared in 1733[3], and to which Hutcheson refers in his *System of Moral Philosophy*[4].

The effect of such intellectual movements and so much criticism, joined with the experience of lecturing upon his system, taught Hutcheson much; and hence soon after his arrival at Glasgow, he is reported to have wished to recast his Philosophy. Wodrow writes that " he [i.e. Hutcheson] sayes, on reflection he sayes, he is not thoroughly satisfyed in the principles or rather some superstructures, upon which his book the *Beauty of Virtue* [is founded], and, if he publish another edition, he designs to alter severall things[5]." Whether the dissatisfaction mentioned extended to principles or details is an important point which may with advantage be discussed below. It has already been mentioned that the mathematical formulae were withdrawn and an addendum, printed in the fourth edition, published in 1738. Besides, beginning with the third edition, 1729, and still more in the fourth edition, there were many important changes made in the text. Several of these were replies to criticisms, and others were designed to bring the fourth edition of the *Inquiry* into line with Hutcheson's new mode of thought; some of these are exceedingly

---

[1] *Moral Philosopher*, I. p. 442.

[2] Cf. Hutcheson's *System of Moral Philosophy*, I. 273, "Precepts of the law of Nature, or these practical observations are deemed immutable and eternal," &c.

[3] *Scottish Philosophy, ut supra*, p. 44.

[4] I. p. 200.

[5] *Analecta*, IV. p. 190—.

important as a commentary upon the *System of Moral Philosophy*, which is, as will be seen, of about the same date. But it was impossible to completely re-create the *Inquiry*, and therefore Hutcheson determined to prepare an altogether new work.

Inasmuch as an investigation of the date of the composition of this book—the *System of Moral Philosophy*—is important in estimating Hutcheson's mental growth, some facts connected with the writing of it deserve to be told in detail.   Dr Martineau very ingeniously conjectures " that the volumes contain internal evidence of a mixed fabrication," which he attributes to the imperfect literary form of the notes from which Hutcheson had lectured, and the consequent necessity imposed upon the editor of filling them up by reference to the reports taken down by his most assiduous students[1].   Hutcheson's own letters show that the manuscript was in a much more complete state than might have been supposed from the date of publication, having been begun in 1734 or 1735, while they confirm the supposition of " mixed fabrication," besides giving an interesting account of the travels of the original rough draught.

Under the date of Sept. 21st, 1737, he writes to Drennan,

"I hope before it will be very long to let you see in print what has employed my leisure hours for several summers past ; but I am at a loss how to get a right printer to employ, being a stranger in London.   I don't incline to put my name to what I print or give any proofs of the author to any wasps in this country.   'Tis a 'System of Morality' in English, larger than both my former books.   You need not talk of this."

Five months later, on February 27th, 1738, he returns to the tale of the MS., now complete—

"You would readily hear that in November last I sent some papers, at Will Bruce's[2] desire, to be perused by Dr Rundle[3]; a *traik*, as they call it here, attends them.   They came to Will only ye 8th of February, by contrary winds ; and, though my design was to get Will's and Abernethy's opinion, he, without looking into them, gave them immediately to the Bishop, where perhaps they may lye a good time to little purpose ; and it may be resented unless Synge sees them too.   But I am in no haste about them."

[1] *Types of Ethical Theory*, II. p. 522.
[2] Hutcheson's cousin, *vide supra*, p. 26.
[3] Rundle, Bishop of Derry.

Again, on April 17th of the same year, he writes,

" About November last I sent a MS. to Will Bruce, chiefly for his and Mr Abernethy's perusal. He shewed it to ye Bishop of Derry, who, it seems, was much pleased with it, and promises me a long epistle soon. I heartily wish you had seen it, but it did not get to Dublin till February and was in the Bishop's hands till the beginning of this month. I believe Will is perusing it now.

I am not expecting it back again speedily. During our College Session I get nothing done ; but, if I get them back during our vacation, with remarks of my friends, I shall endeavour to put the last hand to them."

A letter written on June 15th, 1741, more than three years later, gives a despairing account of the delay in the final touches.

" I shall not leave Glasgow, except about three weeks in July, for this whole vacation, but have more avocations, by too numerous an acquaintance, than you can imagine.

In short Thom, I find old age, not in grey hairs and other trifles, but in an incapacity of mind for such close thinking and composition as I once had, and have pretty much dropped the thoughts of some great designs I had once sketched out.

In running over my papers, I am quite dissatisfied with method, style and some reasonings, tho' I don't repent my labour, as by it and the thoughts suggested by friends, a multitude of which I had from W. Bruce and Synge and still more in number from some excellent hands here, that I am fitter for my business ; but, as to composing in order, I am quite bewildered, and am adding confusedly to a confused book all valuable remarks in a farrago, to refresh my memory in my class lectures on several subjects."

From this time, on to Hutcheson's death, there is no further mention of the *System of Moral Philosophy*. There are several reasons to account for this. The want of " capacity for close thinking" is in all probability to be attributed less to failing powers than to the fact that Hutcheson could only work in solitude and free from all distractions; besides the "too numerous acquaintance," his energies were dissipated by the contest inside the University, which was much in his thoughts. Moreover, the publication of the *System* had been too long delayed. It represents a stage of thought, intermediate between the early works written in Dublin, and the short

Compends written after it, but published earlier.   It is easy to
imagine that, when in 1739 or 1740, he was face to face with
his own MS. it would be irksome to modify it to represent his
later views.   To a man of his impulsive, impatient temperament, it was easier to begin again, and warned by the delay in
the completion of the larger undertaking, he adopted the
refuge of the busy man, of writing a series of short works,
which were to be published as "Compends" or Synopses.
These were originally all written in Latin, and two of them,
the *Metaphysicae Synopsis* and the *Philosophiae Moralis Institutio Compendiaria*, were published in 1742, and the *Logicae
Compendium* in 1756.   Writing to Drennan on Oct. 29th, 1743,
Hutcheson gives an account of the publication of the *Metaphysicae Synopsis* and his own opinion of the books.

"I send you," he writes, "by the bearer, Dr Thompson, two[1] copies of
a trifle which I don't own, as it was first most imperfectly and foolishly
printed without my knowledge, from some loose hastily wrote papers;
and now, tho' much enlarged and altered, yet I have not leisure, either to
examine the whole thoroughly or to correct the Latin.   I am sure it will
match De Vries, and I therefore teach the third part of it *De Deo*.   I see
[upon reading] my *Compound of Morals*, a good many de[fects and]
oversights.   But I am so diverted by vain [jaunts and] business, that
I must do every thing by starts.   [I am...] and have something desultory
in me, [with the tur]n of my mind, besides something of old [age cre]eping
on."

The nature of the "Compends" may be best illustrated by
reference to Hutcheson's relations with Hume, which extended
over a period of six years.   There is a peculiar interest in the
encounter, both of the men and the philosophies—Hutcheson,
the enthusiast in the cause of virtue and universal happiness,
now verging upon middle age, but the more impulsive of the
two; and Hume, the anatomist of human nature, that looked
rather to the articulations of the skeleton, than the beauty
of the flesh tints.   As to the philosophies, whether one ranks
Hutcheson as the most renowned upholder of the old order
that Hume was to overthrow, or as the anticipator of later

[1] He adds at the end, "Pray send, by first safe hand the copy directed to
Bishop Synge.   I had a very fond letter from him, but a very melancholy one,
last summer; he is wanting such elementary books for his son."

answers to scepticism[1], it can scarcely fail to be of interest to see the philosophy of the man of fashion and philanthropist subjected to the disintegrating force of criticism.

In 1737 Hume, at the age of twenty-six, had returned from France with the MS. of the first two parts of his *Treatise on Human Nature.* It is unnecessary to retell his struggles in London, and his disappointment at the chilling reception given to the cherished child of his brain, from which he had expected so much. It was published early in 1739, and in a letter written to Henry Home, afterwards Lord Kames, on Feb. 13, there may be a hint of the chain of events that led to his connection with Hutcheson. Failing to get any public recognition of his work, he writes to his friend,

"If you know anyone that is a judge, you would do me a sensible favour in engaging him to a serious perusal of the book. 'Tis so rare to meet with one that will take pains on a book that does not come recommended by some great name or authority, that I must confess I am as fond of meeting with such a one as if I were sure of his approbation[2]."

Whether this request of Hume's led to his book being brought under Hutcheson's notice, or whether he had already been interested in the young philosopher, we find that the two men were soon engaged in a literary correspondence, and Hutcheson had consented to send Hume his remarks upon the unpublished parts. The promise must have been fulfilled in the summer or autumn of 1739, as Hume replies as follows :

"NINEWELLS,
Sept. 17*th,* 1739.
" SIR,

I am much obliged to you for your reflections on my papers. I have perused them with care, and find they will be of use to me. You have mistaken my meaning in some passages, which, upon examination, I have found to proceed from some ambiguity in my expression.

What affected me most in your remarks, is your observing that there wants a certain warmth in the cause of virtue, which you think all good men would relish and [which] could not displease amidst abstract

[1] This question will be found discussed in Chapter XIII.
[2] *Life and Correspondence of David Hume*, by John Hill Burton. Edinburgh, 1846, I. p. 106.

enquiries. I must own this has not happened by chance, but is the effect of a reasoning good or bad. There are different ways of examining the mind as well as the body. One may consider it either as an anatomist or as a painter[1]: either to discover its most secret springs and principles, or to describe the grace and beauty of its actions. I imagine it impossible to combine these two views. Where you pull off the skin and display all the minute parts, there appears something trivial, even in the noblest attitudes and most vigorous actions ; nor can you ever render the object graceful or engaging, but by clothing the parts again with skin and flesh, and presenting only their bare outside. An anatomist, however, can give very good advice to a painter or statuary. And, in like manner, I am persuaded that a metaphysician may be very helpful to a moralist, though I cannot easily conceive these two characters in the same work. Any warm sentiment of morals I am afraid would have the air of declamation amidst abstract reasonings, and would be esteemed contrary to good taste. And though I am much more ambitious of being esteemed a friend to virtue than a writer of taste, yet I must always carry the latter in my eye, otherwise I must despair of ever being serviceable to virtue. I hope these reasons will satisfy you ; though, at the same time, I intend to make a new trial, if it be possible to make the moralist and metaphysician agree a little better.

I cannot agree to your sense of '*natural*[2].' 'Tis founded on final causes, which is a consideration that appears to me pretty uncertain and unphilosophical. For, pray, what is the end of man ? Is he created for happiness, or for virtue ? for this life, or for the next ? for himself, or for his Maker ? Your definition of natural depends on solving these questions, which are endless and quite wide of my purpose. I have never called justice unnatural, but only artificial. *Atque ipsa utilitas, justi prope mater et æqui*[3], says one of the best moralists of antiquity. Grotius and Puffendorf, to be consistent, must assert the same.

---

[1] It is interesting to note that this letter to Hutcheson formed the germ of the comparison of the "easy" and "profound" philosophies of the opening pages of the *Enquiry 'concerning Human Understanding*; where the simile appears as follows—"The anatomist presents to the eye the most hideous and disagreeable objects ; but his science is useful to the painter in delineating a Venus or a Helen. While the latter employs all the richest colours of his art, and gives his figures the most graceful and engaging airs, he must still carry his attention to the inward structure of the human body, the position of the muscles, the fabrick of the bones, and the use and figure of every part or organ."

[2] In reference to Hutcheson's criticism of the discussion as to whether moral distinctions and justice are "natural" in the *Treatise*, pp. 471—3 (edition edited by Selby-Bigge), evidently Hutcheson's criticism, though not used in the *Treatise*, bore fruit, later, in the *Enquiry*, where in Appendix III and in Note [QQ] Hume re-states his position on the "naturalness" of justice.

[3] Horat. Lib. I. Sat. iii. 98.

Whether natural abilities be virtue, is a dispute of words[1]. I think I follow the common use of language ; *virtus* signified chiefly courage among the Romans. I was just now reading this character of Alexander VI. in Guicciardin, "In Alessandro sesto fu solertia et sagacità singulare ; consiglio eccelente, efficacia a persuadere maravigliosa, et a tute le faciende gravi, sollicitudine, et destrezza incredibile. Ma crano queste virtù avanzate di grande intervallo da vitii." Were benevolence the only virtue, no characters would be mixed, but would depend entirely on their degrees of benevolence. Upon the whole, I desire to take my catalogue of virtue from Cicero's *Offices*, not from *The Whole Duty of Man*. I had indeed the former book in my eye, in all my reasonings.

I have many other reflections to communicate to you but it would be troublesome. I shall therefore conclude by telling you that I intend to follow your advice in altering most of those passages you have remarked as defective in point of prudence ; though I must own, I think you are a little too delicate. Except a man be in orders, or be immediately concerned in the instruction of youth, I do not think his character depends upon his philosophical speculations, as the world is now modelled ; and a little liberty seems requisite to bring into the public notice a book, which is calculated for few readers. I hope you will allow me the freedom of consulting you when I am in any difficulty and believe me &c.

P.S. I cannot forbear recommending another thing to your consideration. Actions are not virtuous nor vicious, but only so far as they are proofs of certain qualities as durable principles in the mind. This is a point I should have established more expressly than I have done[2]. Now, I desire you to consider if there be any quality that is virtuous, without being a tendency either to the public good or the good of the person who possesses it. If there be none without these tendencies, we may conclude that their merit is derived from sympathy. I desire you would only consider the *tendencies* of qualities, not their actual operations which depend on chance. Brutus riveted the chains of Rome faster by his opposition, but the natural tendency of his noble dispositions—his public spirit and magnanimity—was to establish her liberty.

You are a great admirer of Cicero as well as I am. Please to review the fourth book, *De Finibus Bonorum et Malorum*, where you will find him prove against the Stoics, that, if there be no other goods but virtue, 'tis impossible there can be any virtue, because the mind would then want all motives to begin its actions upon ; and 'tis upon the goodness or badness of the motives that the virtue of the action depends. This proves that to every virtuous action there must be a motive or impelling

---

[1] *Treatise*, Bk. III. Pt. III. § 1, i.e. whether "non-artificial" abilities are virtues?

[2] *Treatise, ut supra*, p. 575. Hume returned to this point in the *Enquiry*, Note [DD].

passion, distinct from the virtue, and that virtue can never be the sole motive to any action. You do not assent to this : though I think there can be no proposition more certain or important. I must own my proofs were not distinct enough and must be altered[1]. You see with what reluctance I part with you, though I believe it is time I should ask your pardon for so much trouble[2]."

At first sight it would appear that Hume, while flattered by Hutcheson's notice, was somewhat impatient of his criticism, except upon points of prudence. Yet it is also true that Hutcheson's few suggestions, though not used in the *Treatise on Human Nature*, germinated in his mind, and led to additions in the *Enquiry concerning Human Understanding*, which was published after Hutcheson's death, and this is the more remarkable both because Hume himself considered it to " contain his philosophical sentiments and principles," and also because, as a rule, it is little more than an abridged summary of the earlier work.

In the March of the following year, Hume follows up his acquaintance with Hutcheson, by the request contained in the following letter.

" Ninewells,
March 4th, 1740.

" Dear Sir,

You will find the good nature and friendly disposition which I have experienced in you, is like to occasion you more trouble ; and 'tis very happy that the same good nature which occasions the trouble, will incline you to excuse it.

Since I saw you I have been very busy in correcting and finishing the *Discourse concerning Morals* which you perused ; and I flatter myself, that the alterations I have made have improved it very much, both in point of prudence and Philosophy. I shall set out to London in three weeks or a month, with an intention of publishing it. The bookseller, who printed the first two volumes, is very willing to engage for this ; and he tells me that the sale of the first two volumes, though not very quick, yet it improves. I have no acquaintance among these folks, and very little skill in making bargains. There are, therefore, two favours, I must ask of you, viz. to tell me what copy-money I may reasonably expect for one edition of a thousand of this volume, which will make a four shillings

---

[1] *Treatise, ut supra*, pp. 478—9.
[2] Burton's *Hume, ut supra*, i. pp. 112—115.

book : and, if you know any honest man in this trade, to send me a letter of recommendation to him, that I may have the chance of more than one to bargain with. 'Tis with much reluctance I ask this last favour, tho' I know your authority will go a great way to make the matter easy for me. I am sensible that the matter is a little delicate. Perhaps you may not care to recommend, even to a bookseller, a book that may give offence to religious people. Perhaps you may not think it calculated for public sale. I assure you, therefore, that I shall not take it the least amiss, if you refuse me. I shall only say, with regard to the first article, that the book is pretty much altered since you saw it, and tho' the clergy be always enemys to innovators in Philosophy, yet I do not think they will find any great matter of offence in this volume. On the contrary, I shall be disappointed, if impartial judges be not much pleased with the soundness of my *Morals.*

I have sent you the *Conclusion* as I have altered it, that you may see I desire to keep on good terms even with the strictest and most rigid. You need not return this copy, unless you point out any passage which you think it proper for me to alter[1]."

Hutcheson in the kindness of his heart went over and returned this MS., erasing the words " both our selfishness and pride " in the first sentence of the last paragraph of the *Treatise,* which reads as follows in the MS.: " The same system may help us to form a just notion of our happiness as well as the dignity of Virtue, and may interest every principle of our nature, both our selfishness and pride, in the embracing and cherishing this noble quality[2]."

Hume continues his letter by saying,

" My bookseller has sent Mr Smith a copy of my book, which I hope he has received, as well as your letter. I have not yet heard what he has done with the abstract, perhaps you have. I have got it printed in London, but not in the *Works of the Learned,* there having been an article with regard to my book, somewhat abusive, printed in that work, before I sent up the abstract[3]."

Both Burton and Mr Rae, the biographer of Adam Smith, agree in thinking that this refers to the future economist, who had just been appointed to a Snell exhibition at Oxford, but was probably at this time at home in Kirkcaldy[4]. From

---

[1] Hume MSS., Library, Royal Society of Edinburgh.
[2] Hume MSS.
[3] Burton's *Hume, ut supra,* i. pp. 109—111.
[4] Burton's *Hume,* i. p. 116; Rae's *Life of Adam Smith,* pp. 15—16. The

Carlyle's *Autobiography* we learn that it was customary for Hutcheson and Leechman to require promising members of their classes to prepare abstracts either of new or standard works, and that these summaries often attracted considerable notice in the University[1]. In this case, Hutcheson evidently sent the abstract to Hume, who thought it worthy of being printed. It was an age of young philosophical authors, but, assuming that the "Mr Smith" of the letter was Adam Smith, we have a reviewer of only seventeen years of age. This is not to be taken as tending to discredit the early connection of Adam Smith with Hume, rather, it is a remarkable instance of Hutcheson's success as a teacher, and the enthusiasm with which he inspired his pupils for Philosophy.

It is interesting to notice how Hutcheson, now nearing the end of his labours, was forming the minds of his successors. Adam Smith was his pupil, he was the literary adviser and critic of Hume, and to complete the group of greater thinkers in Scotland of the next generation, it only remains to add that far away at New Machar, near Aberdeen, about this time, the attention of Reid was directed to Philosophy by the impression made upon him through the geometrical method and illustrations of Hutcheson's *Inquiry*, which bridged the gap between his mathematical and metaphysical studies[2]. It is true that Reid, like Kant later, was first wakened from his "dogmatic slumber" by Hume, from whose writings, he says, "he learnt more than from all others put together[3]," but at the same time the existence of his early essay is sufficient to show

following anecdote is important as supporting the conjecture that the Mr Smith of this letter was the future economist. "His modest deportment, and his secret studies, however, provoked, it has been said, the jealousy of or the suspicion of his superiors. It has been mentioned, that the heads of the College having thought proper to visit his chamber found him engaged in perusing Hume's *Treatise of Human Nature*, then recently published. This the reverend inquisitors seized, while they severely reprimanded the young philosopher." *Wealth of Nations, with a Life of the Author.* Edinburgh, 1840, p. ii.

[1] p. 101.

[2] Reid's *Works*, Ed. Sir W. Hamilton, p. 7. McCosh, *Scottish Philosophy*, p. 200. His first work published in the *Transactions of the Royal Society of London* is a direct result of Hutcheson's influence.

[3] Reid's *Works*, p. 91.

that .if the direction of his work is attributable to Hume, the impetus came from Hutcheson.

To return to the fate of Hume's MS. of the latter part of the *Treatise* and his request for help in securing a publisher, it may be remembered that Hutcheson himself, in 1737, had written that "being a stranger in London he was at a loss to get a right printer[1]," still he was able to offer Hume an introduction to Thomas Longman in 1740, to which Hume replies in less than a fortnight from the date of the former letter.

"March 16*th*, 1740.

" DEAR SIR,

I must trouble you to write that letter you were so good as to offer to Longman[2] the bookseller. I concluded somewhat of a hasty bargain with my bookseller, from indolence and an aversion to bargaining : as also because I was told that few or no booksellers would engage for one edition with a new author. I was also determined to keep my name a secret for some time, though I find I have failed in that point. I sold one edition of these two volumes for fifty guineas, and also engaged myself heedlessly in a clause which may prove troublesome, viz. that upon printing a second edition, I shall take all the copies remaining upon hand at the time. 'Tis in order to have some check upon my bookseller, that I would willingly engage with another : and I doubt not, but your recommendation would be very serviceable to me, even though you be not personally acquainted with him.

I wait with some impatience for a second edition, principally on account of alterations I intend to make in my performance[3]. This is an advantage we authors possess since the invention of printing, and renders the *nonum prematur in annum*, not so necessary to us as to the ancients. Without it, I should have been guilty of a very great temerity, to publish, at my years, so many novelties in so delicate a part of philosophy ; and, at any rate, I am afraid that I must plead, as my excuse, that very circumstance of youth which may be urged against me. I assure you, that without running any of the heights of scepticism, I am apt, in a cool hour to suspect, in general, that most of my reasonings will be more useful by furnishing hints and exciting people's curiosity, than as containing any principles that will augment the stock of knowledge that must pass to future ages.

[1] *Supra*, p. 113.
[2] This part was published by Longman in 1740.
[3] The edition of *Treatise*, Part III, 1740, contained an Appendix, with additions to be inserted after certain specified sentences in the earlier parts.

I wish I could discover more fully the particulars wherein I have failed. I admire so much the candour I have observed in Mr Locke, yourself, and a very few more, that I would be extremely ambitious of imitating it by frankly confessing my errors. If I do not imitate it, it proceeds, neither from my being free from errors nor want of inclination, but from my real unaffected ignorance[1].

I shall consider more carefully all the particulars you mention to me : though with regard to *abstract ideas*, 'tis with difficulty I can entertain a doubt on that head, notwithstanding your authority. Our conversation together has furnished me a hint with which I shall augment the second edition. 'Tis this—the word *simple idea* is an abstract term, comprehending different individuals that are similar. Yet the point of their similarity, from the very nature of such ideas, is not distinct nor separable from the rest. Is not this a proof, among many others, that there may be a similarity without any possible separation, even in thought[2] ?

I must consult you in a point of prudence. I have concluded a reasoning with these two sentences : 'When you pronounce any action or character to be vicious, you mean nothing but that, from the particular constitution of your nature, you have a feeling or sentiment of blame, from the contemplation of it. Vice and Virtue, therefore, may be compared to sound, colours, heat and cold, which, according to modern philosophy, are not qualities in objects, but perceptions in the mind. And this discovery in morals, like that other in Physics[3], is to be regarded as a mighty advancement of the speculative sciences, though, like that too, it has little or no influence on practice.'

Is not this laid a little too strong ? I desire your opinion of it, though I cannot entirely promise to conform myself to it[4]. I wish from my heart I could avoid concluding, that, since morality, according to your opinion as well as mine, is determined merely by sentiment, it regards only human nature and human life. This has been often urged against you[5], and the consequences are very momentous. If you make any alterations in your performances, I can assure you there are many who desire you would more fully consider this point, if you think the truth lies on the popular side. Otherwise common prudence, your character, and situation forbid you [to] touch upon it. If morality were determined by reason, *that* is the same to all rational beings, but nothing but

---

[1] Cf. *Treatise*, ed. Selby-Bigge, Appendix, p. 623.

[2] Amongst the additions to the two Parts of the *Treatise*, already published, which appeared as an Appendix to Part III, there is a note "to be added to Part I. § 7," which embodies this line of thought.

[3] Cf. Hutcheson, passages quoted *infra*, p. 194.

[4] *Treatise*, III. § 1, p. 469 (edition of Selby-Bigge). The only alteration is the substitution of "considerable" for the "mighty" of the MS.

[5] E.g. before the Presbytery at Hutcheson's prosecution for heresy, *supra*, p. 84, and *infra*, Chapter XI.

experience can assure us that the sentiments are the same. What experience have we with regard to superior beings ? How can we ascribe to them any sentiment at all ? They have implanted those sentiments in us, for the conduct of life, like our bodily sensations, which they possess not themselves. I expect no answer to these difficulties in the compass of a letter. 'Tis enough if you have patience to read so long a letter as this.

I am, &c."

It is worthy of mention that the difficulty raised by Hume, in the last paragraph of his letter, which might be stated in slightly different language, as the alleged inferiority of the moral sense theory to that of the rational moralists, on the ground of its being dependent on the will of God, mutable, and confined to men only, is answered by Hutcheson in the " Compend" or *Introduction to Moral Philosophy*, published in Latin, in 1742. He endeavours to evade the difficulties by making the moral sense "approve" Benevolence (Benevolence being used almost in the sense of perfection), and that such approval is ordained by a Benevolent or perfect God ; and from these premises he boldly advances the paradox that the various "approbations" (one cannot use the natural expression "decisions") of the Moral Sense "are thus as immutable as the Divine wisdom and goodness." "Cast the consideration of these perfections of God out of the question, and indeed nothing remains certain or immutable[1]." Truly an "Immutable Hedonism" ought to deserve a place in the museum of philosophical monstrosities, with which a recent writer has threatened his opponents.

In 1742 both Hutcheson and Hume published books— Hutcheson the *Compend of Morals* already mentioned, and Hume the second volume of his *Essays, Moral and Political*, the first part having appeared in 1741. In these essays Hume repays his debt to Hutcheson, and it is easy to see how much he owes, from the treatment of *Superstition and Enthusiasm, The Stoic*, and especially *The Standard of Taste*[2], which is almost a reproduction of Hutcheson's early work.

[1] Ed. 1773, pp. 19, 20. Leechman endeavours to get rid of the same difficulty in his *Life of Hutcheson*, Hutcheson's *System*, i. p. xxxviii, note.

[2] Published 1757 as the last of the four dissertations.

With regard to Hume's writings on Moral Philosophy, at this time, he is greatly under Hutcheson's influence, and that, too, in a rather remarkable manner. The chilling reception of and hostility to his philosophical audacities, joined to Hutcheson's hints and "remarks," exercises a restraining force upon his criticism. The destructive tendency of his work seems to contend against an attempt at construction, through which his criticism or philosophical scepticism sometimes comes to the surface. He is dominated by Hutcheson's earnestness in the cause of virtue, but he struggles against the domination. This unconscious struggle was inevitable. With Hutcheson the didactic impulse was always first; with Hume, however, he gave way "to points of prudence,"—Truth, severe and faced unflinchingly, was always of paramount importance.

Upon the issue of the *Philosophiae Moralis Institutio Compendiaria*, Hutcheson had sent a copy to Hume, who makes the following acknowledgment:

"EDIN^R.

Jan. 10*th*, 1743.

"DEAR SIR,

I received your very agreeable present, for which I esteem myself much obliged to you. I think it needless to express to you my esteem of the performance, because both the solidity of your judgment, and the general approbation your writings meet with, instruct you sufficiently what opinion you ought to form of them. Though your good nature might prompt you to encourage me by some praises, the same reason has not place with me, however justice might require them of me. Will not this prove that justice and good nature are not the same?

I am surprised that you should have been so diffident about your Latin. I have not wrote any, in that language, these many years, and cannot pretend to judge of particular words and phrases. But the turn of the whole seems to me very pure, and even easy and elegant.

I have subjoined a few reflections, which occurred to me, in reading over the book. By these, I pretend only to show how much I thought myself obliged to you for the pains you took with me in a like case, and how willing I am to be grateful[1]."

The "few reflections" are of the nature of a critical commentary, and are given, together with the passages to which

---

[1] Burton's *Hume*, i. p. 146.

they refer, in Burton's *Life of Hume*[1]. There are eight of them, of which two refer to Latin phrases, four raise minor points, but the remaining two are of real importance. In one, Hume raises one of the difficulties connected with Hutcheson's benevolence; and in the other, he is acute enough to see how much Hutcheson had fallen under the influence of Butler, which interesting question will be more profitably discussed in its proper place in the sequel[2].

It is unfortunate that a misunderstanding clouded the pleasant relations between the two men. In the next year (1744) there was a rumour that the professorship of "Ethics and Pneumatic Philosophy" at Edinburgh might be vacant. Sir John Pringle, who held the Chair, was a medical doctor, and in 1742 he had been appointed physician to the British troops in the Low Countries. An absentee landlord may be tolerated, but an absentee professor was obviously impossible. The Town Council naturally wished Pringle to resign one or other of the appointments, and it was generally expected that, if his natural affection for a sinecure could be overcome, he would retire from the professorship. Hume mentions in one of his letters that John Coutts, the father of Thomas Coutts, the celebrated banker, was in favour of his coming forward as a candidate[3]; and he was dismayed to find that the influence of Hutcheson's name was being used against him.

"The accusation of heresy, deism, scepticism, atheism, &c. &c. &c.," he writes, "was started against me; but never took, being bore down by the contrary authority of all the good company in town. But what surprised me extremely, was to find that this accusation was supported by the pretended authority of Mr Hutcheson and even Mr Leechman[4], who, 'tis said, agreed that I was a very unfit person for such an office. This appears to me absolutely incredible, especially with regard to the latter gentleman. For, as to Mr Hutcheson, all my friends think that he has been rendering me bad offices, to the utmost extent of his power. And I know that Mr Couts, to whom I said rashly that I thought I could depend upon Mr Hutcheson's friendship and recommendation—I say that Mr Couts now speaks of that Professor rather as my enemy than my friend. What

---

[1] Burton's *Hume*, i. pp. 147—150.
[2] *Infra*, Chapter XII.   [3] Burton's *Hume*, i. p. 165.
[4] This letter is dated August 4, 1744, and Leechman had been elected Professor of Divinity at Glasgow in December, 1743.

can be the meaning of this conduct in that celebrated and benevolent moralist I cannot imagine. I shall be glad to find, for the honour of Philosophy, that I am mistaken : and, indeed, I hope so too : and beg of you to enquire a little into the matter ;- but very cautiously, lest I make him my open and professed enemy, which I would willingly avoid. Here, then, it behoves you to be very discreet.

'Tis probable Mr Murray of Broughton may consult Mr Hutcheson and the other Professors of Glasgow, before he fix, absolutely, on a tutor for his son. We shall see then whether he really entertains a bad opinion of my orthodoxy, or is only unwilling that I should be Professor of Ethics in Edinburgh ; lest that town, being in the neighbourhood of Glasgow, should spread its contagion all around it, and even infect the students of the latter university[1]."

This letter of Hume's is difficult to harmonize with Hutcheson's known character. However much allowance may be made for the indiscretions of friends and exaggeration on the part of Hume himself, it probably remains true that Hutcheson was opposed to Hume's success in his candidature for this particular Chair. When, as will be seen, the post was offered to Hutcheson, it would almost appear that here is an instance of jealousy or a desire of the older man to retard the advancement of the younger. Such unworthy motives are, however, altogether inconsistent with the many sacrifices he had already made, and his general desire to be of use to his friends. The true explanation can readily be obtained from Hutcheson's views and confirmed from Hume's own letters, and it will be seen that the opposition was a logical necessity of their respective positions. It must be remembered that the Professorship was that of Ethics and that Hutcheson held strong and individual views upon the teaching of the subject. The fittest candidate, from his point of view, would be the best *preacher* of Philosophy—and one can scarcely imagine Hume in this character. Further, he had, in conformity with this, objected to Hume's "lack of warmth in the cause of virtue[2]," and he had condemned certain lapses from prudence. Hume's defence against this charge is his own condemnation and Hutcheson's justification, for had he not written to Hutcheson in September, 1739, that a man's philosophical opinions do not affect his

[1] Burton's *Hume*, i. p. 167.
[2] *Supra*, p. 116.

reputation "*unless immediately concerned in the instruction of youth*[1]"—the very position which he now sought? Therefore while Hutcheson encouraged Hume's researches for reading in the study, he could hardly fail to look upon his influence as a University teacher as pernicious; and so it no doubt appeared to him to be his duty to advise against Hume's election as a "teacher of morality."

On March 27th, 1745, Pringle actually resigned the Chair, and the deliberations of the Town Council are thus recorded: "Baillie Hamilton reported that, pursuant to appointment of last Sederunt, he had conveened the ministers of this City, for their advisamentum[2], with regard to the Professorship, vacant by Doctor Pringle's resignation, and had likewise intimate to them the Councill's choice of Mr Francis Hutcheson, Professor in the Colledge of Glasgow, with which choice they seemed all well pleased. But [they] hoped the honourable Councill, for hereafter, would order the ministers' advisamentum to be held, prior to any choice, and that such advisamentum should be taken by the whole Councill, and not by a Committee, as heretofore has been the practice.

Further, the said Baillie Gavin Hamilton reported that, in consequence of the Council's recommendation of last Sederunt, he had wrote to Mr Hutcheson and sent him his commission

---

[1] *Supra*, p. 118.

[2] There seems to be some doubt as to what the "Advisamentum" of the ministers was. From the Town Council Records it appears that a Committee or the whole Council chose one or more names, and that the ministers had a customary or legal right to revise this list. Whether this advisamentum amounted to a right of veto does not appear.

During the course of the arguments in the celebrated "Leslie case" both sides were agreed that the Town Council should have the advice of the ministers (the exact phrase of the charter being "cum advisamento tamen eorum ministrorum"), but there are two ways of "having" advice, either, simply *hearing it* (as contended by the supporters of Leslie's election) or *following it* (as contended by his opponents). The balance of argument as well as the final vote is in favour of the former alternative.

It may be noted, too, that one of the speakers asserted that it was owing to the advisamentum of the ministers that Hume had been kept out of the University, but this statement, as will be seen below, is erroneous. Cf. *Report of the Proceedings and Debate in the General Assembly of the Church of Scotland, respecting the Election to the Mathematical Chair in the University of Edinburgh.* Edinburgh, 1805, pp. 4, 20, 53, 120, 155, 192, 217.

for being Professor of Moral Philosophy in this City's University and had likewise got Mr Hutcheson's answer declining to accept of the office; which, having been read in Councill, the same was ordered to be engrosst in the Council minutes, and of which answer or missive the tenor follows:

'GLASGOW,
April 8th, 1745.

'SIR,

I received your letter of the 4th instant, along with an extract of the Councill's act electing me Professor of Morall Philosophy in the University of Edinburgh.

I must, in the first place, return my most humble acknowledgments of gratitude to the honourable the magistrates and Councill of Edinb^r. for their kind intentions, and favourable opinion they are pleased to entertain of me: and assure them that it is with sincere regret that I find it impossible for me to answer their expectations.   But, as I had heard of their design some time agoe, and thus had full leisure to consider it, I could not keep the Councill any time in suspense by any expectation of my acceptance of a charge which, in my present stage of life, I cannot undertake.

I must, therefore, request it of you to communicate this letter to the Council, to let them know that I cannot undertake the said office: which, accordingly, I do hereby decline, that they may not be retarded in proceeding to a new election.

I heartily wish the City good success in their next choice, and in all their affairs, and that the University may flourish in all parts of Literature,

I am, Sir,

Your most obliged and most obedient humble Servant,

FRANCIS HUTCHESON.

To Baily Gavin Hamilton and the Councill of the City of Edinburgh[1].' "

After delaying to obtain a second "advisamentum," the Town Council on June 5th elected a William Cleghorn, who had been Pringle's *locum tenens,* Hume having withdrawn, either through finding his case hopeless or having lost interest in the matter, owing to his being away, in a less advantageous position, as tutor to the Marquis of Annandale.

[1] *MS. Council Records of the Burgh of Edinburgh.*

Whether the coldness occasioned by Hume's suspicions of Hutcheson's attitude to his candidature had led to an open rupture cannot be determined. There is no trace of any further correspondence between them; and none of Hume's letters about the time of Hutcheson's death have been preserved, so that it is impossible to form any opinion as to their attitude to each other after Hume left Edinburgh.

The letters from Hume give the last traces of Hutcheson's literary activity. His other occupations seem to have prevented his carrying on any literary work in 1745, for besides the demands upon his time through University politics, he had, as will be seen, a considerable amount of private business to attend to, and then there was the anxiety connected with the Rebellion and occupation of Glasgow by the Highland clans. These facts will explain why the *Compends* are his latest works, and also why it is extremely probable that few, if any, alterations were made in the *System* after the publication of the shorter works.

CHAPTER VII.

PERSONAL CHARACTERISTICS.

THE main events in Hutcheson's life at Glasgow group themselves naturally round the professional and literary activities recorded in the preceding chapters. To follow out such imperfect traces of his life-history as survive, it only remains to add a brief mention of some disjointed personal experiences and opinions, which throw a considerable light upon his character.

To bring Hutcheson's career at Glasgow into chronological focus, it may be worth remarking that, as far as can be ascertained, the first four or five years were marked by the preparation of the class-lectures, and the writing of them in the *System of Moral Philosophy* occupied a year or two more. About 1737–8 this work was finished, though afterwards altered and added to. From 1739 to 1743 there followed the composition of the *Compends* and the correspondence with Hume. After 1743 Hutcheson's literary productiveness ceased, and he gave his best energies to his campaign against the " zealots " in the University, as well as devoting a considerable amount of his time to business affairs, upon behalf of his friends.

Running through these various public duties, one notices Hutcheson's marked individuality as a firm friend ; and this side of his personality may be best described by random extracts from his correspondence.

It was one trait of his character neither to forget a friend, nor to lose sight of his Irish acquaintances. Even though some of them, like Drennan and Arbuckle, were far from being good correspondents, Hutcheson generally managed to write to them several times in the year—not the scrappy modern note that seems doomed to degenerate into the post-card, but substantial epistles discussing various questions of literary and personal interest—a form of letter killed by the daily paper.

To his friend Drennan he writes as an elder brother might to a younger, giving good advice, and sometimes betraying flashes of humour that are scarcely to be expected from the character of his published writings. The following part of a letter (written Jan. 1, 1737) is an instance of a cordial invitation to Glasgow, which was one of many :

"I am glad your present situation is agreeable to you. I must insist on your promise of a visit, whenever you find honest Mr Haliday in good health, that he could take the burden of the whole preaching for a moneth or six weeks. Robt Simson with you and Charles Moor would be wondrous happy till 3 in a morning. I would be with you from five till ten."

Again, on June 1, 1741, he repeats his invitation still more warmly :

"Matt. Morthland tells me that Cousin Alexander Young and you are talking of a visit to us this Summer. I assure you it would give us great joy, but 'tis too good to be true. Pray, if you do, let us know by a letter, some time before, so that we may not be out of the way, on any jaunt."

A letter written to congratulate Drennan upon his marriage shows a very happy and humorous turn :

"Glasgow,
July 8, 1741.
"Dear Thom,
          Tho' I have often heard the rumour of your courtship without believing it, as I never thought your talent lay in fortune-hunting ; yet, of late, I have had such assurances that you're actually married, as I could not question it any longer. My wife and I congratulate you most heartily, and wish you all the joys of that new relation, and with the same to Mrs Drennan, who shews a more valuable turn of mind by her conduct than most young ladies, in such circumstances. We both long to see you both, and rejoice that we shall find another family of hearty friends in Belfast. If any interposal of mine be necessary to promote or hasten an entire satisfaction of other friends, with this step you have taken, pray let me know and it shall not be wanting.

And now, dear Thom, that you have at last executed what you so often threatened, with Charles Moore, in your swift indignation at the foolish metamorphoses of your comerads by marriage ; display to us the glorious example ; let us see how we should behave. Away to Dublin every quarter : leave the wife behind you : or, if you take her along, don't mind her : stay at the Walshe's Head till 2 in the morning : saunter in Jack's shop[1] all day, among books : dine abroad : and then to the Walshe's Head again, to Charles' great consolation and edification. I'm sure you cannot be so foolishly fond, or so stupid, as to quit all Comerads, and sacrifice all merry conversation for one woman[2] !

*　　　*　　　*　　　*　　　*　　　*

You are sensible how much the fortune you get is the sacred right of another and her descendants : and your friends should be sensible of the same and not presume upon account of it to enlarge their demands on you ... Dear Thom, I just write to you as I would talk to you, if we were walking in Hackmer or on the Long Bridge, where I hope before I am many years older to have some pleasant walks with you and Mrs Drennan. Pray write me soon."

In the next letter Hutcheson reproaches his friend for failing to reply :

" You are such a lazy wretch," he says, " that I should never write you more. Not one word of answer to my congratulatory epistle, you got six weeks before you were married ! Not one word of godly admonitions about spending an evening with friends at the Walshe's Head, and other pious sentiments about the vanity and folly of staying at home in the evenings."

These letters show Hutcheson at his best, before worry, and, perhaps, failing health had clouded his spirits. The following one may be taken as his own judgment, on his life at Glasgow, in a more serious mood.

" *To the Revd. Mr Thomas Steward* (*Minister in St Edmondsbury*).

GLASGOW,

Feb. 12, 1740.

" SIR,

I received by a very worthy sober studious young gentleman, Mr Armstrong, your most obliging letter in October last ; and would have

---

[1] John Smith—the partner of William Bruce—Hutcheson's cousin, who published Hutcheson's two first books. The house was the Philosopher's Head on the Blind Quay.

[2] The next sentence is imperfect in the MS. It alludes to prudence in money matters.

sooner acknowledged the receipt of it and my obligations to you for your most agreeable present of your sermons had I not been disappointed by a private hand, I expected to have wrote by. Your sermons must be acceptable to all who have a just sense of piety and Virtue, to promote which they are so much adapted. The perusal of them gave me an additional pleasure as they revived a lively memory of my old worthy friend, whom I ever sincerely esteemed.

I have the most tender sympathy with you in the fortunes of your family, and particularly the loss of your son, if such a death should be called a loss, the bitter sense of which can endure but for a short time, and be succeeded by eternal joy, when we return along with him, to our Heavenly Father, the source of all that's amiable and excellent.

I have the more tender feeling with you in this matter that I have often experienced the like accidents of mortality, having been married now 15 years, and having only one boy surviving of seven children, born to me by a very agreeable woman. I bless God for the one he has spared to me, and that he has no bad genius. If he proves a wise and good man, I am very well in this world.

Since my settlement in this College, I have had an agreeable, and, I hope, not an useless life ; pretty much hurried with study and business, but such as is not unpleasant. I hope I am contributing to promote the more moderate and charitable sentiments in religious matters, in this country ; where yet there remains too much warmth and animosity about matters of no great consequence to reall Religion. We must make allowances for the power of Education and have indulgence to the weaknesses of our brethren.

It will always give me pleasure to hear of your welfare. Our poor old Professor died about ten days ago. I am in much fear about getting a good successor to him and wholly uncertain upon whom our choice shall fall.

> I am Reverend and dear Sir,
>
>> Your most obliged and most obedient Servant,
>>
>>> FRAN. HUTCHESON[1]."

It is probably to this period that the portraits of Hutcheson, now in existence, are to be attributed. There is a full-length picture in the Senate Room at Glasgow University. At first sight it is somewhat disappointing, and there appears nothing but the gown to suggest the Professor. The face is something of what is known as the Saxon type, regular in feature, rather florid and redeemed only by the arched forehead and mobile mouth, that is found amongst the orators of the last century.

[1] MSS., Magee College, Londonderry.

There is a second smaller picture in the Hunterian Museum, which is more striking and certainly a better painting[1]. Having escaped the drastic methods of the unskilled "restorer," it is much more life-like. Besides these a bas-relief was struck by Foulis, during the existence of the ill-fated Glasgow Academy. At one time another portrait was in existence, at Newry, where Hutcheson's elder brother lived. At the beginning of the century it was in the possession of the Ogles of Drumalaine, who were Hutcheson's collateral descendants, but recent enquiries have failed to trace the family or the picture. It is thus described by Stuart, who wrote the *History of Armagh*; in it Hutcheson is represented "as a man of fair and somewhat florid complexion. His forehead is remarkably capacious, his eyebrows, lips and dark blue eyes peculiarly expressive, and every feature of his countenance indicative of good temper and intelligence[2]." Probably the best impression of his appearance would be obtained by looking at the Glasgow portraits in the light of the following description, given by Leechman. "A stature above middle size, a gesture and manner negligent and easy, but decent and manly, gave a dignity to his appearance. His complexion was fair and sanguine, and his features regular. His countenance and look bespoke sense, spirit, kindness and joy of heart. His whole person and manner raised a strong prejudice in his favour at first sight[3]."

In dealing with Hutcheson's relation to the University mention was made of his business capacity, and one learns from his letters that he was equally successful in the management of his own affairs. Though he had property in Ireland he managed to keep in touch with it, and to check the proceedings of his agent — this being just what absentee landowners generally fail to do. In fact, hearing that his agent was in difficulties, he writes[4]:—

[1] This picture came from the Hope family. There is a tradition that Hutcheson had been tutor to the great-grandfather of the donor, Dunbar, fourth Earl of Selkirk.

[2] p. 492.

[3] Leechman's *Life of Hutcheson*, ut supra, p. xliii.

[4] To Drennan, Oct. 18, 1744.

"I take such precautions, as to my own affairs, that I cannot lose anything considerable in his hands, and I found him such an obliging friend to me that I would not grudge a little loss to relieve him."

Such business matters led to his visiting Ireland with comparative frequency. In the first years after his arrival at Glasgow he had been at least once in Dublin[1], and from his own letters it appears that he had been there afterwards in 1736[2], and at Newry in the summer of 1745[3]. As happens with most capable persons his own business was but a small part of the total amount that fell to his share. Many of his friends frequently availed themselves of his advice, and no doubt occasioned him no little trouble, as several of them were far from being "men of affairs." Leechman says, "He was sparing indeed of the external professions of friendship, but liberal in the most important offices of it: he was the refuge of his friends for advice and assistance in all cases of perplexity and distress[4]." Besides the trouble he took to help poor or giddy students and his attention to the business of his friends in Scotland and Ireland, he was always ready with help to those who needed it, delicately offered and freely given. When a cousin was charged with manslaughter, probably as the result of a duel, it is Hutcheson who makes plans for the support of the family, inducing his own brother to take charge of one of the boys and some other relatives to provide for a young child or two, he himself undertaking "to club for transporting the rest to Pensylvania[5]." Mention of Pennsylvania is connected with another instance of his kindness of heart :

"I had this day" [April 16, 1746], he writes, "a letter from a Presbytery of Pensilvania, of a very good turn, regreting their want of proper ministers and books ; [and] expecting some assistance here. I shall speak to some wise men here, but would as soon speak to the Roman conclave as to our Presbytery. The Pensilvanians regret the want of true literature : [they write] that Whitefield has promoted a contempt for it among his followers and bewailing some wretched contention among themselves.

[1] Wodrow's *Analecta*, iv. p. 298.

[2] Letter quoted from p. 83.

[3] Letter written to Drennan (upon business matters) from Newry dated July 19, 1745.

[4] Leechman's *Life of Hutcheson*, p. xxv.

[5] Letter to Drennan, Sept. 21, 1737.

The only help to be expected from you is the sending of some wise men, if possible. I shall send them my best advice about books and Philosophy, and hope to be employed to buy them books [which are] cheaper here than they are to be got anywhere else."

This episode is a distant parallel to Berkeley's gifts to the Universities of Harvard and Yale.

In this case it is unlikely that Hutcheson was able to carry out his intention, owing to his death soon afterwards, and it is only fair to him to add that it was rare for him to stop with mere advice, which he generally followed by more tangible assistance. The following is a case in point :

[*Nov.* 24–29, 1743.]

"DEAR THOM,

Having this opportunity, I must trouble you with a small affair. Upon conversation with Mr Brown, who came lately from Ireland, along with Mr Alexander Haliday, about the circumstances of some ministers, some very worthy men, in your Presbytery ; it occurred to me that a little liberality could not be better exercised than among them. I am concerned that, in my prosperous circumstances, I did not think of it sooner.

If you have any litle contributions, made towards such as are more distressed than the rest, you may mark me as a subscriber for £5 per annum, and take the above £10 as my payment for the two years past.

Alex. Young will advance it, as I wrote him lately, that I would probably draw such a bill, without telling him the circumstances.

I think it altogether proper you should not mention my name to your Brethren but conceal it. I am already called ' New Light' here. I don't value it for myself, but I see it hurts some ministers here who are most intimate with me."

Quite another side of Hutcheson's generosity to his friends lay in supplying them with notes for sermons ; and, of all the calls upon his good nature, this was acceded to most readily, for he was by nature a preacher. The following letter is evidently written in reply to one of Drennan's, asking for help in the preparation of a funeral sermon, and is of great interest in confirming Leechman's account of what Hutcheson recommended as the best mode of preaching.

"GLASGOW,

March 5, 1739.

"DEAR THOM,

I had yours of the 26th of Feb. on Friday and could not answer sooner. I had resolved, when I first read yours, to have replied in the negative, being in as much hurry, at present, as I have been this Session, by many letters of business as well as by my ordinary work. I have got on my hands almost the whole paternal care of my old pupil, Lord Kilmarnock's three sons here. But upon reading over your letter this morning, with the deepest concern for that worthy, friendly, generous man, I could not refuse you, altogether, what you desire, tho' I conclude, it must be much either an unreasonable diffidence in yourself or an unjust value your friendship makes you put on what comes from me, that occasions such requests. I shall be forced to work in starts and with many interruptions, which never succeeds right with me. I beseech you be as busy, as you can, with some plan of your own, and don't take any sudden interrupted attempts of mine, as fit for all the purposes, you say, are expected by friends on this occasion. I hint to you my plan that you may work upon it, and be the readier to patch up a right thing out of the two. A consideration of what sort of life is most worthy and best suited to a being capable of such high endowments and improvements and actions, destined to an immortal existence, and yet subjected for a certain space to a mortal existence in this world, and then, without drawing a character, leaving it to the audience to recollect, how much of this appeared in our friend's life.

I hope Jack Smith has sent you down to your town *A Serious Address to the Kirk of Scotland*, lately published in London. It has run like lightning here, and is producing some effect. The author is unknown. 'Tis wrote with anger of the Kirk and Confession, which, I imagine, few will have the brow to answer.

My most hearty respects to all friends.

I am, dear Thom, Yours most affectionately,

FRAN. HUTCHESON.

I really sympathize with you most heartily on the loss of your worthy friend : you will miss him exceedingly and so will your cause."

It is a matter for regret that only one of Hutcheson's letters written in the year 1745 is extant. Unfortunately it was written in July from Newry, and therefore we miss his views upon the Rebellion, and the obscure chapter of Scottish history, dealing with the panic at Glasgow, towards the close of the year.

As early as the 2nd of September Cochrane, the Provost, speaks of "great alarum and disquiet" in the city, and a few days later the citizens urged that "all accounts agree that the Rebels were to march by Glasgow, if not stopt[1]." To this the Government replied through the Lord Advocate: "I am very sensible of the defenceless state of your city, in case of a visit of the rebels ; and I wish it were in the power of anybody that I have access to, to give you a better defence, but you know as well as I the present state of the King's forces in this country[2]." From this time till the end of the year the condition of the city was lamentable. Business was suspended and the people seem to have been panic-stricken. The vicinity of the Highland forces in September paralyzed the citizens, and when they were given a respite by the movement of the army to the South, they still neglected the precautions taken in 1715. Practically deserted by the Government, the leading men seem to have recognized that the wealth of the city, added to its defencelessness, would sooner or later tempt the Prince's army to seize it. In November Cochrane says there had been "no business for the past eight weeks, our custom-house is shut up, our manufactures at a stand for want of sale and money, no payments of any kind and no execution[3]." At this stage of panic it was the University that struck the key-note of defence. On Oct. 31st, that there might be no doubt as to its position, the Professors went in processions to the Town Hall and drank the King's health, on the anniversary of his accession, and towards the end of November the Senatus decided upon taking active measures in support of the Government[4]. Some three weeks later, that is by December 16th, it was decided to barricade the town and arm the militia. Unfortunately these measures were taken too late, as the Rebel army was then almost within striking distance of the town and the vanguard entered into occupation upon Christmas Day, being followed by the main body on the 27th. The city was only saved from pillage by the

---

[1] *The Cochrane Correspondence*, Glasgow, 1836, pp. 6—8.
[2] *Ibid.*, p. 10.   [3] *Ibid.*, p. 26.
[4] MS. Records, Univ. of Glasgow.

payment of a large indemnity, and during the negotiations
the Pretender had promised to take the University under "his
special protection[1]." Evidently this offer failed to secure the
support of the Professors, for there is a tradition that the
University narrowly escaped being burnt by the Highlanders[2].
The lot of the inhabitants must have been an unhappy one
during the eight or ten days[3] of the occupation, as the clans
were quartered upon them to the number of 10, 15, or 20 men
to each house, where, of course, they exacted free quarters,
besides burning goods and furniture belonging to prominent
Anti-Jacobites[4]. Cochrane gives a highly-coloured description
of the distress of the people. "You see what was our unhappy
situation under a government worse than the French—nay even
worse than the Turkish. It may be said of him [the Pre-
tender] and his ministers that they have the arbitrariness of
tyrants and the genius of slaves ... To sum all up never was
a place so harassed and abused... we suffer more than all
Scotland beside, in a stop of trade, sales of goods, and payments,
bad debts and otherwise...The lower and even middling inhabitants ruined by want of business, entertaining from 10 to 20 of
these guests at free quarters[5]."

Evidently Hutcheson must have suffered with the rest, but
it is extremely probable that he escaped better than most,
owing to the fact that his old pupil, Lord Kilmarnock, was in
command of a troop of horse in the Pretender's army[6], and
consequently it is likely that his influence would be exerted in
favour of his former tutor, in whose charge his sons had been
only a few years before. This surmise is confirmed by the tone
of his letters written early in 1746, as if the occupation had
been no more than a distraction in an otherwise dull winter.

---

[1] *The Cochrane Correspondence*, p. 133.

[2] Macgregor's *History of Glasgow*, p. 323.

[3] There is some discrepancy in the accounts of the length of the occupation
of Glasgow, varying from eight days to ten. Probably it was ten days from the
time of arrival of the vanguard to the evacuation by the rearguard : while the
army was only in occupation for the eight days.

[4] *The Cochrane Correspondence*, p. 62; *London Gazette*, Jan. 4, 1746.

[5] *Ibid.*, pp. 63—65.

[6] Macgregor's *History of Glasgow*, p. 322.

The first letter after the occupation of Glasgow is dated March 17th, 1746, and he writes:

"We have had a dull winter, more so after the departure of the vagabonds than before, as my wife and I have both been tender but I hope we are recruiting.

The Duke is advancing from Aberdeen to attack the rebels, who are to dispute the passage of a very deep river with bad fords, the Spey. If we get more news to-morrow you shall have a postscript.

Pray let Mr McCartney know that his of 17th came to hand only this night, to-morrow it shall go to Greenock in case the French ship is not arrived, that notice may be sent to our ships of force on this coast.

P.S. There is no news of consequence, only the ship Mr McCartney wrote about came into [the] Clyde, as she said for tobaccos, where she will get double what she wants."

On April 15th of the same year he writes further on the same subject:

"Our publick news of the 15th from Edinburgh was that the Duke had passed the Spey, that 2,000 rebels on the banks fled precipitately upon his pointing his cannon at them. They may reassemble, and as they are very cunning, may yet have some artifice to surprise; but, I cannot but hope, that they are dispersing and their chiefs making their escape[1].

You have heard, no doubt, of our taking from them the Harvard sloop they had taken at Montrose. She returned from France with 150 men and arms and amunition and had landed them. But Lord Rea very boldly attacked them with a smaller number and took them all prisoners, with £13,000 sterling. The same man-of-war took another of their ships, with arms and amunition, which had seized twelve small merchantmen in [the] Orkneys for their use.

The Duke has endeared himself to some of his very enemies by his good sense and humanity, void of all state or pride."

In the spring and early summer Hutcheson was distracted, as already mentioned, by the contest for the Chair of Greek, and besides this he suffered considerable anxiety owing to illness in his family. His wife's relatives, the Wilsons of Longford, had come on a long visit about 1744. Hutcheson speaks of them with great affection. "Mrs Wilson is a discreet friend her daughter a very agreeable girl and her son Joseph one of my idols. I never knew a better genius, a sweeter temper or more prudence, in such years; his body does not

---

[1] One fancies Hutcheson's anxiety for Lord Kilmarnock speaks here.

belie his mind." About the time the Jacobite army was in Glasgow both Joseph and Miss Wilson had been ill; and in April he writes in much distress, saying:—

"I am in a great deal of private distresses about Jo. Wilson and his sister, the latter [is] in the utmost danger ; and the former, scarce recovered from death ; my wife too is very tender.

I am intending to take them over, if I am alive, this summer; but by a set of most intricate business, upon which the soul of this College depends, and all may be ruined by the want of one vote, I cannot leave this till after the 26th of June, and we go to Dublin first."

This is Hutcheson's last letter to Drennan. Moor was elected Professor of Greek on June 27th, and soon afterwards Hutcheson left Glasgow for Dublin, where he contracted a fever and died upon August 8th (1746)[1]. He was buried in St Mary's Churchyard, Dublin, his great friend and cousin, William Bruce, being buried in the same grave in 1755. Gabriel Cornwall, whose name appears in Hutcheson's letters, composed a joint epitaph, in Latin, for a proposed monument, but it proved too lengthy for the purpose; and the memories of the friends are preserved by a broken and defaced gravestone. Cornwall's epitaph appears to have perished. It was in the possession of Dr William Bruce, who contributed his articles on the "Non-Subscription to Creeds" to the *Christian Moderator* in 1828, but his descendants have lost all traces of it.

A minute in a volume of the Glasgow University Records dated September the 22nd speaks of "Mr Hutcheson's much regreted death" at Dublin and appoints Leechman to teach the "Bachelor" classes until the election of a new Professor. Hutcheson was succeeded by Thomas Craigie before the end of the year, and after his death in 1752 Adam Smith was elected to the Chair, being transferred from that of Logic to which he had succeeded in 1751, upon the death of Hutcheson's old teacher and antagonist, John Loudon. Adam Smith was followed by Reid.

It is rather a puzzle why Hutcheson's friends allowed an interval of nine years to elapse between his death and the

[1] Possibly it is worth drawing attention to this date, as in almost all histories of Philosophy it is given as 1747, though all the authorities agree in giving 1746.

publication of the works he had left in manuscript. It cannot have been the need of collecting the notes of students as Dr Martineau suggests[1], since it has been seen that the MS. was complete some years before his death, nor could it have been due to a need of revision, for it was a "confused book" then, and a confused book it remains. The real reason is that the work would naturally devolve upon the only child, who was also named Francis—the "Frankey" of the letters—who was a mere youth at the time of his father's death—he took his M.A. Degree in 1744 and the M.D. in 1750. Francis the second settled in Dublin soon afterwards as a physician, and in 1760 became Professor of Chemistry at Trinity College, Dublin. He left a son, also called Francis, who became Rector of Donaghadee in Co. Down. Hutcheson's son seems to have been urged by friends of his father to publish the works left in MS. at his death, and in this he succeeded, with the aid of Leechman, who wrote the introductory life and estimate, which has been quoted from so frequently in the preceding pages. The work appeared in 1755, published by R. and A. Foulis, and in London by Longman, with the following title—*A System of Moral Philosophy in three Books, written by the late Francis Hutcheson, LL.D., Professor of Philosophy in the University of Glasgow, published from the Original Manuscript, by his Son Francis Hutcheson, M.D. To which is prefixed some account of the Life, Writings and Character of the Author by the Reverend William Leechman, D.D., Professor of Divinity in the same University.* The two volumes are appropriately dedicated to Edward Synge, who was then Bishop of Elphin. In the following year, 1756, the *Logicae Compendium* was issued anonymously.

As showing how enduring was Hutcheson's fame as a writer, it may not be out of place to enumerate some of the chief editions of his various works.

Inquiry into the Original of our Ideas of Beauty and Virtue.

London, 1725: 2nd Edition, 1726: 3rd, 1729: 4th, 1738 (with addendum): 5th, 1753: Glasgow, 1772 (with corrections

---

[1] *Supra*, p. 113.

and additions in their proper places).   Translated into French, Amsterdam, 1749 : into German, Frankfurt, 1762.

Reflections upon Laughter and *Remarks on the Fable of the Bees.*

In *Dublin Journal*, No. 11 (June 5th, 1725) : No. 12 (June 12th) : No. 13 (June 19th), and No. 45 (Feb. 5th, 1726) : No. 46 (Feb. 12th) : No. 47 (Feb. 19th).

In *Hibernicus's Letters*, 1729 : 2nd Ed. 1734.

Separately, Glasgow, 1750, 1758. 1772, also containing Burnet Correspondence.

Essay on the Nature and Conduct of the Passions, with Illustrations upon the Moral Sense.

London and Dublin, 1728: 3rd, 1742 : 1756. Glasgow, 1769: 3rd, 1772.

Letters between the late Mr G. Burnet and Mr Hutcheson. London Journal, 1728.

Separately, 1735, 1772 (with Letters upon Laughter, &c.).

Hutchesoni Oratio Inauguralis, 1730, 1756.

Considerations on Patronage addressed to the Gentlemen of Scotland, 1735.

The Meditations of M. Aurelius Antoninus.   Newly Translated from the Greek, with Notes and an Account of his Life.

Glasgow, 1742 : 2nd Ed. 1749 : 3rd, 1752 : 1764.

N.B.   There is the following Note in Foulis's Catalogue of Books, "The two first books by Professor Moor, and the rest by Dr Francis Hutcheson[1]."

Philosophiae Moralis Institutio Compendiaria, Ethices et Jurisprudentiae Naturalis Elementa continens, Libri Tres.

Glasgow, 1742 : 2nd Edition ["auctior et emendatior" (see p. 115)], 1745 : 3rd, 1755.   Rotterdam, 1745.   Strasburg, 1772. Dublin, 1787.

The same translated into English and published as *A Short Introduction to Moral Philosophy in Three Books, containing the Elements of Ethics and the Law of Nature.*

Glasgow, 1747 : 2nd Edition, 1753 : 3rd, 1764 : 4th, 1772.

Metaphysicae Synopsis Ontologiam et Pneumatologiam complectens.

[1] *Notices and Documents Illustrative of the Literary History of Glasgow*, p. 49.

Glasgow, 1742 : 2nd Edition, 1744 : 3rd, 1749 : 4th, 1756 : 5th, 1762 : 6th, 1774. Strasburg, 1772.

A System of Moral Philosophy in Three Books, written by the late Francis Hutcheson, LL.D., Professor of Moral Philosophy in the University of Glasgow. Published from the original MS. by his son Francis Hutcheson, &c.

Glasgow, 1755.

Logicæ Compendium, &c.

Glasgow, 1756 : 2nd Edition ("Præfixa est Dissertatio de Philosophiae Origine, ejusque inventoribus aut excultoribus praecipuis"), 1759 : 5th, 1764, 1772. Strasburg, 1772.

Perhaps a clearer proof of Hutcheson's popularity than the foregoing dry enumeration of dates will be found in the fact that Foulis' Catalogue records eight publications for the year 1772 and of these no less than five are editions of various works by Hutcheson. It may possibly be of interest to record the published price of some of these books. The first edition of the *Essay on the Passions* was sold in London at 5s. 5d., the Dublin edition at 2 "British Shillings"; Foulis' third edition, "fine" copies 2s. 6d., "common" 1s. 2d. Foulis' "common" copies of the *Inquiry* were also 1s. 2d., the "fine" ones being 2s. 3d. The *System* cost 15s., the reprint of the Burnet Correspondence (Foulis) "fine" copies 1s. 2d., "common" 9d. and the *Oratio Inauguralis* 9d.[1]

---

[1] *Mem. Glas., ut supra.*

CHAPTER VIII.

HELLENIC AND PHILANTHROPIC IDEALS.

THE whole tenour of Hutcheson's life produces a vivid impression of the power of his personality. He was one of the rare spirits who exercise a gracious influence over those they meet. His ideal of life was high, and his exposition of it, alike by word and deed, made both friends and students desirous of following his example. In Scotland he introduced—or rather revived—a spirit of culture and broadmindedness, and at the same time his own character was a living exemplar of lofty aims and noble aspirations. Therefore it is, that a distinct and definite influence is traceable to his personal magnetism, beyond that of most other thinkers and writers. The word that was spoken and, at the same time, *lived*, was the true vehicle in which he clothed his ideal; and, to this, his writings were of merely secondary importance. What he wrote seems to have an accidental character. All his works are mere *obiter dicta*, some "hastily written and published without his knowledge," and others—such as the *System* and *Compendium Logicae*—he does not appear to have considered worthy of publication. With him Philosophy was essentially *living* and organic, it was an enthusiasm for the ideal, and as such, was always active expression and endeavour, always free and fresh, and not to be stereotyped in the printed book. In fact, he shared with Shaftesbury the Stoic conception of Philosophy as the "Art of Life"; and under the analogy of the arts, which so powerfully dominated the outlook of both, Hutcheson recognised that Philosophy, being an art, cannot be taught, and all that can be done is to show right examples. Just as Æsthetic culture

grows out of the study of masterpieces, so he endeavoured to
"teach morality," by exhibiting a gallery of the world's heroes,
giving in place of a metaphysic of ethics, a cult of hero-worship.
In this his quick sympathy with what was noble made his
subject near and living, while his eloquence fired the imagination
of all who came in contact with him. Thus he understood
teaching—partly, from his general position, as culture by familiarity with the most perfect originals; partly, perhaps, through
a personal peculiarity, he needed an actual audience. The
"reading public" was too vague and also too cold to fire his
enthusiasm as a writer, and, therefore, from all that one can
gather, his books are merely skeleton outlines of his real
teaching. It was the power of this personal teaching that
made his fame in Scotland, and that left permanent traces
upon the education and thought of the country. Such an
influence is difficult, if not impossible, to deal with. It
remains apart from the books written by the man who exerts
it; from contemporary evidence it is recognised as real at the
time, yet in looking back from an interval it will be found to
have been absorbed and assimilated, so that but few instances of
its existence can be isolated and exhibited. How this influence
operated, and how Hutcheson himself so lived to make his life
his strongest argument, may perhaps be faintly gathered from
the account already given of the main facts of his various
activities; and it is to be regretted that the information available still leaves the data all too scanty.

Though Hutcheson's literary expression of his views was
altogether secondary to the purely personal one, still it exerted
a considerable power outside the more favoured circle that he
addressed by word of mouth—just as the sermons of a great
preacher carry weight primarily as delivered, with all the power
of oratory and religious accessories of time and place, and
secondarily as printed in book form. Such a comparison too
may be less inapt, when it is remembered that Hutcheson was,
before all else, a preacher of morals, or as he himself would
have said, of philosophy. This aspect of his character forces a
comparison, or rather a contrast, between his writings and those
of his greater contemporary, Butler. Hutcheson, nominally a

Professor, was in reality a preacher in the University; and it was in this character that his influence was most widely felt; while that of his books was of less importance. Butler, on the other hand, though a preacher by profession, has exerted a vastly greater power by his writings than by his *Sermons* as actually delivered—Hutcheson's influence in fact passed directly into men; Butler's remained in his books.

To estimate Hutcheson's published works it is necessary to set him in his due historical perspective and especially to trace his relations to Shaftesbury and to note the attitude of both to the problems of the age.

Though Shaftesbury laid great claims to cosmopolitanism his Philosophy was, in reality, called forth by an English need; and, to say the need was English, is to implicitly affirm that it was an ethical one, and consequently the prevailing character of Shaftesbury's Philosophy is ethical. Further, like every system called forth by a national need, it begins by a series of revolts against tendencies either exaggerated so as to be hurtful, or on the other hand harmless in practice but erroneous in theory.

In the first place Shaftesbury lived at a time when the more extreme tendencies of Puritanism had become exhausted. The ideal of a Theocracy or God-governed state was impregnated with the "subjectivity" of the Reformation, and only the iron hand of Cromwell had mitigated the confusion of contradictory interpretations of the will of Heaven. In the politico-religious movement of the Civil Wars there was an inevitable lack of unity. Even in the revolt against oppressive religious and civil enactments, there was no fixed policy amongst the supporters of the Parliament, as to how far the revolt should extend, and when the time came for political reconstruction the views of the various sectaries were still more diverse. Carlyle has shown Puritanism as heroic—"the last heroic age"— "because it had declared war to the death with quackeries and knaveries, and would have neither truce nor treaty with these; and went forth flame-crowned, as with bared sword, and called the Most High to witness that it could not endure these[1]." This strength of a nation's uprising, "by wager of battle, is the

---

[1] *Life and Letters of Oliver Cromwell*, vol. I. p. 72.

measure of all worth[1]," from which the "lightnings" of
Carlyle's eloquence make a nimbus for the spirit of Puritanism.
Side by side with the genius of idealised Puritanism are many
less heroic spirits, forming part of the broad Puritan revolt.
The combination of all these appeared one tendency to the
thinkers of the age, who rushed to the opposite extreme after
the Restoration.

Now Puritanism, in its most thoroughgoing forms, had
changed the religious and social life of Britain.   It had
banished Beauty and martyrized the whole sensuous man.   In
place of these, it gave a profound religious and mystic nearness
to the world to come, towards which the present life is a "weary
pilgrimage," but in which the pilgrim is always a soldier, either
actually at war or merely resting between two battles.   This
state is necessary owing to the magnitude of the opposing
forces.   Everything is at war with the elect, and the Christian
life is one long vista of battlefields—not merely metaphorically
but in many cases actually, when Puritanism was forced to send
its Ironsides to destroy utterly "root and branch" the licence
represented by roistering malignants.   One cannot but admire
the readiness of the conscientious Puritan to follow the guidance
of an idea and the stern unbending tenacity of purpose arising
out of a religious enthusiasm, "with its undying wrath at evil...
its spirit of indignation against every form of oppression and
injustice, especially when they touch the religious life of the
individual[2]."   To such a spirit the world is not merely coupled
with the flesh and the devil, it *is* both flesh and devil; something to which the soldier-soul is alien and hostile.   Hence
some of the Puritans used the world as an enemy's country, to
be plundered and despoiled, but never enjoyed; for enjoyment
was a snare of the enemy.   Therefore, however much it is to be
regretted, one cannot help admitting the severe logic of the
destruction of pictures, statuary, church decorations of all kinds,
laces, fine textile work and historic architecture.   Such things
were dangerous and therefore better burnt.   Thus the whole

[1] *Heroes and Hero Worship*, p. 132.
[2] *The Evolution of Religion, Gifford Lectures, St Andrews*, 1890—2, by
Edward Caird, LL.D., D.C.L., vol. II. pp. 81, 304.

spirit of a certain section of the Puritan movement was at war with Beauty and enjoyment. It was wholly ascetic ; and not merely inartistic but hostile to Art. Therefore a first national need to be answered by Shaftesbury's Philosophy was the protest against the unloveliness of Puritanism, to relieve life of its predominant greyness and restore colour and harmony of outline—after the Restoration of the dynasty must come the restoration of the graces of life.

There are several aspects of the protest against unloveliness of life. The need for a counter doctrine to the condemnation of the æsthetic standpoint by ascetics goes back far beyond the Puritanism of the seventeenth century. The cry for mortification of the flesh had found its way into the early Church, possibly as a relic of Neo-Pythagoreanism, and had continued through the long line of hermits into the Monasteries, and again on to the various Protestant Churches. "Through Sense came corruption and through the mortification of sense, alone, can the corruption be purged" seems to have been the general tendency of religious history. Hence almost every fresh revival and purification of the Churches finds the Senses lowered and with them the Æsthetic feelings. It is this long-standing campaign against Beauty, in the Mediæval and Modern World, that gives more permanence to the protest against it by Shaftesbury, than it could have had, were it only directed against the asceticism of Puritanism.

Another aspect of the protest against unloveliness of life is wider than the controversy with the asceticism of Puritanism. Hitherto Art had been a chance visitor to Great Britain ; it was an imported, not yet a native product. Though the country had shared in the general revival, originated by the Renaissance, in renewed culture, freedom of thought and material advantages, the progress of the Arts had lagged behind. From the time of Henry VIII., all the artists of any renown were foreigners, either refugees from their own countries or tempted by offers of patronage. Thus in the reign of Henry VIII. we have Holbein and Lucas Cornellius ; in that of Mary, Joas Van Cleeve and Sir Antonio More of Utrecht ; under Elizabeth, Zucchero, Lucas de Heere, Cornelius Ketler,

Garrard of Bruges; under James I., Paul Vansomer of Antwerp, Cornelius Jansen, Daniel Mytens. Charles I. was a munificent patron of Art and his Court was celebrated as including Van Dyck, Rubens, Henry Stienwyck the younger, Cornelius Polenberg, Abraham Diepenbeck, besides a host of other foreigners of inferior merit. Naturally, Art was in slight request under Cromwell, when the Protector himself was able to acquire the Raphael Cartoons for £300 and a Holy Family by Van Dyck for £40[1]. If Painting was despised during the Commonwealth, it was degraded after the Restoration, and the artists of the Court of Charles II.—such as Simon Varelst and Antonio Verrio—would be best passed over in silence—were it not for the names of Lely and the Van-der-Veldes. With the accession of William III. came a fresh troop of foreigners, amongst whom were Kneller, Godfrey Schalken and Marco and Sebastian Ricci. Plainly Britain was neglectful of Art. Amongst so many strangers there was the merest sprinkling of native painters, and none of these of great importance. The Olivers, the Coopers—all miniature painters—George Jameson—"the Van Dyck of Scotland," John Hoskins, William Dobson and Robert Streater were little more than imitators. In fact, so far Art was an exotic, and as yet the work of the Renaissance was incomplete. Not only must the appreciation of Beauty be restored, but the cultivation of it in Art required to be made indigenous—indeed both expressions are merely variants of the same historical fact; if Beauty were appreciated Art would have been native to the country and *vice versâ*. Therefore concurrently with the defence of Beauty must come the last step of the Renaissance, the awakening of the country to the value of Art and hence the formation of a National School of painting[2].

Yet another aspect of the revolt against Puritanism was the demand for a return to the Literature and thought of the past. The more extreme Puritans had condemned all non-Biblical Literatures, in reaction against the "Paganised

---

[1] *Anecdotes of Painting in England*, by H. Walpole, 1826, II. 137, 138.

[2] It is interesting to note that Shaftesbury, in his *Letter concerning the Art or Science of Design*, predicts the formation of a national Art in "United Britain." Cf. Fowler's *Shaftesbury*, pp. 60, 61.

Christianity" of the Mediæval Church. As the Children of
Israel were the historical prototypes of the religious soldiers
of the Parliament, so the Old Testament was their favourite
reading. All Literature, outside the Bible, was "profane,"
and to the more thoroughgoing sectaries it could teach
nothing. In this banishment of pagan thought, Classical
writings were of course included; and so England was in danger
of losing much that had only just been learnt after the Revival
of Learning. The Greek ideal of life especially was not merely
incomprehensible, but was also condemned in the strongest
terms by the Puritans. After the Civil Wars there was no
place left for it. It was heathen and all the more reprehensible
because its authors were civilized and not savages. Yet,
though the yearning for the reposeful Beauty of a well-ordered
simplicity may be temporarily repressed, it breaks forth again
all the more insistently, after the ecstatic enthusiasms of a
faith that over-rides the world and man. The Greek spirit
takes its revenge in demanding a more unquestioning desire for
its supreme calm—a calm that can never come to the modern
world in its fulness, for it has been always sought as a reaction
after undue spiritual exaltation or sensuous excitement. After
a one-sided activity people long for the duly ordered activity of
the whole man as one unity, with each part or faculty of his
nature performing its own proper function—τὸ τὰ αὐτοῦ
πράττειν, as Plato happily expresses it.

Therefore with the reinstatement of Beauty must come the
parallel reinstatement of the fairest expression of it, primarily
in the Greek life, and in a lesser degree in Greek Art.

In the second place another clamorous British need was
that of a reply to the prevailing selfishness of life and the
reiterated demands of Self-Love as the only Ethical principle.
Not to go further back than the seventeenth century, Hobbes
had denied the objective reality of morality, giving in return no
basis, save a subjective convention. Prior to this convention
every man fought for his own hand, and the ultimate result of
Hobbes' theory was the definition of practical life as an Ishmael-
state, in which everyone claimed all that he had power to hold.
In this view, too, life was a battle, in which the fighter strove,

not for any spiritual end, but merely for his own personal good, under whatever shape he had conceived it. Self-Love, in fact, was not merely the "master-passion," as Pope later characterized it, but also the one primary synthesis of desires, from which all others, though apparently independent, had been originally derived.

These views created a great sensation. "The answers to the Leviathan alone would form a library[1]"; Warburton says that "the Philosopher of Malmesbury was the terror of the last age, as Tindal and Collins had been of this. The Press sweat with controversy, and every young Churchman militant would needs try his arms in thundering upon Hobbes's steel cap[2]." In this controversy, especially after the Restoration, the "Church Militant" made certain concessions and a tendency gradually became manifest to reinforce the claims of religion, by laying emphasis on future rewards and punishments. Thus, to the Hobbist, men were moral upon purely selfish grounds, through dread of the punishments of the State; while to the Restoration Divines they were moral through the greater dread of eternal sufferings. In either case the "soldier" was a mere mercenary, fighting "the good fight" for the sake of the pay, in the one case to be taken hedonistically in the present; and in the other, in the future[3]; the latter being but a system of deferred payment; as the matter has been profanely expressed in modern commercial phraseology, as a "fire insurance policy."

Against both views Shaftesbury contended with vehemence —against the latter especially. It was not so much the doctrine itself, that aroused his indignation, as some of its implied consequences, which Mr Leslie Stephen has generalised as "the blasphemy of God, the World and Man[4]." This view blasphemed God, because "representing Him as angry with His

[1] *Dissertation on the Progress of Ethical Philosophy*, Sir James Mackintosh, p. 133.

[2] *The Divine Legation of Moses*, Books IV.—VI., Preface, Works, IV. p. 31. Cf. *Hobbes*, by G. Croom Robertson, pp. 207—222.

[3] Shaftesbury's *Moralists*, Part 2, § 3.

[4] Article on Shaftesbury's *Characteristics* in *Fraser's Magazine*, January, 1873, vol. VII. New Series, p. 88.

creatures, as punishing the innocent for the guilty, and appeased by the sufferings of the virtuous." It "paints the world in the darkest colours, in order to throw a future world into relief." "But, most of all, it blasphemes man." "In its zeal to vindicate God, it pronounced all our own qualities to be essentially vile. It gave our virtues to God, and left us merely the refuse of selfishness and sensuality[1]." This triple blasphemy roused Shaftesbury to the bitterest indignation. His main polemic against self-love is an integral part of his system, but the violence of his attack upon the consequences, drawn from the hedonistic conclusions of the current theology, may well be isolated from his general standpoint. Such a view, he holds, is fit only for slaves, not for free men, much less for the moral exquisite with whom he generally deals[2]. So far from being an argument in favour of Morality, it is absolutely "fatal" to its very existence[3]; for a virtue that needs reward is not worth rewarding[4]. With regard to the subordinate position, that punishment is valuable, as a deterrent from vicious conduct, he is even more emphatic. "Those who have no better a reason for being honest than the fear of a gibbet or a jail—I should not, I confess, much covet their company or acquaintance...If a saint had no other virtue than what was raised in him by the same objects of reward and punishment in a more distant state ; I know not whose love or esteem he might gain besides ; but for my own part, I should never think him worthy of mine[5]." "There is no more of rectitude in a person thus reformed [i.e. by fear of punishment] than there is of meekness or gentleness in a tiger strongly chained, or innocence or sobriety in a monkey under the discipline of the whip[6]."

Both these forms of Egoism have several consequences. Practical life to them is essentially atomic, each pleasure-giving or pain-bearing state has value in itself as a component part of

[1] *Fraser's Magazine*, 1873, p. 88.   [2] *Moralists*, Part 2, § 3.

[3] *Inquiry*, Book i. Part 3, § 3.

[4] *Essay on the Freedom of Wit and Humour*, Part 2, § 3.

[5] *Ibid.* Part 3, § 4.

[6] *Inquiry*, Book i. Part 3, § 3. The relation of Shaftesbury's Philosophy to the religious thought of the time is fully dealt with in *Die Philosophie des Grafen von Shaftesbury von Dr Gideon Spicker*, Friburg, 1872, Erster Theil.

the mass of satisfactions, either present or future. Further, just as each state stands alone, so each man is a distinct practical atom, hedonistically isolated. Thus the tendency of both views was eminently individualistic.

Again, to each of them life is purely mechanical. As a last result everything is to be interpretable in hedonistic terms, and as such knows nothing of Teleology. The practical world is pure mechanism, or at best susceptible of dynamic explanation. The causal nexus—as efficient cause—rules all actions, and therefore when the logical conclusion is boldly drawn, as by Hobbes, nothing remains but the most complete Determinism. Teleology finds no place amid the rigour of an universal mechanism.

Such then were the two main problems confronting Shaftesbury—the need for protests against the neglect of Beauty and against the prevailing selfishness of the current views of life. It is difficult to determine which need he felt to be the more imperative, and the question is of some importance for the right understanding of his point of view, since his double answer contains inconsistent elements, and the ascertaining of the priority of one of the two problems, will explain a corresponding preponderance of one element, and its consequences, in the solution. Shaftesbury's whole outlook and personal peculiarities tend to show that the Renaissance of Beauty and Art was prior in order of time if not of importance. With a double question to face he had only one way open to seek the answer, namely by a return to the past. As a lover of Greek Literature and the Fine Arts he found little, if any guidance, in the works of his contemporaries, and therefore his inclination and training forced him back to the Greek world for inspiration. Now Greek thought only gave him aid towards the restoration of the appreciation of Beauty, and therefore it is that of the two problems, this is first to be dealt with.

Such a return to the ancient world naturally suggests a comparison with the Cambridge Platonists, who also sought old world inspiration against the " heresies " of Hobbes. Yet the difference is no less marked than the resemblance. The whole force of the position of the Cambridge Platonists depends upon the validity of their identification of the ethical teaching of

Hobbes with that of the Sophists. Plato destroyed the Sophistic position, therefore his arguments are of equal force against that of Hobbes. Consequently much of the work of the Cambridge Platonists is little more than a restatement of certain arguments of Plato's. It is not even that the Philosophy of Hobbes is confronted by Plato's system as a whole, but rather that isolated parts of his polemic against the Sophists are quoted; since Hobbes and the Sophists represent identical tendencies, and what was efficacious against the latter must, *ipso facto*, hold good against the former. Quite apart from the weakness involved in the identification of the two tendencies, there is the further want of power in reproducing Plato piecemeal. This was avoided by Shaftesbury. He does not borrow the mere arguments or even the spirit of Plato, but rather the broad outlines of the Hellenic spirit—" the mind of Plato is not to be exhibited by a Chinese catalogue, but is to be apprehended by an original mind in the exercise of its original power[1]." To reinstate Beauty in the modern world is to reproduce the Greek life, and show it as it was in outward manifestation and inner meaning.

Shaftesbury was unable to win his way to a full comprehension of the Hellenic Ideal, yet he saw it in many aspects. It gave him primarily a great peace for the existing warfare between the world and man, and relieved things of sense both from degradation on the one hand and from over-valuation on the other. In Great Britain, before his time, the outer world had been only partially reinstated. At the Baconian revival it had been opened up to all the early scientific enquiries connected with utility, but beyond utility remained Beauty and Art, both of which were far from being indigenous. To naturalise both Shaftesbury gives rather an æsthetic cult than a Philosophy proper. He endeavours to restore the Greek "worldliness" by reviving the conviction of the nearness of man and Nature. To the true Greek, in the best days of his history, there was no breach between the two, and Beauty was an integral part of himself and his environment. Natural and artistic Beauty went hand in hand, each expressing and supplementing the other. Nature was half-human and man was an

---

[1] *Emerson's Works*, George Bell and Sons, I. p. 296.

artist to his finger-tips, not merely reproducing his ideals in material form, but in the institutions of the state and especially in life.   This was the highest art—namely that whose vehicle was man himself.   It was not only an ideal of a lovely environment; but, further, this environment was the background for a beautiful and self-complete life.   Thus there is a rhythm running through all expressions of Greek life, at once a harmony in variety, never allowed to dissipate itself in vagueness but always centralised.   The ruling ideas throughout are the laws and restraints of artistic expression; so that together with a complete centralisation there is, at the same time, perfect freedom— "each alike was Greek, alike was free."   Just because the keynote of action was a regard for the Beautiful, everything worked under æsthetic rules, subject to law, yet without consciousness of restraint.   What was inwardly ideal, materialised itself outwardly; and the outer world was idealised by a spiritual interpretation.   Thus the two spheres, so sharply distinguished in the modern world, each interpenetrated the other, and that too automatically.   There was no duality, only an all-pervading unity.

This unity was not individualistic but universal—the generality or breadth, which Mr Pater called "the supreme characteristic of the Hellenic ideal[1]," is the unity of the various parts of man's nature and further of man with the world.   It is a complex wholeness of differences, never sufficiently accentuated to become opposites; and therefore the artistic synthesis has neither thesis nor antithesis, it is rather a series of graduated transitions.

The result of this unity is a "blitheness" of life, a wide serenity, a reposeful calm.   Life is satisfying like any other perfect work of art, executed under the canons of a severe simplicity, in which nothing is superfluous, nothing redundant. This "everlasting calm" of the highest Greek Art is based upon the wholeness of the many-sided Greek life.   Each individual falls into his proper place spontaneously, so that the state or a group of individuals or a single life is a work of art, graceful and artistically satisfying throughout.

Underlying the Greek breadth and calm is the ruling idea

_____
[1] *The Renaissance*, p. 226.

of a Cosmos, in which each part performs its proper function and works organically for the good of the whole. This fitness for its proper task is the basis for the due performance which, when carried out in unison, becomes the excellence of both whole and part.

Such graduated excellences of function give the calm satisfaction of balance, symmetry, proportion, order, harmony; all of which are expressions for various relations within any given Cosmos.

These ideas are of great importance to Shaftesbury, since they form the basis of his general cult of Beauty. The Universe as a whole is a Cosmos, so also is human life. Therefore all the due performances of the different functions manifest innumerable harmonies; the appreciation of which was less a matter of argument than of insight. Harmony, excellence, τὸ καλόν were everywhere; and he, who was rightly constituted and trained, could not fail to experience the joyous emotions, due to this universal loveliness. All that was needed was the right point of view; given that, appreciation was inevitably rewarded.

Shaftesbury was much perplexed for want of a terminology. As a man of fashion and keen critic of " dry-as-dust " academicism, he could not perpetrate the barbarisms of Cudworth, in loading his essays with Greek terms, so he is in want of a word to express the idea of a Cosmos; he most often uses " System," which Butler afterwards made so celebrated, " Œconomy " or " Whole and Parts[1]." " Whatever things have order, the same have unity of design, and concur in one, are parts of one Whole, or are in themselves intire Systems ... Now in this, which we call the Universe, whatever the perfection may be of any particular systems; or whatever single parts may have Proportion, Unity or Form within themselves; yet if they are not united, all in general, in one System, but are in respect of one another, as the driven sands, or clouds or breaking waves; then —there being no Coherency in the whole—there can be inferred no order, no proportion, and consequently no project or design[2]." " Nothing," he continues, " is more strongly imprinted on our

---

[1] These terms were derived from the later Stoics: vide infra, ch. XIV.

[2] Moralists, Part 2, § 4.

minds, or more closely interwoven with our souls than the idea
or sense of Order and Proportion...What a difference there is
between Harmony and Discord ! between composed and ordered
motion, and that which is ungoverned and accidental ! between
the regular and uniform pile of some architect and a heap of
sand or stones ! and between an organiz'd body and a mist or
cloud driven by the wind[1]!" " The Ballance of Europe, of
trade, of power is strictly sought after, while few have heard of
the ballance of the passions, or thought of holding these scales
even. Few are acquainted with this province, or knowing in
these affairs. But were we more so (as this Inquiry would
make us) we should then see Beauty and Decorum here, as
well as elsewhere in Nature ; and the order of the Moral
World would equal that of the natural[2]." Elsewhere he
writes, " Knowing as you [i.e. Palemon] are, well knowing and
experienced in all the degrees and orders of Beauty, in all the
mysterious charms of the particular forms, you rise to what is
more general; and, with a larger heart and mind more comprehensive, you generously seek that which is highest in the
kind. Not captivated by the lineaments of a fair face or the
well-drawn proportions of a human body, you view the life
itself, and embrace rather the mind that adds the lustre and
renders chiefly amiable. Nor is the enjoyment of such a single
Beauty sufficient to satisfy such an aspiring soul. It seeks
how to combine more Beautys, and by what Coalition of these
to form a beautiful society. It views communitys, friendships,
relations, dutys ; and considers by what Harmony of particular
minds the general harmony is composed[3]." This excellence of
the Cosmos is fundamentally artistic ; and it is from this side
that Shaftesbury speaks of " the consummate Art exhibited
through all the works of Nature. Our weak eyes, helped by
mechanick Art, discover in these works a hidden scene of
wonders ; worlds within worlds, of infinite minuteness, though,
as to Art, equal to the greatest, and pregnant with more
wonders than the most discerning sense, joined with the greatest
Art, or the acutest reason, can penetrate or unfold[4]." The
whole universe is the masterpiece of an infinite artist, and it is

---

[1] *Moralists*, Part 2, § 4.   [2] *Ibid.*
[3] *Ibid.* Part 1, § 3.   [4] *Ibid.* Part 3, § 1.

sharply defined as the perfect example of the Greek Ideal,
being, like all art, sublimely simple in conception without
redundancy in execution, even to the minutest particular[1].

Shaftesbury's whole system revolves round the idea of a
Cosmos, beautiful and perfect, in which there is room, not
merely for natural Beauty, but also for loveliness of life, which
is the higher type of the two. This restoration of the Hellenic
ideal of life is Shaftesbury's reply to the banishment of beauty
by the Puritans. As already stated, it is less a theory than a
cult; indeed, appealing, as it does, to the æsthetic sense, it
tends to be exclusive, or rather it will not condescend to argue
with those who have failed to realise its conditions of attaining
to the right point of view.

But it is one thing to protest and quite another to maintain
the validity of one's protest, and Shaftesbury laboured under
the disadvantage of requiring a return to an impossible state.
The Greek life was a *phase* in the history of humanity not its
goal. To regain it would be to reproduce all the multifarious
conditions of the Age of Pericles, natural, social, racial, linguistic
and economic. This would be as gigantic a task as a fresh
creation *ex nihilo*. The reason that the way is barred for any
complete return to the Greek life is well characterized by
Mr Pater, when he said, " The Greek mind had advanced to a
peculiar stage of self-reflexion, but was careful never to pass
beyond it. In Greek thought, the 'lordship of the soul' is
recognised; that lordship gives authority and divinity to human
hands and eyes and feet; inanimate nature is thrown into the
back-ground. But just here Greek thought finds its happy
limit[2]." Even amongst the later Greeks this happy limit was
passed; and therefore much more had modern life gone beyond
it. Further, there could be no real return. The devotion of
the Greeks to youth for the sake of its grace and beauty had
passed with the youthfulness of the world, and any attempted
revival of it is as out of place, as age, enamelled and tight-laced,
dancing in short-frocks with school girls. The modern world has
succeeded to a heritage of problems, which leave life divided
into sharply defined and often contradictory parts, for which

---

[1] *Advice to an Author*, Part 1, § 3.
[2] *The Renaissance*, p. 218.

reconciliations must be found; and in its complexity such solutions present no small difficulty. Therefore the unity that was unquestioned amongst the Greeks can only come to us with toil and pain. Thus it is that the *spontaneity* of the Greek ideal is unattainable, and the progress of time stands for the flaming sword that for ever bars humanity from this lost Eden.

If Shaftesbury had followed out his renaissance of the idea of a Cosmos throughout, he would have been able to deduce a system of Ethics in several directions as the excellence of human action, and thereby have endeavoured to confute the " Selfish " moralists[1]. Yet the problem he had to face carried him beyond the Hellenic outlook, to which man played his part in the theatre of the Cosmos without a desired precedence over the other non-human actors. From the æsthetic point of view, man was seen from the outside, and the question was less *why* he acted in a certain way, than *how* he acted, and, further, *how* his acts harmonized in a general scheme. The Greeks had avoided abstruse introspection and casuistic analysis of motive; what concerned them was τὸ ἔργον—man's deed, and this should be excellent. As Dryden expresses it, the diapason of universal harmony, " closes full in man " ; there is no jarring note in the human part of the chorus nor any too obtrusive minor key.

Now hedonistic systems had passed this limit—just as if a child had broken all the strings of an instrument, then twisted them together, and expected harmony by a simple process of eliminating, not overcoming, differences. Hence, when Shaftesbury stands face to face with the second great national need— the necessity for a reply to the prevailing selfishness in life and theory—he finds that the Greek ideal can no longer help him, since his opponents had already passed beyond it. Man's " lordship " in the world had been questioned and to assert it he had long been at war with the world, so that the old alliance had gone never to return.

Still the problem confronted Shaftesbury, and some solution was required. Fortunately he lived just at the end of a period of historical anachronisms. If poets and painters had found

---

[1] Cf. Hutcheson's "third period" in chapter XI.

nothing incongruous in mixing Greek sages with Jewish Apostles, it was unlikely that Shaftesbury would find any incongruity in blending a precept of exclusively Christian Ethics into a Greek ideal of a cosmos.   Thus the maxim " Thou shalt love thy neighbour as thyself" becomes the root of Shaftesbury's reply to the Egoist.   To selfishness he opposes unselfishness, to Egoism, Benevolence.   To the pagan conception of the life beautiful, he adds the Christmas message of " Good-will to men."   That is—he is first forced to break into his system of harmony, in deference to the spirit of his age, then he endeavours to heal the breach by introducing an altogether foreign conception.   Nature and God are still contemplated each as expressed, both are viewed from the outside, while man, on the contrary, is to be seen from within in his character or " temper."   This is the same inconsistency as if an artist painted all the persons of a group, except one, in the usual way and that one as seen by the Röntgen Rays !

Obviously the æsthetic and ethical views were in conflict ; and Shaftesbury, by identifying the two, ignores the difference. Benevolence is beautiful, and all beauty in human action is due to a benevolent disposition.   Yet even here the inconsistency is only concealed, for " the good kind affections " are no longer spontaneous.   The harmony of Beauty is reached only indirectly through a step in the dark, altogether outside the view of æstheticism.   Another difficulty consists in the manner of apprehension of moral states.   This is to be intuitive.   Now, if the rightness of an affection be the object of immediate perception, it is dealt with in isolation, and the whole cosmic theory is lost with its harmony and symmetry, and we have ethical atomism ; on the other hand, if the act is to be approved of, in the long series of its effects, the intuitive side of the theory must go by the board ; and with it Shaftesbury's main defence against the Hobbist.

Such difficulties were concealed by the fact that the ideal of the comely life was rather a cult than a theory, while in the Benevolent interpretation of it, argumentation preponderates— the first Shaftesbury had borrowed, the second was more his own, and besides it was more necessary to defend, owing to the

exigencies of controversy. Further, he endeavoured to find a
point of union in showing the benevolent life as the beautiful
life. Having already justified Beauty by appeal to the Æsthetic
sense, he then shows the man of good impulses—nature's gentleman—and asks "Is not his life also beautiful?" Elsewhere,
in dealing with Beauty, Shaftesbury is satisfied to show the
existence of harmonious and symmetrical relations, but in
human character the mere existence of relations is not sufficient;
they must be of a certain kind, namely dispositions of character
that lead to the good of the "system" as a whole. Thus, in
human character, there is to be a censorship, not required elsewhere.

The necessity for such censorship is, as far as possible,
concealed, and the identification of the beautiful with the
benevolent life is skilfully made by directing the reader's attention to the Harmony of the benevolent character. First of all
Shaftesbury clearly explains that what he calls goodness has to
do exclusively with character or "temper." "That which is
not done through any affection at all, makes neither Good nor
Ill in the nature of that creature; who, then, is only supposed
good, when the good or ill of the System, to which he has
relation, is the immediate object of some passion or affection
moving him[1]." "Nothing therefore being properly either
goodness or illness, in a creature, but what is *natural temper*; a
good creature is such a one as by the natural temper or bent of
his affections is carried *primarily and immediately*, and not
secondarily and accidentally, to Good and against Ill : and an
ill creature is just the contrary—viz. one who is wanting in
right affections, of force enough to carry him *directly* towards
Good ; or who is carried by other affections to Ill and against
Good. When in general all the affections or passions are suited
to the Publick Good or Good of the Species, as above mentioned,
then is the *natural temper* intirely good[2]." Further, Shaftesbury distinguishes between isolated affections and the union of
these in a good character, which is possessed of that sound and
well-established Reason, " which alone constitutes a just affec-

---

[1] *Inquiry*, Book I. Part 2, § 1.
[2] *Ibid.* § 2.

tion, a uniform and steddy [sic] will and resolution[1]." Such a
fixed character is that of a " rational being," who is able to
attain to " virtue in itself."

The following is Shaftesbury's account of the rise and scope
of the public affections. " If any appetite or sense be natural,
the sense of fellowship is the same. If there be anything of
Nature in that affection, which is between the sexes, the affection is certainly as natural towards the consequent offspring;
and so again between the offspring themselves, as kinsmen and
companions, bred under the same discipline and œconomy.
And thus a clan or tribe is gradually formed; a Public is recognised, and besides the pleasure found in social entertainment,
language and discourse, there is so apparent a necessity for
continuing this good correspondency and union, that to have no
sense or feeling of this kind, no love of Country, Community, or
anything in Common, would be the same as to be insensible,
even of the plainest means of self-preservation, and most
necessary condition of self-enjoyment...Universal good or the
interest of the *world in general* is a kind of remote Philosophical object. That greater community falls not easily under
the eye[2]. Nor is a national interest, or that of a whole people
or body politick, so readily apprehended. In less parties, men
may be intimately conversant and acquainted with one another.
They can there better taste society, and enjoy the common
good and interest in a more contracted publick. They view the
whole compass and extent of their community, and see and
know particularly whom 'tis they serve and to what end
they associate and conspire. All men have naturally their
share of this associating and combining principle: and they,
who are of the sprightliest and most active faculties, have so
large a share of it that, unless it be happily directed by right
Reason, it can never find exercise for itself in so remote a
sphere as that of the body politick at large. For, here, perhaps
the thousandth part of those whose interests are concerned are
scarce as much as known by sight. No visible band is formed,
no strict alliance, but the conjunction is made with different

[1] *Inquiry*, Book I. Part 2, § 4.
[2] Contrast Hutcheson's "second and third periods," chapters x. and xi.

persons, orders, and ranks of men, not sensibly, but *in idea*, according to the general view or notion of a state or Commonwealth[1]."

That "universal good is a kind of remote philosophical object" sufficiently differentiates Shaftesbury's Philanthropy from Stoic Cosmopolitanism. Even, in the eclectic form, in which Cicero reproduced the theory—for it must be remembered that "Tully" was a household word amongst people of culture during the first half of last century—the firmest bond of union was that amongst the Wise[2]. The Stoic "citizenship of the world" was an ideal for the Philosopher and too much inclined to despise the rights and interests of the rest of mankind, mostly, if not all, fools: it was an abstract universal working downwards, yet failing to reach the particular: it was, to borrow a phrase of Kant's, rational, not pathological, love. Shaftesbury's philanthropy, on the contrary, started from the family grouping of individuals; and from this basis found it difficult to reach "the greater community that falls not easily under the eye," because it was founded on actual affection and love for the individual as such.

Shaftesbury's expressions in favour of altruism are not to be understood in the sense that the "self-affections" are to be suppressed, though they are to be kept in bounds; they are to be used to make the individual as efficient as possible for the service of the community. He is to be, from the Greek point of view, excellent throughout. From Shaftesbury's position, what he calls "self-affections," are to be held in trust for the public good[3]. The moral state of the individual is a fiduciary one, his nature, in itself a microcosm, might be compared to a joint-stock Company, which would be a "system," in Shaftesbury's sense, though sometimes, perhaps, not a very

---

[1] *Essay on the Freedom of Wit and Humour*, Part 3, § 2. Cf. *Butler's Sermons*, Oxford, p. 12. "Men are so much one body, that, in a peculiar manner, they feel for each other, shame, sudden anger, resentment, prosperity, distress; one or another or all of these, from the social nature in general, from Benevolence, upon the occasion of natural relation, protection, acquaintance, dependence—each of these being distinct cements of Society."

[2] *De Officiis*, i. ch. xvii.

[3] *Inquiry*, Book i. Part 2, § 2.

"harmonious" one.   A director's private advantage in any contract in which both he and the Company were concerned would correspond to the Self-affections, while the interests of the general body of Shareholders might be compared to the objects of the Public affections.   Now as according to recent legal decisions in such a case, the Director is a trustee for the Shareholders, so the moral man uses his self-affections as a trustee for the community at large.   Individual excellence is not an end-in-itself for the individual, and is only his end, rightly, in so far as it is serviceable to the community.   Here then is a second censorship, since the Self-affections must be approved of by the Public ones, before resulting in right conduct; and, conversely, the Public stimulate the Self-affections after the latter have been unreservedly approved. Obviously this is a refinement of the theory, and not a very stable one; for the "immediate object of an affection" which is originally approved becomes the approval by the public affections of a remote object of the self-affections—that is in fact the affection of an affection.

Having explained the nature of affections towards the public good, and supplemented the pagan life by the Ethics of Philanthropy, it remains for Shaftesbury to make the two cohere together.   This, as already hinted, is effected by exhibiting kind affections as excellent and also as instances of harmony and order.   This excellent ethical condition is the "due ballance and counterpoise of the affections.   In every different creature and distinct sex, there is a different and distinct order, set or suit of Passions, proportionable to the different order of life and different functions and capacities assigned to each.   As the operations and effects are different, so are the springs and causes in each System.   The inside work is fitted to the outward action and performance[1]."   This same idea is developed under all the alternative expressions of union, order, symmetry and harmony—in the latter case by the simile of the lyre, which is in proper tune, each string ready to give due expression to its appropriate note of melody[2].

[1] *Inquiry*, Book II. Part 2, § 1.   [2] *Ibid.* Part 1, § 3.

This symmetry of affection, then further, is beautiful. " No sooner," Shaftesbury says, "are human affections and passions discerned (and they are most of them as soon discerned as felt) than straight *an inward eye* distinguishes, and sees *the fair* and *shapely*, the *amiable* and *admirable*, apart from the *deformed*, the *foul*, the *odious* or the *despicable*[1]." " Whoever has any impression of what we call gentility or politeness is already so acquainted with the decorum and grace of things that he will readily confess a pleasure and enjoyment in the very survey and contemplation of this kind.   Now, if, in the way of polite pleasure, the study and love of Beauty be essential, the study and love of Symmetry and Order, on which Beauty depends must also be essential in the same respect... Should not this (one would imagine) be still the same case and hold equally as to the Mind ?   Is there no natural tenour, tone or order of the passions or affections ?   No Beauty or Deformity in this moral kind ?   Will it not be found, in this respect, above all ' That what is beautiful is harmonious and proportionable : What is harmonious and proportionable is true: and what is, at once, both beautiful and true, is, of consequence, agreeable and good[2]' ".   " The true poet," he says elsewhere, " is indeed a second Maker : a just Prometheus under Jove.   Like that sovereign Artist, or universal Plastick Nature, he forms a whole, co-herent and proportioned in itself, with due subjection and subordinacy of constituent parts. He notes the boundaries of the passions and knows their exact tones and measures ; by which he justly represents them, marks the sublime of sentiment and actions, and distinguishes the Beautiful from the Deformed, the amiable from the odious. The Moral Artist, who can thus imitate the Creator, and is thus knowing in the inward form and structure of his fellow creature, will hardly, I presume, be found unknowing, in himself, or at a loss in those numbers which make the harmony of a mind.   For knavery is mere dessonance and disproportion[3]."   Besides the poet, " the real ' honest' man, however plain or simple he

[1] *Moralists*, Part 3, § 2.
[2] *Miscellaneous Reflections*, No. 3, ch. II.
[3] *Advice to an Author*, Part 1, § 3.

appears, has that highest species of 'honesty' itself in view
(i.e. the Honestum, Pulchrum, τὸ καλὸν, πρέπον) and instead
of *outward* forms of symmetries, is struck with that of *inward* character, "the harmony and numbers of the heart
and beauty of the affections, which form the manners and conduct of a truly social life[1]." In the same spirit Virtue is
described "as the chief of all Beauties and excellencies" and is
characterized, in the effects flowing from the kind affections, as
"the prop and ornament of human affairs, which upholds com-
munities, maintains union, friendship and correspondence
amongst men, [it is] that by which countries, as well as
private families, flourish and are happy, and for want of
which everything comely, conspicuous, great and worthy
must perish and go to ruin[2]."

Obviously from Shaftesbury's general point of view the
kind affections which are virtuous are harmonious and symmetrical, and therefore beautiful. It is by these affections that
the microcosm of the individual is orderly connected with the
macrocosm of society at large. Thus Shaftesbury, following
the later Stoics, passes from the purely Hellenic to the organic
view of the universe. Man and society are organically connected, for each individual is a member of the whole social body.

This position introduces a slight modification of the former
one. Beauty, as applied to the social macrocosm, tends to lose
its most essential characters. In dealing with natural and
artistic Beauty, Shaftesbury finds place for the characteristics
of form, colour and movement[3], but plainly these do not apply
in the so-called Beauty of the social organism, which is a
symmetry without material form (except in a metaphorical
sense). This widening of the term is exceedingly fruitful to
Shaftesbury by the introduction of the idea of *end*; and thus
when Virtue, as a kindly disposition, is called beautiful, we are
to understand the expression in reference to the end of the
system as a whole, and virtue is interpreted as ἀρετή, the
excellence of function towards its object—such object being
again the larger excellence of the macrocosm. From this

---

[1] *Miscellaneous Reflections*, No. 2, ch. i.
[2] *Inquiry*, Book ii. Part 2, § 3.   [3] *Moralists*, Part 3, § 2.

aspect we see the reverse side of the renaissance of Greek life in an universal teleology, from which Shaftesbury deduces the existence of an intelligent First Cause.

Though the results of the substitution of Teleology for Beauty are fruitful, they are reached at the expense of an inconsistency already mentioned. The artistic spontaneity and unconsciousness of the Greek ideal of life are lost. The excellence attained is not the untrammelled success of Art, but rather a laboured one, where the end tends more and more to be obtruded. Man ceases to be an artist fashioning his own character, blithely and happily; but on the contrary painfully struggling with dissention inside the microcosm, and endeavouring to guide the different affections towards the end they should seek spontaneously. Thus the modern spirit really renders a return to the Hellenic ideal an impossibility. The life beautiful after all turns out to be a quest for a life of philanthropy; if it be artistic in any sense, it is only in that of Art with a purpose; and if there is a rhythm in living, it can but be followed with a constant eye upon the moral, which is to be expected somewhere in every movement.

In Shaftesbury's balance of a system of affections, one is forcibly reminded of Green's universe of desires; and in one passage the language of the *Prolegomena to Ethics* is strikingly anticipated. " We find," he says, " that there is no expression more generally used, in a way of compliment to great men and princes, than that plain one which is so often verified, and may be falsely pronounced for truth on most occasions, ' That they have acted *like themselves* and suitably to their own genius and character....' Such is the natural affection of all mankind towards moral Beauty and Perfection, that they never fail in making this presumption in behalf of themselves—' That, by nature they have something estimable and worthy in respect of others of their kind; and that their *genuine true* and *natural Self* is, as it ought to be, of real value in society and justly honourable for the sake of its merit and good qualities.' They conclude therefore they have the height of praise allotted them when they are assured by anyone that they have done nothing *below themselves*, or that in some particular action they have

exceeded the ordinary tenour of their character. Thus is
everyone convinced of a *better Self*, and of the cult or homage
due to it[1]." From Shaftesbury's standpoint the higher or
better self is that in harmony with the end of the macrocosm;
and, as will be seen, he is forced to postulate a pre-established
harmony between the end of the individual and that of the
social organism. The suppression of the rights of the self as
personal is an intelligible exaggeration as a protest against
Hobbes, but it really vests the interests of the Self in the social
organism, and thus in Green's language, Shaftesbury's ideal
might be formulated as " realise the end of society and thereby
the self is realised."

The revival of the Hellenic ideal of life, gradually passing
from an æsthetic to a teleological interpretation of the Cosmos,
is the resultant of the two great national needs which originated Shaftesbury's Philosophy, and this remedy outlines the
main features of his manner of thinking. There remain, however, a few further influences of an accidental or personal
nature, which account for certain minor portions of his work.

First of these is the superficial resemblance between some
of his results and the system of Leibniz. Though Shaftesbury
professed a thorough contempt for the usual academic Philosophy—which he calls pedantic and useless—he was attracted
by the courtier-metaphysician in Leibniz, who had sent him
very flattering comments upon his writings[2]. In the symmetry
and minute gradations of the Monads, there was a certain
resemblance to the symmetry and harmony of Shaftesbury's
"system or Œconomy." On the other hand, the English thinker,
being unaffected by the Cartesian tendency, escaped the need
for the isolation and repulsion that characterizes the Monad.
Nevertheless Shaftesbury found an opposition in his own system,
and one might hazard the guess that it was to Leibniz he owed
the idea of a Pre-established Harmony between the excellence
of self-regarding and that of other-regarding affections—true
self good and true public good are identical—the end of the

---

[1] *Advice to an Author*, Part 3, § 1. (The italics are those of the edition
published 1711.)

[2] Fowler's *Shaftesbury*, p. 137.

microcosm is subsumed under that of the macrocosm[1]. Therefore it is indifferent from which of the two points one approaches the question of excellence. It is true that Shaftesbury endeavours to prove this thesis, and therefore he has been charged with the paradox of Hedonism : since if each man follows his public affections, the motive may be merely a conviction of the justness of the argument that by so doing he secures his own happiness. In part at least Shaftesbury escapes this criticism ; for he differs from the Universalistic Hedonist in that it is not the effects of the action that are approved, but the emotive spring that prompts it; and the latter must be an immediate affection, whose object is the social good—if there were any reference to "self-good" the harmony would be lost, for the end would not be social, and not even personal in the best sense, it would be a discord, a deformity. As to the further question, how casuistical cases are to be decided, Shaftesbury is careful to keep a discreet silence. He takes his stand on the broad principle that excellence of character consists in the brotherhood of man and the cultivation of a brother's love for every fellow-creature. He gives us, in fact, the Ethics of Philanthropy not merely in good offices, but in universalised good-will.

Another personal relation is that of Shaftesbury to Locke, who had been his tutor. Possibly the teacher had been a stern disciplinarian, or it may be that he had to join the other despised Philosophers in the limbo of pedants—at all events, Shaftesbury rarely speaks of him except with bitterness. At the same time, whether he was aware of it or not, he was indebted to Locke for several ideas—though, in truth, these are far from strengthening his Philosophy. The most important instance of his indebtedness is in connection with the terminology, by which he describes the act of approval of the correspondence between individual and social ends. Whether he is indebted to Locke for more than the terminology is a question of some difficulty. He clearly states that the approval of kind affections is the work of a " reflex Sense " or affection. " In a creature capable of forming general notions of things, not only the outward beings which offer themselves to the sense,

---

[1] It is from this point that Shaftesbury starts to establish his optimism.

are the objects of the affection, but the very actions themselves and the affections of Pity, Kindness, Gratitude, and their contraries, being brought before the mind by Reflection, become objects. So that by means of this reflected sense, there arises another kind of affection towards those very affections themselves, which have already been felt, and are now become the subject of a new liking or dislike.

"The case is the same here as in the ordinary bodies or common subjects of Sense. The shapes, motions, colours and proportions of these being presented to our eye, there necessarily results a Beauty or deformity, according to the different measure, arrangement and disposition of their several parts. So in behaviour and actions, [in which] when presented to our understanding there must be found of necessity an apparent difference, according to the regularity or irregularity of the subjects.

"The mind, which is the spectator or auditor of other minds, cannot be without its eye and ear, so as to discern Proportion, distinguish sound, and scan each sentiment or thought that comes before it. It can let nothing escape its censure. It feels the soft, the harsh, the agreeable and disagreeable in the affections; and finds a foul and a fair, a harmonious and dissonant, as really and truly here, as in the outward forms or representations of sensible things.

"As in the sensible kind, the species or images of bodies, colours and sounds, are perpetually moving before our eyes and acting on our senses even in sleep, and when the real objects themselves are absent, so in the moral and intellectual kind the forms and images of things are no less active and incumbent on the mind.

"In these vagrant characters or pictures of manners, which the mind of necessity figures to itself, and carries still about with it, the heart cannot possibly remain neutral; but constantly takes part, one way or other. However false or corrupt it be within itself, it finds the difference, as to Beauty and Comeliness, between one heart and another, one turn of affection, one behaviour, one sentiment and another; and accordingly, in all disinterested cases, must approve in some measure what is natural and honest, and disapprove what is dishonest and corrupt.

"Thus the several motions, inclinations, passions, dispositions and consequent carriage and behaviour of creatures, in the various parts of life, being in several views or perspectives represented to the mind, which readily discerns the good or ill towards the species or publick; there arises a new trial or exercise of the Heart, which must either rightly and soundly affect what is just and right and disaffect what is contrary; or corruptly affect what is ill, and disaffect what is worthy and good[1]."

Here we have the language of Locke, expressing his naïve view of the world, and its effect upon the mental *tabula rasa*. "Things" affect the mind, which proceeds "to compound, enlarge and abstract" the simple ideas already given. These functions Shaftesbury, when he speaks in Locke's language, assigns to Reason which is only discursive. There are thus two divisions of ideas, those due to Reason which are arbitrary, since it is a matter of choice whether the faculty shall be employed or not, and the non-rational ideas, including all the rest. Shaftesbury's constant use of metaphor in speaking of the sense of beauty of character or moral beauty, his use of expressions, such as "the eye" and "ear of the mind," "the taste" for Moral Beauty, "a relish" for it, "sensations" of it, have led to his theory being classed as crudely hedonistic. Possibly the two points of view, which he never succeeded in reconciling, may throw some light upon the difficulty and show that he did not consciously maintain the disinterestedness of virtue against the egoist, only to be himself an egoist of the egoists, in showing that disinterestedness was egoistically twice-blessed, first by the "Pre-established Harmony" already mentioned and secondly by the pleasant approval of the "Sense."

It must be remembered that in reading the passage quoted above from the *Inquiry*, Shaftesbury speaks from the first of his two points of view. He is the "spectator of other minds" and characters, the critic of excellence of temper and behaviour, and thus he pronounces a "judgment of taste" upon

---

[1] *Inquiry*, Book i. Part 2, § 3.

the rightly-ordered life. Such a life is, from the Hellenic
standpoint, a work of art, and as such produces æsthetic
pleasure in the person who views it. So each "sensitive" or
"rational" being—Shaftesbury uses both expressions—is, or
ought to be, artistically satisfying to the other spectators, and
therefore the sense of Beauty of character looks at life from an
outside point of view. Behind the beautiful life is the beautiful character, the existence of which is inferred, and this, as
that which "means, intends, regulates and orders," is the true
principle of Beauty[1]. Beauty, however, has been resolved into
the teleological idea of a Cosmos of rightly-ordered affections,
and so behind or beyond the judgments of taste upon conduct,
which are passed by others, rather than by the agent himself,
there is the value of affections and dispositions to the social
organism. Shaftesbury never speaks in any very precise terms
of the act or state by which the harmony of the will of the
microcosm and the end of the macrocosm is perceived. The
general drift of his expressions tends to show that such apprehension is intuitive in the widest sense in which Prof. Sidgwick
uses the expression[2]—that is, it is not "rational" or mediate or
arbitrary, but immediate. Whether this immediate perception
is active or passive, emotional or intellectual, or again partaking
of both characteristics, there is little evidence. Shaftesbury
frequently speaks of the subjectivity of sense in quite a Platonic
strain (that is, of sense as a state of feeling); while in the case
of this intuitive perception of harmony of the system of affections
in reference to their end, he often uses the expression that
it gives us access to Virtue "in itself"—that is, that the
harmony of the individual and the macrocosm is known objectively or absolutely. Further he even uses somewhat
Platonic language in saying such harmony of ends is known by
" pre-conceptions " or "anticipations[3]." He even goes so far as
to call it "instinct" in the sense of that "which is exclusive of
art, culture or discipline." He appears to be groping after
some expression like *a priori*, though it is difficult to determine

[1] *Moralists*, Part 3, § 2.
[2] *The Methods of Ethics*, p. 97.
[3] *Moralists*, Part 3, § 2.

whether a "pre-conception" is to be prior to all experience or only to all experience save the æsthetic feelings.

These "pre-conceptions" are founded upon an original, inderivative power of mind, and cannot be resolved by any psychological solvent. This is what Shaftesbury means by so frequently maintaining that certain mental facts are "natural," —that is φύσει not νόμῳ. From his point of view every mental state that was "natural" in this sense was direct or immediate, as opposed to the mediacy of the discursive reason, and "necessary," as opposed to the arbitrariness of anything conventional. Thus the affections (the social ones, especially as against Hobbes) are natural; so is the perception of symmetry and the joy of contemplating the harmonious life.

With regard to the power of making moral distinctions, there is primarily a natural foundation which is capable of rudimentary approval, this may develope in many directions; first, it may blunder on without special training, as a part of a mediocre character, either good in a limited degree or bad in a limited degree—this is the condition of the "vulgar,"—secondly, it may be trained by the virtuoso by careful cultivation and familiarity with masterpieces of moral excellence. This addition of frequent exercises of the natural power gives rise to an individual and general standard, besides accounting for wide variations of standard from time to time[1]. The "better self" is always growing, and the standard grows and deepens with its growth. It is thus that training makes the moral exquisite, who in Shaftesbury's Philosophy corresponds in some degree to the Ideal of the Wise Man with the Stoics, or the Happy Man of the Epicureans. With the virtuoso the original natural capacity or faculty has been so thoroughly developed, that he can unfailingly detect the least discord in character or admire any traces of harmony he may discover. With him the original intuitive power has passed through such a course of training that the developed critical faculty has become apparently intuitive again. The necessity of "nature" has now been cultivated into the inevitableness of artistic insight.

If the *Questio quid juris* be asked with regard to this moral

---

[1] *Moralists*, Part 3, § 2.

virtuosoship, Shaftesbury can scarcely rely, without contradiction, upon the æsthetic satisfaction of judgments of taste as applied to systematic or cosmic harmony of character.   In fact such an interpretation is foreign to his whole outlook.   The *primary* object of this satisfaction is the character of others, and therefore if it is to be a motive to any given individual, he could only live an excellent life, so as to provide others with the opportunity of gaining satisfaction from the contemplation of it, or in a lesser degree by making himself his own morally artistic vehicle for his own satisfaction.   This, as a motive, would be much too nebulous for the egoist.   In this connection it is noteworthy that Shaftesbury very rarely uses the expression "moral sense"—and that, except in one or two instances, only in his marginal notes; while "conscience" occurs still more rarely.   These two expressions are not to be confounded, for they meant different states of mind, "moral sense" with "sense" generally, as applied to Beauty of Character, standing for the æsthetic "contemplation" already mentioned; while Conscience[1] generally implies a consciousness of demerit, being nearly akin to Remorse.

Rather than in either of these, the moral principle with Shaftesbury is to be found in the more obscure and deeper perception of conformity to the ends of the Cosmos as related to the individual[2].   It is justified first in its "natural" or pure state, and, afterwards, as cultured by the consciousness of the endeavour to attain a parallelism between the individual and the social organism.   All the main ideas of the whole mode of thought draw together to reinforce it, in the Cosmic ideal, which Shaftesbury calls the "faith of Theism."   "I am convinced," he says, "of my own being and of this self of mine. That 'tis a real self, drawn out and copied from another principal and original Self—the great one of the world.   I endeavour to be really one with it, and conformable to it, as far as I am able.   I consider that, as there is *one* general mass, one body of the whole; so this body then is an order, to this order

---

[1] *Inquiry*, Book II. Part 2, § 1.

[2] Cf. Mansel's theory of "Moral Perception" and "Moral Sensation," *Psychology*, p. 163.

a mind—that to this general mind, each particular one must have relation, as being of like Substance (as much as we can understand of Substance), alike active upon body, original to motion and order—alike simple, uncompounded, individual—of like energy, effect, operation—and more like still if it cooperates with *It* to general good, and strives to *will* according to that best of Wills[1]."

This consciousness of the identity of the ends of the microcosm and macrocosm has another side in the further consciousness of Dignity or Worth of the microcosm. "Worth and Merit," Shaftesbury says, "are substantial, and not variable by fancy or will, and Honour is as much *itself*, when acting *by itself* and unseen, as when seen and applauded by all the world." "Should one," he continues, "who had the countenance of a gentlemen, ask me—'Why I should avoid being nasty, when no one was present?' In the first place, I should be fully satisfied that he himself was a very nasty gentleman who could ask this question, and that it would be a hard matter for me to make him ever conceive what true cleanliness was. However, I might notwithstanding this, be contented to give him a slight answer, and say, ''Twas because I had a nose.' Should he trouble me further, and ask again, 'What if I had a cold?' 'Or what if, naturally, I had no such nice smell?' I might answer perhaps, 'That I cared as little to see myself nasty as that others should see me in that condition.' But what if it were in the dark? Why even then, though I had neither nose nor eyes, my sense of the matter would be still the same, my nature would rise at the thought of what is sordid, or if it did not, I should have a wretched nature and hate myself for a beast. Honour myself I never could, whilst I had no better a sense of what, in reality, I owed myself, and what became me as a human creature[2]." Elsewhere he shows that the consciousness of worth is the foundation of self-respect or self-esteem, which, when abused, becomes conceit and pride. "Does anyone who has pride think meanly or indifferently of himself? No, but honourably. And how this, if there be no

---

[1] *Moralists*, Part 3, § 1.
[2] *Essay on the Freedom of Wit and Humour*, Part 3, § 4.

real Honour or Dignity presupposed? For self-valuation presupposes "Self-Worth"; and in a person conscious of real
worth is either no pride, or a just and noble one[1]."

Finally, another aspect of Shaftesbury's mode of thought is
purely accidental and personal. It arises out of the peculiar
views he held of the semi-æsthetic cultivation of the original
inderivative power of making moral distinctions. He supposes
the person of true moral culture to go through a regular
æsthetic or teleological training; and, therefore, he must be a
man of leisure. Hence his mode of expression is exceedingly
exclusive—it is aristocratically esoteric—and one finds he
addresses himself to "gentlemen of fashion," "fine gentlemen,"
"virtuosi," those living in the "polite world" or the "beau
monde." To these moral exquisites, are opposed the vulgar,
who are to be constrained to do what the virtuosi do from high
and noble motives. Hence Schleiermacher calls the whole
system one of "Moral Etiquette[2]."

This exclusiveness gives an artificial cast to the moral
doctrine, which is strikingly incongruous, when compared with
the precepts inculcating the universal brotherhood of man. It
is an ethical primogeniture with a vengeance, where all the
privileges go to the first-born. All men are *terrae filii*, but the
virtuoso leaves little more than the husks for the less fortunate
children. In fact the love of man is not true brotherly love,
but rather something the ideal gentleman owes, not to his
fellows out of kindness of heart, but to his own higher nature
and the Cosmos generally. The kindly affections, in fact, tend
not to rest directly upon their immediate objects, but upon the
harmony of the social organism as a whole.

This artificiality is to a certain extent reflected in Shaftesbury's style. One thinks of him as a Watteau rustic or, to
borrow an expression from Mr George Meredith, as a "Dresden
shepherd." Throughout there is the want of spontaneity,
already noticed, and a certain straining after effect. Still it
scarcely deserves the following scathing criticism of Mr Leslie
Stephen. "Whenever he tries to be facetious he is intoler-

---

[1] *Moralists*, Part 3, § 2.
[2] *Die Philosophie Shaftesbury's von Dr Georg von Giżycki*, p. 127.

able... Yet Shaftesbury is less annoying, when he is writhing his grave face into a contorted grimace, than when the muse, whom he is in the habit of invoking, permits him to get upon stilts. His rhapsodies then are truly dismal.... His prose at excited moments becomes a kind of breccia of blank verse.... No English critic can witness his native language tortured into this hideous parody of verse without disgust.... No Philosophy can persuade us out of our ears, and Shaftesbury's mouthing is simply detestable.... Shaftesbury in short is deficient in the cardinal virtues of clearness and order; and the consequence is, that working upon abstruse topics, he tries his readers beyond all ordinary bearing. Perhaps this is a sufficient reason for the neglect which has overtaken him, for the writers are few and fortunate, who have succeeded in reaching posterity without the charm of a beautiful style[1]." This seems to be rather a harsh judgment, pronounced upon the principles of Matthew Arnold, and yet it narrowly escapes being what Arnold calls "saugrenu." It is founded on the same error that Arnold himself makes in condemning some of Burke's oratory as "Asiatic," by isolating it from its context and the circumstances which occasioned it. Similarly Mr Stephen here condemns Shaftesbury for expressions which occur at the conclusion of the *Moralists*—these are the Rhapsodies or Soliloquies for which the whole book has, from the artistic point of view, been written, and which constitute its peroration. It is scarcely fair to isolate them from the context, and censure Shaftesbury for his endeavour after eloquence. In fact there are two sides to the style of a philosophical work—whether it is considered as Literature or as Philosophy proper. It is evidently as Literature that Mr Stephen holds that Shaftesbury's writings are deservedly neglected; but it must always be remembered that much of his mode of thought was versified by Pope, and that in this more compact form a large number of lines in the *Essay on Man,* derived directly from Shaftesbury, are more frequently quoted than those of any other poet— except Shakespeare. In this way, Shaftesbury received in a remarkable manner both the reward and the penalty of his

[1] *Fraser's Magazine*, vol. VII. pp. 77—79.

popularity in his own day. Had his mode of thought and his own expression of it not been widely admired, Pope would not have versified it; but once turned into such verse, which, however "rhetorical" or "laboured," or unsuitable to the subject, is still admirably terse and epigrammatic—it can readily be understood that the poetic reproduction stole the recognition of posterity from the original[1]. Most readers of Shaftesbury's works will admit that the style is brighter and more "sprightly" than in most philosophical writings of the time. There is humour, irony and sarcasm beyond what is generally met with in productions of the kind. His very eccentricities and mannerisms help the reader's attention, and give a variety that is not met with in similar compositions[2]. Sometimes too Shaftesbury is really eloquent, without breaking into the rhythm of blank verse. Against this is to be set the defect that his allusions sometimes miss the point, and instead of reaching the Sublime, he narrowly escapes an anticlimax. Evidently he had a high ideal of a style that would have something of the grace and poetry of Plato's; and, as is so frequently the case in attempts of this kind, his successes make his failures all the more conspicuous,—still is it not better to fail to attain such an ideal than to be altogether without it?

In the same article Mr Stephen makes an exceedingly luminous comparison between Shaftesbury and Matthew Arnold, mentioning as similar characteristics the desire of both for intellectual sanity and light, and the hostility of both to the Philistinism of their respective times. Such a parallel throws more light upon Shaftesbury's relation to the general progress of culture than pages of explanation. At the same time such a comparison should not be extended too far. Shaftesbury's enthusiasm—his interpretation of the Platonic ἔρως—was altogether foreign to Matthew Arnold's temperament, and leaves no room for suspense of judgment. In this respect Shaftesbury was the more virile writer of the two, since it is to be feared that Arnold would leave one no language in which to

---

[1] Cf. *supra*, p. 101.

[2] Cf. Rendall's *Marcus Aurelius*, p. vi. "Marcus hits off phrases and combinations, which, if not quite felicitous strike the mind and stick."

express condemnation of a great wrong, lest such expression might not be "Attic"—Shaftesbury on the contrary, not only held pronounced opinions but also dared to express them in strong language[1]. Another difference is one due to the lapse of time. Shaftesbury is an aristocrat, Arnold has much of the bourgeois spirit—despite his polemic against "respectability"—that seeks "light" by rule of majorities and finds "what is best" more readily when marked by a well-known name. This difference is a result of the political Zeitgeist—for since Shaftesbury's day we have had the French Revolution and the Reform Bill.

If Shaftesbury's historical position is to be defined by a modern instance, in some respects his resemblance to Mr Ruskin is more marked than to Matthew Arnold. He is to be compared to the former in his contempt for academic Philosophy—for has not Mr Ruskin excluded all modern speculative works from his list of "best books," except Mill's *Logic*?—in his enthusiasm and philanthropy, in the cult of æstheticism and maintenance of ethical and national art, in his Platonism and contempt of rigid method, even too in the fact that there are utterances of both which appear flat contradictions to the general reader. At the same time this comparison, like the other, should not be pushed too far, for it would be criticism worthy of Laputa to find any resemblance between the style of the *Moralists* and that of *Modern Painters* or the *Stones of Venice*. Shaftesbury's expression of the Beauty of Nature and of Art is half-inarticulate, it only *strives* to speak and most frequently fails, in his own words it is too often "a cloud driven by the wind"—of rhetoric.

---

[1] 'John Oliver Hobbes' speaks of "the dogmatic assurance, which all men dislike in each other, which, nevertheless, no man who is earnest may lack. Strong convictions alone can lead to strong deeds, and a man who is timorous in uttering an opinion will be even weaker in his attempt to act upon it." *The School for Saints*, pp. 96, 97.

CHAPTER IX.

HUTCHESON'S PHILOSOPHY—FIRST FORM IN THE *INQUIRY* AND "LETTERS" TO *DUBLIN JOURNAL*, UNDER THE INFLUENCE OF SHAFTESBURY AND CICERO.

IT is obvious that Shaftesbury's treatment of the moral problem, left a number of important ethical questions unanswered. Several of these will be found to obtrude themselves upon his followers, and other thinkers, who without being professed disciples, were influenced by him.

The various steps which led to the formation of a Shaftesbury *coterie* at Dublin have already been detailed[1]; and, in view of the protest against the Puritan banishment of Beauty, it is exceedingly interesting to notice that all Shaftesbury's followers had had Puritan connections. Molesworth had served the Commonwealth, Arbuckle and Hutcheson were the sons of Presbyterian clergymen, and Butler, who has many points of contact with Shaftesbury, though he afterwards became a Bishop of the Church of England, was also born of Presbyterian parents and was himself educated for the ministry of that Church[2]. Thus the protest against extreme Puritan tendencies was accepted by the younger men of a body that had given backbone to the original movement.

Arbuckle and Hutcheson begin by being "incomplete" followers of Shaftesbury. Their point of contact with their teacher is the difficulty he had found in reconciling the Hellenic and Philanthropic views of life. With Shaftesbury, Virtue, as the beautiful life, consists in neglecting the idea of end, as in any other work of art; while, on the other hand, in

---

[1] *Supra*, pp. 28—33.
[2] *Butler's Works*, Oxford, vol. I. p. xliii.

the harmony of the temper of the microcosm with the end of
the macrocosm this very idea becomes of primary importance.
The question in fact was whether the character of kind affections is approved because *internally* harmonious or beautiful, or
because *externally* harmonious with the social good.   Broadly
speaking, Arbuckle adopts the former line of thought, Hutcheson
the latter.

Arbuckle, as a man of poetic temperament, naturally endeavoured to further strengthen the Æsthetic view of life.   He
slightly developes Shaftesbury's ideas of natural Beauty, and
adds considerably to the theory of Poetry and Art.   With him
the Artistic imagination is the most important faculty.   Running
through Shaftesbury's work there is often an implied analogy
to the work of a sculptor or artist; with Arbuckle there is a
similar metaphorical idea, except that the poet takes the place
of the exponent of the plastic and graphic arts, as a type of the
worker, who makes his own life beautiful.   Imagination tempers
and recreates the whole character, and displaces Shaftesbury's
intuitive sense as the power of moral approbation.   Arbuckle
strongly holds that this power is "natural," but the whole drift
of his writings tends to differentiate him from both Shaftesbury
and Hutcheson.   While it is difficult to determine whether
Shaftesbury held a theory of moral perception as well as
intuitive moral emotion, there is no doubt that to Arbuckle
moral approval was thoroughly æsthetic, in that it was accom-
panied by, or formed part of, an imaginative *act*, which framed
an ideal of a beautiful personality.   Thus Shaftesbury's isolated
expressions, concerning the "better Self," constitute the germ of
Arbuckle's ideal of a harmonious and beautiful character, which
externalises itself in action.   Even more than Shaftesbury, he
holds that the approval is primarily from the outside; we first
approve the beautiful life in others, then the individual character
must be de-personalised and projected out, and as such is
disinterestedly approved or condemned as a work of art.   In
this way Arbuckle converts Shaftesbury's disinterested trustee-
ship of the "Self-affections" into æsthetic disinterestedness.
With regard to the further question of the harmony of the
individual character with the end of the macrocosm, Arbuckle

has little to say. From Shaftesbury he learnt the expression "public good," and from Hutcheson "Benevolence," but he repeats them like a formula, and his only real concern is that the character and actions of others should prove capable of forming a fitting framework for the beautiful life.

It is a matter for regret that Arbuckle published nothing after his *Letters to the Dublin Journal* of a philosophical nature, as he undoubtedly had the opportunity of laying the foundation of modern Æsthetics, an honour which is usually attributed to Hutcheson. With regard to priority both may be said to run a dead heat, since the "Letters" began to appear within a few weeks of the publication of Hutcheson's *Inquiry*, and, in the first of the series, Arbuckle expressly states that they had been composed for some time[1]. With regard to both thought and style, Arbuckle is the more vigorous and interesting of the two, if allowance be made for the disconnected form of his work, occasioned by the exigencies of essay-writing. He is much more at home in dealing with matters relating to Æsthetics than Hutcheson; for he caught the Greek spirit more fully, and he has a more thorough grasp of his subject-matter. Beauty, as it will be seen presently, with Hutcheson, is mathematical—if such can be imagined—the uniformity of ideas; a Sorites or Proposition of Euclid is as true and average an example as the glory of a summer sunset or the Sistine Madonna. Arbuckle has avoided this error—for him Beauty means colour, life, the play of feature, the complete and centralised character. It is in fact æsthetic harmony with him, while Hutcheson only gives us metaphysical symmetry[2].

Hutcheson's *Inquiry* and Essays contributed to the *Dublin Journal* are the exact complement of Arbuckle's work. His sympathies are moral rather than æsthetic, and it is from the practical side that he proceeds to develope and interpret Shaftesbury as a follower and disciple. It is important to note here that the *Inquiry* was much changed in the later editions, which thus become exceedingly puzzling, owing to the juxta-

---

[1] Hibernicus's *Letters, ut supra*, I. p. 4.
[2] A fuller account of Arbuckle will be found in *Mind*, N. S. No. 30 (April, 1899), pp. 194—215.

position of earlier with later views, so that it frequently occurs that one section is contradicted by the following one. In every case of this kind it will be found that the earlier view has been contrasted with an altogether different one, though it is difficult to understand how Hutcheson failed to appreciate his own change of opinion, especially as he prided himself upon the candour (which Hume commends) of confessing his philosophical shortcomings[1]. Therefore it is important to isolate the different works, which naturally belong to each phase of thought, and consider them separately, especially as the neglect of this simple expedient has somewhat confused the summaries of Hutcheson's Philosophy, given by Fowler, McCosh, and Dr Martineau. Therefore the *Inquiry* and *Dublin Journal* "Letters" must be taken separately, as representing the first stage of Hutcheson's Philosophy, extending in time from 1723 to 1726; and, after the later dates there are abundant reasons to explain the different form of his theory, contained in the *Essay on the Passions*, which was published in 1728.

In this first phase of thought, Hutcheson is confessedly the follower of Shaftesbury, but he follows independently, not blindly. How much of his independency is due to Molesworth and how much is his own, it is impossible to decide. Even the fact of similar divergencies from Shaftesbury, appearing in Arbuckle's "Letters" is not sufficient evidence to trace such innovations back to Molesworth, since Hutcheson and Arbuckle might have influenced each other during the time they were together before their respective works were published.

In the first place, Hutcheson made a much needed improvement upon Shaftesbury by disowning all sarcastic references to Revealed Religion. As he explicitly stated, later, " It is indeed to be wished that he [*i.e.* Shaftesbury] had abstained from mixing with such noble performances, some prejudices, he had received against Christianity....How would it have moved the indignation of that ingenious nobleman, to have found a dissolute set of men, who relish nothing in life but the most sordid pleasures, searching into his writings for those insinuations against Christianity, that they might be less restrained

[1] *Supra*, p. 123.

from their debaucheries; when, at the same time, their low minds are incapable of relishing those noble sentiments which he has placed in so lovely a light[1]"! It is true that Shaftesbury's polemic was directed chiefly against egoistic errors of theologians; but it was scarcely to be expected that opponents would care to notice this, nor that Hutcheson, a man with clerical connections and sympathies, should emphasize this aspect of the Hellenic revival.

In the second place, Hutcheson begins to democraticize Shaftesbury's Philosophy. In the early editions of the *Inquiry* there are occasional references to virtuosi and the fashionable world, but these are mere unconscious reproductions of Shaftesbury, and they were expunged in the later editions. The general tone is broader and more human. Morality is possible for all, not merely for the exquisite. Behind this democratic tendency there is a necessity of thought; for Hutcheson is anxious to maintain the universality of a natural capacity for moral approbation, and therefore is ready to appeal to the farmer or the savage.

In the third place, Hutcheson felt the necessity for some further explanation of the two species of harmony or symmetry. Either one must be absorbed in the other, or else the two must be distinguished, and separate spheres assigned to each. With Hutcheson, the harmony—or, as he named it, the "uniformity" of the individual character with the social good takes precedence of the "Beauty of action." He effected this change by making explicit what had remained implicit with Shaftesbury; at the same time adding certain qualifications, necessitated by the new division. Both are intuitively perceived; but the "internal Sense" is now divided into a Sense for Beauty and the Moral Sense[2]. Hutcheson leaves his reader without the possibility of mistaking the meaning in which he uses the term Sense, it is the passive side of the mind as opposed to "Reason," and

---

[1] Hutcheson's *Inquiry*, Ed. 4, pp. xix, xx.

[2] *Inquiry*, Ed. 1, Preface. This division is probably due to a study of Cicero, e.g. Nec vero illa parva vis naturae est rationisque, quod unum hoc animal sentit quid sit ordo, quid sit quod deceat, in factis dictisque, quid modus....Quibus ex rebus conflatur et efficitur, id quod quaerimus, honestum. *De Officiis*, I. ch. IV.

"internal sense" "is a natural power of perception, or determination of the mind to receive necessarily certain ideas, from the presence of objects. The internal Sense is a passive power of receiving ideas of Beauty from all objects in which there is uniformity amidst variety[1]." The whole tone of the *Inquiry* in dealing with the "Internal Sense" is undisguisedly Hedonistic; and therefore, at the start, Hutcheson has missed the purport of Shaftesbury's hints about immediate knowledge as distinct from mere feeling. Though he expressed this somewhat barbarously by the term Egoity (as an equivalent for the *Cogito, ergo Sum*, thereby partially anticipating Fichte's "Ich-heit,") still there are sufficient indications to have pointed the way to a "complete" follower. There is nothing answering to this idea in Hutcheson's early work. His whole anxiety is to saturate internal sense in emotion. Pleasure and terms of pleasure are his magic formulæ for solving every difficulty and explaining all problems.

Such unnecessary hedonism led to a further lost opportunity of developing Shaftesbury's higher meaning. He had often spoken of Virtue being "in itself," and it might have been possible to have developed these isolated expressions into an objective theory of Harmony between the character of the microcosm and the end of the macrocosm: but Hutcheson shuts himself out from this by not only speaking the language of Locke, but also adopting his meaning. Internal Sense is a capacity for feeling and nothing more, but feeling is altogether subjective, and therefore the æsthetic and moral feelings must also be subjective—if subjective, they are not far removed from being conventional, and therefore all the elaborate proofs of the feelings of the two "Senses" being natural or φύσει seem to be beside the point.

The Sense of Beauty being separated from the Moral Sense, Hutcheson endeavours to distinguish the appropriate object of each. That of the Sense for Beauty is to be found where "uniformity amidst variety is observed[2]," and the substitution of this expression for Shaftesbury's "Harmony" is significant.

---

[1] *Inquiry*, Treatise I, § 6 (Edition 1), p. 75.

[2] *Ibid.* Treatise I, § 2 (Edition 1), p. 5.

Hutcheson had little or no appreciation of colour—for instance, speaking of the prevalence of green "on the dry part of the surface of our globe" he can find nothing better to say than that it is a "very pleasant inoffensive colour[1]"; and, similarly, when writing of Art, with the exception, perhaps, of Statuary, he is unable to draw any distinction between fine art and mechanical contrivances. His sense of form or outline everywhere predominates, and so he might be said to write in chiaroscuro; indeed there is nothing in the *Inquiry* to show that he would have more appreciation for Titian's colour than for the outline of the same picture with the light and shade of an engraving. This point of view also explains his calling geometrical figures beautiful; in fact this is the type of his conception of Beauty. He even goes so far as to instance the 47th Proposition of Euclid, Bk. I., as an example, adding that there is "another Beauty when one Theorem contains a great multitude of corollaries easily deducible from it[2]." Thus, of the various characteristics of Beauty enumerated by Shaftesbury, Hutcheson gradually accentuates order and proportion; and, of the many aspects of the Hellenic revival, he is most influenced by those summed up in sculpture. In Nature and Art, regularity of outline and its concomitants, light and shade, chiefly appealed to him. In fact, when ultimately analysed, "Beauty" means little more than the geometrical uniformity of figures, composing the different objects, and so "uniformity" or regularity tends to displace variety in the formula[3]. The whole mental tendency consists in discovering new uniformities and thereby reducing the variety, still this process must have a limit, for variety can never be altogether eliminated; and, in this connection, Hutcheson anticipates the language of Hamilton in deploring the errors of Philosophers in pushing the search for unity too far. "It is no less easy to see into what absurd attempts men have been led by this Sense of Beauty....'Twas this probably which set Descartes on that hopeful project of deducing all human knowledge from one proposition, viz. *Cogito, ergo Sum*....This observation is a strong proof that men perceive the Beauty of Uniformity in the Sciences, since they are led

---

[1] *Inquiry*, p. 20.   [2] *Ibid.* § 3, p. 29.   [3] *Vide infra*, p. 216.

into unnatural deductions by pursuing it too far[1]." To
Hutcheson the form of the Cosmos was everything, and
"Beauty," as he understands it, finds its highest natural ex-
pression in the reign of law, and a comprehensive type in the
Uniformity of Nature.

In this wide signification of Beauty there are many interesting and suggestive remarks, several of which may be
grouped together under certain distinctions which eventually
found their way into Kant's æsthetical theory[2]. With
Hutcheson, as also with Arbuckle, the appreciation of Beauty
has the characteristics of being disinterested, necessary and
universal, but the remaining characteristic of the Judgments
of Taste does not appear with either of the earlier thinkers,
since Teleology was not separated from Æsthetics proper[3].
The identity of language is striking, but there is not so great
an identity of thought; as in many other cases Kant used
a current terminology in a new meaning. While Hutcheson
and Kant would agree with regard to the characteristic of
disinterestedness, they would differ materially in their respective interpretations of the other two. According to Hutcheson,
the "necessity" of æsthetic appreciation means, that given
"uniformity amidst variety" a pleasant feeling results, independently of the will; in fact it is only another expression for
the contention that the Sense is natural[4]. Universality, again,
is mere empirical universality, as he says, for "the universal
agreement of mankind in their sense of Beauty, we must
consult experience[5]."

[1] *Inquiry* (Edition 1), p. 31.

[2] Cf. Schwegler's *History of Philosophy*, translated by Dr James Hutcheson
Stirling, Translator's Note, p. 416.

It is worth mentioning that Hutcheson anticipated Kant's distinction between
moral good and gifts of fortune, in terms nearly resembling those of the first
section of the *Grundlegung zur Metaphysik der Sitten*. "How differently men
are affected towards those they suppose possessed of Honesty, Faith, Generosity,
Kindness, even when they expect no benefit from these admired qualities;
and those who are possessed of the natural goods, such as houses, lands, gardens,
vineyards, health, strength, sagacity? We shall find that we necessarily love and
approve the possessors of the former, but the possession of the latter procures
no love at all toward the possessor." *Inquiry*, Tr. II. Intr. Ed. 1, p. 102.

[3] *Infra*, ch. XI.   [4] *Inquiry*, § 1, p. 11.   [5] *Ibid.* § 6, p. 68.

Apparently, the object of the Moral Sense differs widely from that of the Sense of Beauty. "By a Superior Sense," Hutcheson writes, "which I call a moral one, we perceive pleasure, in the contemplation of such [*i.e.* good] actions in others, and are determined to love the agent (and much more do we perceive pleasure in being conscious of having done such actions ourselves) without any view of further natural advantage from them." It may also appear " That what excites us to these actions, which we call virtuous, is not an intention to obtain even this sensible pleasure, much less the future rewards from Sanctions of laws or any other natural good which may be the consequence of the virtuous action, but an entirely different principle of action from Self-Love[1]." Further, it is not so much "actions," which are the object of the Sense, as the character from which they flow—" the love, humanity, gratitude, compassion, a study of the good of others and a deep delight in their happiness[2]." This is called the Benevolent character and it is really *this* that gives the " perception of pleasure," since "the most useful action imaginable loses all appearance of Benevolence as soon as we discern that it only flowed from Self-Love or Interest[3]." The extent and scope of Benevolence is exactly specified in terms anticipatory of Mill, as follows:—" We may see what actions our Moral Sense would most recommend to our election as the most perfectly virtuous, viz. such as appear to have the most universal unlimited tendency to the greatest and most extensive Happiness of all the rational agents to whom our influence can extend[4]."

It will be noticed that Hutcheson is in doubt whether to assign the good affections or kindly actions as the object of the Moral Sense. During his earlier work he wavers between the

---

[1] *Inquiry*, Tr. ii. Introduction, p. 106. The first sentence quoted is an instance of the alterations made in later editions. In the fourth edition it read as follows—expressions altered being italicised:—"By a superior sense, which I call a moral one, we *approve* the actions of others *and perceive them to be their Perfection and Dignity*, and are determined to love the agent: *a like perception we have in reflecting on such actions of our own*, without any view of Natural advantage from them."

[2] *Ibid.* § 1, p. 113.   [3] *Ibid.* § 2, p. 129.

[4] *Ibid.* § 3, p. 165.

two positions, but, to be consistent with himself, he must make character, rather than its effects, the object. Though he expresses himself very loosely, this is the general drift of the *Inquiry*, and the ambiguity is occasioned by his interpreting acts as signs or symbols of character in others, and retaining the same form of expression, when speaking of the Moral Sense of the individual, applied to his own disposition.

Though Hutcheson appears to have separated the objects of his Æsthetic and Moral Senses, as a matter of fact, they are more closely related than the different kinds of Beauty, which Shaftesbury embraced under the province of his single sense. Beauty, understood as regularity or uniformity, has always with Hutcheson a precise reference to an end, conceived by some intelligent "designer"; and hence the engineer is his type of the producer of "Beauty" so called, rather than the Artist proper, as with Shaftesbury. Every ordered scheme of parts has relation to the idea of a Cosmos, in which it finds its proper place; and, so the whole is to be interpreted in relation to the part or *vice versâ*, as effects of the *design* of some intelligent agent. As Hutcheson expresses it:—" We see this confirmed by our constant experience, that regularity never arises from any undesigned force of ours; and from this we conclude, that wherever there is any regularity in the disposition of a system, capable of many other positions, there must have been Design in the Cause; and the force of this evidence increases, according to the multiplicity of parts employed[1]."

...“The recurrence of any effect, oftener than the laws of hazard do determine, gives presumption of Design; and the combinations, which no undesigned force could give us reason to expect, must necessarily prove the same; and with superior probability, as the multitude of cases in which the contrary might possibly happen, surpass all the cases in which this could happen, which appears to be, in the simplest cases at least, as infinity does to unity[2]." In this way the regularity of each cosmos or system, and especially the regularity of the whole macrocosm, proves the existence of an intelligent "artificer" of it. Hutcheson, at first, claims no "apodictic" rigour

---

[1] *Inquiry*, Tr. i. § 5, p. 44.   [2] *Ibid.* pp. 50, 51.

for his proof, which is simply based upon an enormous number
of observed instances of uniformity, but afterwards, he gives it
a demonstrative aspect, when formulating, mathematically, the
overwhelming evidence in favour of his argument. The chances
against are not even one to infinity, but barely one to infinity
to the third power, and finally one to infinity to the nth
power—still the "one" chance remains experience's irreducible
minimum, that stamps the conclusion with the birth-mark
of its origin.

Further "Beauty" or uniformity is more than an argument
for an intelligent artificer; it also proves that the designer has
wisdom and Benevolence. For the fact that regularity is
pleasing to the appropriate sense, forces us to suppose that
" the Happiness of mankind is desirable or good to the Supreme
Cause, and that this form pleases us in an argument of his
Wisdom,"...and, "upon the supposition of a Benevolent Deity,
all the apparent Beauty produced is an evidence of the execution of a Benevolent design, to give them [i.e. Rational agents]
the pleasures of Beauty. But what more immediately proves
Wisdom, is this; when we see any machine with a vast
complication of parts actually obtaining an End, we justly
conclude, 'That, since this could not have been the effect of
Chance, it must have been intended for that End which is
obtained by it, and then, the Ends or intentions, being in part
known, the complication of Organs and their nice disposition
adapted to this end, is an evidence of a comprehensive, large
understanding in the Cause, according to the multiplicity of
Parts and the Appositeness of their structure, even when we do
not know the intention of the Whole[1].'"

Thus, by two brief steps, Hutcheson's æsthetics pass into
Teleology and from Teleology to the Metaphysic of Ethics; for
regularity presupposes design and design a Benevolent Cause.
In effecting this transition, Shaftesbury's Hellenic ideal is
largely displaced by his Christian one. The supreme artist
passes into the background, to give place to the good and
benevolent God of Hutcheson's Ballyrae sermon. It follows,
therefore, that the object of the sense of "Beauty" is the series

[1] Inquiry, pp. 60, 61.

of acts of the Benevolent first cause, as regular and uniform ; and so the pleasures of Beauty constitute human hedonistic recognition of all such acts; and Æsthetics become a species of Divine ethics. Similarly, the object of the Moral Sense is found by applying the same thought within the sphere of the microcosm, namely man's recognition of human acts and dispositions, which, as benevolent, are also regular and uniform. Under this form, Shaftesbury's harmony of the character of the microcosm with the end of the macrocosm, reappears in man, who becomes a parvus Deus Benevolens. The chief difference between the two kinds of regularity is that the Sense of Beauty only gives pleasure, " it is designed to give us positive Pleasure, but not a positive Pain or disgust, any farther than what arises from disappointment[1]." The inner reason of this depends upon the implied optimism of the world as the product of a benevolent First Cause ; whereas, in the microcosm, the regularity of action and character tending towards public good, is not always attained, and therefore the Moral Sense is not only a capacity for pleasure, but also for pain.

The general drift of Hutcheson's thought tends to make the objects of the Moral Sense a subdivision of those of the Sense of " Beauty "; and so, though he starts by dividing Internal Sense, he virtually ends in subsuming the second Sense under the first. Such a cosmic theory of Ethics naturally sacrifices the microcosm to the macrocosm and therefore it is not surprising to find Hutcheson reducing the moral import of Self-Love still more than Shaftesbury. " Actions which flow solely from Self-Love," he writes, " and yet evidence no want of Benevolence, having no hurtful effects upon others, seem *perfectly indifferent in a moral sense*[2]."

From this point of view, things and actions become intelligible, as instances of Benevolence—things as examples of divine, and actions of human, Benevolence—and therefore the macrocosm as a whole, is uniform, because ruled by ethical springs. Thus the true " Welt-anschauung " is an ethical idealism. This ethical idealism is painfully embarrassed by

---

[1] *Inquiry*, Tr. I. § 6, p. 66.
[2] *Ibid.* Tr. II. § 3, p. 160.

Lockian pre-suppositions. Hutcheson can give his reader no help in explaining the genesis of the idea of an end. Besides the æsthetic and Moral Senses, there are only the "Ideas of Sensation" and Reason, as a faculty for compounding them. Reason has no power to add anything to the given material, and the only possible supposition is that the idea of end is interpolated. Not only so, but Hutcheson is face to face with a very pressing difficulty in the apprehension of this idea, however obtained. The "Internal Senses" are only capacities for feeling, as he himself says, they are "faculties of perceiving pleasure[1]," and how is an end to be apprehended hedonistically? Reason, even in the limited sense in which the term is used, can only discover the presence of adaptation, and therefore, reason must re-arrange the elements originally presented, and when this process is carried out (of which no account is given), Internal Sense is pleasantly affected. But suppose the same steps be traced in the opposite direction and a start is made from the actual feeling. Feeling is generically the same, and how is a given feeling to indicate the presentation of a cosmos or system rather than some quite different source? Hutcheson, too, was convinced of the subjectivity of feeling as such and with Locke he held that the Secondary Qualities "denote the Sensations in our minds, to which perhaps there is no re-semblance in the objects which excite these ideas in us[2]"; while Primary Qualities "*may*" have a "*nearer*" resemblance to objects. Now it is obvious that, even if the pleasure of Internal Sense were analogous to the Primary Qualities, it could only give a guarantee of contingent objectivity; while, on the contrary, being feeling and feeling only, it finds its analogue in the "Secondary Sensations" "as a modification of the perceiving mind[3]." If this be so, granting that *ends* may be expressed hedonistically, there is no guarantee for the accuracy of the re-translation of feeling back to ends. In fact the Self, being wholly passive, absorbs everything and gives back nothing.

Hutcheson was conscious of this difficulty and made some attempt to meet it, by asserting that Uniformity depends upon

[1] *Inquiry*, Tr. I. § 8, p. 88.   [2] *Ibid.* Tr. I. § 1, pp. 13, 14.   [3] *Ibid.*

the perception of some Primary Quality[1], but this is altogether beside the point. Even if the Regularity were due to a re-grouping of the elements of a Primary Quality, its objectivity would remain doubtful. Besides, the only Uniformity, derived from Primary Qualities, is that of a geometrical nature, and this is a type, not the whole of Beauty. It leaves no room for the regularity of character and action, which is the object of the Moral Sense. In fact, the Moral Sense is in the dilemma of dealing either with a hypothetical object or else being left without any object—for, if character be the object, it can only be *guessed* from the actions which express it; on the other hand, actions constitute no object at all, in Hutcheson's sense, since, as has been seen, actions apparently attributable to Benevolence may be morally vitiated, by being afterwards proved the results of an undetected egoistic motive. Conse-quently the Moral Sense is even less objective than the Æsthetic one. Further, the object of the Internal Senses, being subjective, the hedonistic register of it is doubly sub-jective as feeling and feeling only, and therefore it can give no possible criterion.

Quite apart from the general difficulties of a Sensationalistic theory, Hutcheson has left himself no outlet from the indi-vidual subjectivity as solely sensitive. All uniformity is uniformity of *Ideas* of Sensation, and therefore all conclusions founded upon it remain conclusions "in idea." Further, feelings, either æsthetic or moral, are merely signals of certain dis-positions or groupings of others already experienced, and as repetitions are objectively weaker.

Therefore, neither the uniformity of ideas nor the feeling occasioned by them is any guarantee of objective design and hence the whole " physico-theological " proof of the existence of a supreme Benevolent Designer falls to pieces. If the Hedonistic effects upon the Sense are alone considered, Hutche-son is imprisoned within the disconnected consciousnesses of minima of feeling; if he bursts through these, there is a *petitio principii.* He saw that his standpoint involved some such difficulty, and he endeavours to solve it by declaring it to be

[1] *Inquiry,* p. 13.

no difficulty at all. After saying all "Beauty is relative to
the Sense of some mind perceiving it[1]"—that is hedonistically
relative—he continues, "the preceding reasoning, from the
frequency of regular bodies and the combination of various
bodies is entirely independent of any perception of Beauty,
and would equally prove design in the Cause, although there
were no being which perceived Beauty in any form whatsoever[2]." It is true that the æsthetic and moral feelings add
nothing to the cogency of the proof since they are feelings
from an end not *of* an end. But Hutcheson has overlooked
his previous statements which place the Uniformity from which
the feeling results amongst the ideas of Sensation and consequently it cannot be more objective than the ideas of which it
is a relation. Thus Locke's idea of the mind as a *tabula rasa*,
supplemented by doubts as to the objectivity of the Primary
Qualities confines uniformity to the subjective sphere, while
the hypothetical derivation of character from actions never
brings the Moral Sense into immediate contact with its object.

The hedonistic deliverances of the Moral Sense may indeed
authenticate themselves as feelings but not the object which is
to be presumed or imagined before being presented; and so, it
will be found, that followers of Clarke, such as Gilbert Burnet,
drew attention to the difficulties attending an "instinctive"
moral criterion. To meet such objections, Hutcheson in the
Essay on the Passions (1728) gives up much of his original
Hedonistic position by borrowing from Butler, whose *Sermons*
had appeared in 1726.

Before investigating Hutcheson's theory as recast, it may
not be out of place to determine Butler's relation to Shaftesbury in order to ascertain how far Hutcheson in borrowing
from Butler returned to Shaftesbury, and how far he modified
his adaptation of Shaftesbury's theory by additions foreign
to it.

Butler was at once a critic and pupil of the two contemporary tendencies of his time. From the rational moralists he
learnt the need for an authoritative principle that could justify

---

[1] *Inquiry*, Tr. I. § 4, also § 6, pp. 35, 65.
[2] *Ibid.* § 5, p. 50.

itself and give fixity to the moral code. On the other hand, he held that Moral Philosophy is something more than an ethical geometry, and he was therefore opposed to the bold speculative flights of Clarke. At the same time, he would not accept the popular hedonistic interpretation of the Moral Sense, while he followed Shaftesbury in his moral teleology. Butler, therefore, mediated between the two opposite tendencies; but there are two kinds of mediation—either eclectic or by the resolution of differences in a higher unity. Butler's mediation partakes of both characteristics, since he failed in thoroughly synthesizing the two groups of opponents, through his neglect of a true Metaphysic. In Ethics proper, he partly overcomes the opposition by uniting thoughts from both sides in a higher theory, partly by adapting eclectically portions of the respective theories for his own purposes.

CHAPTER X.

HUTCHESON'S PHILOSOPHY—SECOND FORM, IN THE *TREATISE ON THE PASSIONS* AND *ILLUSTRATIONS OF THE MORAL SENSE*, BEING THE BEGINNING OF THE INFLUENCE OF BUTLER.

IN many respects, the *Treatise on the Passions* and *Illustrations of the Moral Sense*, which were published together in one volume (1728), constitute an exceedingly interesting book. As a contribution to the Psychology of the emotions, the former treatise has still an historical value; while the work, as a whole, is important as explaining the alteration in Hutcheson's standpoint. Running all through, there is the general position of the *Inquiry* overlaid by a different theory due to the influence of Butler and others. If the rationale of each can be disentangled, it will to a large degree explain the various inconsistencies by tracing them to necessities of Hutcheson's general outlook.

The whole inner tendency of the *Essay on the Passions*, is to give content to expressions of the *Inquiry*. These may be grouped under two heads, namely the System, as individual, and the System, as a whole—in other words, the microcosm and the macrocosm. In fact, the *Inquiry* had effected little more than to accept Shaftesbury's statement that the microcosm *was* a system, without even giving Shaftesbury's reasons for such assertion. With regard to the macrocosm, the difficulty was exactly the opposite—for Hutcheson had gone farther than Shaftesbury in establishing its cosmical character; but, on the other hand, in developing the Moral Sense, he had, unfortunately, by "hedonizing" it, isolated the individual, or at least endangered his connection with the whole of which he formed a constituent part.

With regard to the Microcosm, which is now not to be merely so described but *proved* to be such, Hutcheson begins by entirely adopting the results of Butler's *Sermons*, with a reservation as to the supreme authority of Conscience. In the *Inquiry*, the various Springs of action are mentioned by name, as for instance, Malice, Friendship, Gratitude, Compassion, &c., without any attempt at classification, whereas, *now*, they are ranked in a hierarchy, up to a certain point, exactly with Butler's Terminology. First, or rather lowest in rank, are the "Propensions" or Instincts, then the Particular Affections, both of which classes again are capable of subdivision as tending directly, in some instances to private, in other instances to public good. Hutcheson, even, goes slightly beyond Butler ; since the latter only contends that "there are as real and the same kind of indications in human nature, that we were made for society, and to do good to our fellow creatures, as that we were intended to take care of our own life and health and private good[1]," while Hutcheson claims that there is an exact "Balance." "With this balance of public passions against the private...we find that human nature may be really amiable... provided we vigorously exercise the powers we have, in keeping this balance of Affections, and checking any passion that grows so violent, as to be inconsistent with the Public Good. If we have selfish passions for our own preservation, we have also Public passions which may engage us into vigorous and laborious services to offspring, friends, Countries." In this division also, one notes how quickly Hutcheson learnt, from the Sermons on Resentment, to find in Anger "one of the cements of society." Further, following Butler, Hutcheson distinguishes Reason as applied to unify the two classes under the heads of Self-Love and Benevolence. In following Butler so far, Hutcheson has contradicted his previous expressions, since if there is to be a "balance," it would follow that Self-Love should have equal rights with Benevolence, in case of any conflict arising.

---

[1] *Sermons*, Oxford, p. 4.

Having followed Butler to this point, Hutcheson's original position returns upon him, and he has a sword of Brennus to throw into the " balance " in favour of Benevolence. Self-Love unifies particular affections according to a scale of *natural good* merely, that is pleasure and pleasure only. Benevolence, on the other hand, deals with *moral good*, which is not individual pleasure but universalistic happiness with a reference to perfection. Thus, Happiness, as a result of Self-Love, is a sum of personal or individual pleasures—it " denotes pleasant sensation of any kind or a continued state of such Sensations[1] "—and, as such, the individual is looked upon as isolated, and his relation to the macrocosm is destroyed. On the other hand, the Happiness which Benevolence seeks, is the union of the individual with the system *as a whole;* and, being universalistic, includes a reference to the perfection of that whole[2]. Further the perfection of the individual is not only included as that of a part of the Macrocosm, but also the perfection of the individual as in himself a microcosm. In fact, by following Self-Love, the individual cannot be perfect since he is no longer a system or microcosm, while, by acting benevolently, he realises the cosmic relation and thereby perfects himself[3]. In the *Treatise on the Passions*, the references to Perfection are slight and are rather hints of a theory to come, than the theory itself in actual realisation.

Not only does the object of Benevolence take precedence of that of Self-Love, but the principle of Benevolence is assigned a distinct superiority. Hutcheson in fact further weights the altruistic side of his balance by introducing two new " Senses "— the one a " Public Sense," viz. " our determination to be pleased with the Happiness of others, and to be uneasy at their misery[4]"; and the other, " a Sense of Honour, which makes the Approbation or gratitude of others for any good action we have done, the necessary occasion of pleasure." The latter in fact is a correlative of the Moral Sense, which primarily ap-

---

[1] *Essay on the Passions*, p. 205.

[2] The idea of Perfection is incidental in the *Essay on the Passions*, but in the next period it becomes of cardinal importance.

[3] *Essay on the Passions*, 1728, pp. 200—203.   [4] *Ibid.* p. 5.

proves the character inferred from the actions of others, while the Sense of Honour is the agent's recognition of the action of the Moral Sense of those benefited by him. Obviously, therefore, it constitutes a hedonistic *quid pro quo*, and is a survival of the position of the *Inquiry*. Now, the Public Sense is pleased with any affection tending to the interests of others, however conceived, or however contracted the sphere of those included by it—it constitutes in fact a " natural " *solatium* for all donors of misdirected charities. Therefore, it follows that, since admittedly all altruistic impulses do not contribute "to the greatest moment of good toward the most extensive system to which they can reach[1]," a further principle is needed "so as to limit and counteract not only the selfish Passions, but even the particular kind affections." This principle is " *universal calm Benevolence*," which is "the perfection of Virtue."

To fully appreciate the import of this admission, it is necessary to digress very briefly, in order to investigate Hutcheson's view of the distinction between the different springs of action. These are broadly three, namely "affection," passion and desire. By affection is meant the " Perceptions of Pleasure or pain, not directly raised by the presence or operation of the event or object, but by our reflection upon, or apprehension of their present or certainly future existence ; so that we may be sure the object or event will raise the direct sensations in us[2]." Passions constitute a sub-class of Affections, including "a confused sensation, either of pleasure or pain, occasioned or attended by some violent bodily motions, which keeps the mind much employed upon the present affair, to the exclusion of everything else, and prolongs or strengthens the affections, sometimes to such a degree, as to prevent all deliberate reasoning about our conduct[3]." Opposed to these are the Calm or " pure " Affections which are without this confusion—in this distinction Hutcheson is following Malebranche and Butler, with a return to Shaftesbury's " rational affection." Green, when writing of Hutcheson, seems to think that he made no distinction between desire and affection or Passion[4]. Evidently

[1] *Essay on the Passions*, p. xvii. [2] *Ibid*. p. 28. [3] *Ibid*. p. 29.
[4] Green's *Works*, I. p. 326.

Green had the *Inquiry* and *System* in his mind, at the time: for, in the *Essay on the Passions*, a distinction is repeatedly drawn. Desire begins where affection ends. Having "an apprehension of good or evil in objects, actions or events" desires arise "from the frame of our nature to obtain for ourselves or others, the agreeable sensation, when the object or event is good or to prevent the uneasy sensation when it is evil[1]." This definition only includes part of what Hutcheson means by desire, since it leaves no room for the idea of the good of others as perfection, and it affords a striking example of how far exceptions are to prove the rule, when, as afterwards appears, the "agreeable Sensation" is shown to be inadmissible, and the definition is revised as follows, namely, that "the apprehension of good, either to ourselves or others, *as attainable*, raises Desire[2]." The reason for the change is that Hutcheson often follows Butler, in making all Desire terminate upon its object, which thus constitutes its end, and he clearly differentiates it from the uneasiness preceding it on the one hand, and from the personal pleasure attending its gratification, on the other[3]. "It is certain," he writes, "that Desire of the Happiness of others, which we account virtuous, is not directly excited by prospects of any secular advantages, Wealth, Power, Pleasure of the external Senses, reward from the Deity or future pleasures of Self-Approbation." By this reservation, Hutcheson here endeavours to establish the disinterestedness of Desire, that is, that its object is *not* the pleasure of the individual, but it remains an open question, whether beyond the direct object, there may, or may not be, the pleasure of the particular system towards whose "good" the desire is directed. Further Desires may be either "confused" and "passionate" or pure and calm. There appear to be finally only two "calm" desires, Self-Love and Benevolence. Self-Love, being morally, in so far as legitimated, instead of the balanced antithesis of Benevolence, subsumed by it; and thus the sole morally right desire becomes "calm Benevolence." Since it is "pure desire" the element of uneasiness is reduced to a minimum, or indeed

---

[1] *Essay on the Passions*, p. 7.   [2] *Ibid.* p. 61.
[3] *Ibid.* p. 16.

may disappear altogether—"if we consult ourselves, and not the common systems, we shall perhaps find that the noblest desire in our nature, that of universal Happiness, is generally calm, and wholly free from any confused uneasiness[1]."

This Desire of Universal Happiness is a somewhat complicated product. Acting upon the basis of some particular public affections, it first of all sees how these cohere with the idea or ideal of the Macrocosm, whether conceived in its entirety or as that "universe" to which the individual is immediately related by means of imagination and reason, and Hutcheson even goes so far as to state that "we obtain *command* over the particular passions, principally by strengthening the general desires [these being further resolved into universal calm Benevolence], through frequent reflection and making them habitual, so as to obtain strength superior to the particular passions[2]." "Discipline of our passions is in general necessary...And, consequently, it must be of the highest importance to all, to strengthen as much as possible, by frequent meditation and reflection, the calm desires, either public or private, rather than the particular passions and to make the calm universal Benevolence superior to them[3]." The function of reason, understanding or wisdom is important, as these faculties ascertain "the tendency" of actions. Green accepts the expressions "tendency" or "tending to" as equivalent to the motive[4]; and, undoubtedly, this meaning is often intended, but more frequently there is a double reference, on one side to the harmony of the character or act of the microcosm with the end of the macrocosm, and, on the other side, as expressing the consequences of an action in terms of general Happiness. For instance, "Our Passions are often matters of uneasiness to ourselves, and sometimes occasion misery to others, when any one is indulged into a degree of strength beyond its proportion...They are by nature balanced against each other, like the antagonistic muscles of the body; either of which separately would have occasioned distortion and irregular motion, yet jointly they form a machine, most accurately subservient to the necessities, convenience and

[1] *Essay on the Passions*, p. 44.　　　[2] *Ibid.* p. 30.
[3] *Ibid.* p. 167.　　　[4] Green's *Works*, I. p. 328.

Happiness of a Rational System. We have a power of reason and reflection, by which we may see what course of action will tend to procure us the most valuable gratifications of our Desires, and prevent any intolerable or unnecessary pains, or provide some support under them. We have wisdom, sufficient to form Ideas of Rights, Laws, Constitutions, so as to preserve large societies in peace and prosperity and promote a general good amidst all the private interests[1]." " In governing our Moral Sense and desires of Virtue, nothing is more necessary than to study the nature and tendencies of actions, and to extend our views to the whole species, or to all sensitive natures, as far as they can be affected by our conduct[2]." "When the Moral Sense is thus assisted by a sound under-standing and application, our own actions may be a constant source of solid pleasure[3]." " It cannot be an indifferent matter to an agent with a Moral Sense, what opinions he forms of the tendencies of actions; what partial attachments of Love he has towards parties or factions. If he has true opinions of the tendencies of actions, if he carefully examines the real dignity of persons and causes, he may be sure the conduct which he now approves he shall always approve[4]." It will thus be seen that Hutcheson assigns an important if somewhat vague position to reason in the process attending moral decisions. In fact so far from reason being " expressly excluded[5]," it has the function of " assisting," even of " governing " the Moral Sense and " commanding " particular affections. Further, if wisdom can form the idea of a political constitution or a " system " of individuals with harmonized rights, there does not appear to be any cause why the same faculty should not form the idea of a universal system, or that of the Macrocosm as a whole, with a clear view, as to its supreme end. This is clearly inconsistent with the frequently expressed dictum that reason gives no *ultimate* end, but the real contradiction results from the instability of the hedonistic view of the Moral Sense, repeated from the *Inquiry*. In fact it now appears, the

---

[1] *Essay on the Passions*, p. 181.   [2] *Ibid*. p. 191.
[3] *Ibid*. p. 109.   [4] *Ibid*. p. 106.
[5] Green's *Works*, I. pp. 328, 331.

culture of Benevolence is the condition of the stability of the Moral Sense—" the Moral Sense," Hutcheson says, " if we form true opinions of the tendencies of actions and the affections whence they spring, as it is the fountain of the most intense pleasure, so it is, in itself, constant, not subject to caprice or change[1]." It is "universal calm Benevolence," as a reasoned view of the relation of the individual to the Macrocosm, that is the true faculty of moral decision, since it is both chronologically and logically prior to the Moral Sense. This desire, now, does the whole work and it only remains for the Moral Sense to "approve" of it, as presented. If there is any error "in examination" the blame rests wholly with the calculating faculty; and therefore it should be entitled to any credit there may be, when it has come to a right decision. From this point of view, the pleasure resulting from the Moral Sense is a "hall-mark" and that only; while the whole "assaying" has been done by the various steps, which generate the universal desire of calm Benevolence. Benevolence then takes the place of the Moral Sense as the Moral faculty. This is obviously a conclusion unconsciously developed from Butler. " When Benevolence is said to be the sum of virtue it is not spoken of as a blind propension, but as a principle in reasonable creatures, for reason and reflection come into our notion of a moral agent...Thus upon supposition that it were in the strictest sense true, without limitation, that Benevolence includes in it all virtues, yet reason must come in as its guide and director, in order to attain its own end, the end of Benevolence, the greatest public good[2]." Thus Benevolence becomes the cuckoo in the nest that eventually thrusts out the Moral Sense and usurps its original function.

Benevolence then gains more than the Moral Sense loses. In the *Inquiry*, the Moral Sense was "superior"—a species of Psychological labour-saving machine—and its main use was to render Reason, as applied to action, unnecessary—"Must a man," Hutcheson asks in the *Inquiry*, "have the reflection of Cumberland or Puffendorf to admire generosity, faith,

---

[1] *Essay on the Passions*, p. 158.
[2] Butler's *Sermons*, Ser. xii. (Oxford Edition, pp. 166—167).

humanity, gratitude ?   Or reason so nicely to apprehend the evil in cruelty, treachery, ingratitude ?   Do not the former excite our admiration and love and study of imitation, wherever we see them, without any such Reflection, and the latter are contempt and abhorrence ?   Unhappy would it be for mankind, if a Sense of Virtue was of as narrow an extent as a capacity for such Metaphysics[1] ! "   In the *Treatise on the Passions* Benevolence, which now does the work of the Moral Sense of the *Inquiry, in making moral decisions*, requires reason, reflection, suspense of judgment and command over the particular affections, while it is no longer "a kind of Ithuriel's spear, which, when brought in contact with our affections, reveals their true quality, showing the angelic nature of those which are conducive to the public good and the diabolical character of those which are opposed to it. Or it resembles the fabulous cups which detected the poison lurking in any drink poured into them ; and enables us to reject the anti-social and accept the social[2]."   In fact the *comparison* of the imagined results of carrying out any particular altruistic affection with the agent's idea of a macrocosm, constitutes the essential element in the mental state preceding action ; and, if Benevolence gives a favourable verdict, the Moral Sense experiences those refined pleasures which Hutcheson calls the perfection of the Self, because they are wholly its own[3].

Such additions to the scope of Benevolence mark a wide divergence from the idea of a symmetrically balanced microcosm, in the interests of which they are introduced.   The result is that Hutcheson is forced to expel one order of the powers in Butler's "hierarchy," namely Self-Love and (Butler's) Benevolence.   There remain then egoistic and altruistic instincts and affections, which may be unified by a modified Self-Love and a partial Benevolence, while both these and the original affections are judged by Universal Calm Benevolence ; and the Moral Sense becomes a supernumerary, called in not to

[1] *Inquiry*, Tr. ii. § 1.   (Ed. i. p. 115).

[2] *History of English Thought in the Eighteenth Century*, by Leslie Stephen, London, 1876, ii. p. 62.

[3] *Treatise on the Passions*, p. 160.

ratify the decision of Benevolence, but to merely grace the occasion and provide an unsought reward. Notwithstanding the many defects of psychology, here Hutcheson has stumbled on a clue to extricate himself from the labyrinth of the microcosm, but unfortunately he refuses to recognise the rational element in the presentation of cosmic good by Benevolence to the Moral Sense. He cannot reconcile himself to making the Moral Sense a supernumerary and he still insists that it does the work really performed by the genesis of a Benevolent desire. Consequently when he is asked by the Rational Moralists to justify the Moral Sense, he can only reiterate his claim that its action is a fact, but he is unable to provide any explanation.

Towards the objectivity of physical and moral order he contributes several new distinctions, clearly pointing out that Reflection ought to rank equally with Sensation as a " power of Perception" or source of ideas[1], and he adds several important remarks upon the "universal concomitant ideas" or Primary Qualities "which are reputed images of something external[2]." Instead of Internal Senses being mere "determinations" as in the *Inquiry* (though the old definition is repeated in another place) they are now the "pleasures perceived upon the previous reception and comparison of various sensible perceptions, with their concomitant ideas or intellectual ideas, when we find uniformity or resemblance among them[3]." Yet the reinstatement of Reflection is profitless, since Hutcheson deliberately gives away his whole case by denying the objectivity of all ideas of Relation, amongst which uniformity is included, "That, upon comparing two ideas there arises a relative idea, generally when the two ideas compared have in them any modes of the same Simple Idea, is obvious.... This may let us see that Relations are not real qualities inherent in external natures, but only ideas necessarily accompanying our Perception of two objects at once and comparing them[4]." Thus, as in the *Inquiry*, there is no escape from the Microcosm to the Macrocosm; and

---

[1] *Treatise on the Passions*, p. xi.
[2] *Ibid.* p. 4. [3] *Ibid.*
[4] *Ibid.* p. 246.

therefore there is no reliance to be placed either on the world-order or the world-orderer.

It is somewhat remarkable that Hutcheson does not even attempt to maintain the universality of the Moral Sense, apart from the rational process involved in the formation of the universally benevolent character. "Everyone," he says, "judges the affections of others by his own Sense, so that it seems not impossible that in these Senses men may differ as they do in Taste[1]." "Whether our Moral Sense be subject to such a disorder, as to have different perceptions from the same apprehended affections, in an agent at different times, as the eye may have of the colours of an unaltered object, 'tis not easy to determine. Perhaps it will be hard to find any instance of such a change[2]." This subjectivity of the Moral Sense is the penalty Hutcheson has to pay for his enlistment of Pleasure on the side of Virtue, and for his extensive critique of all pleasures according to their intensity and duration to prove the superiority of those of the moral sense[3] and finally for his rhapsodies on the delights of right living. "These pleasures cannot indeed wholly secure us against all kinds of uneasiness, yet they never tend naturally to increase them. On the contrary their tendency is to lead the virtuous agent into all pleasures, in the highest degree, in which they are consistent with each other.... Where Virtue costs us much its own pleasures are the more sublime. It directly advances the pleasures of the Public Sense, by leading us to promote the Public Happiness, and Honour is its natural and ordinary attendant. If it cannot remove the necessary pains of life yet it is the best support under them. These moral pleasures do some way more nearly affect us than any other. They make us delight in ourselves and relish our very nature. By these we perceive an internal dignity and worth and seem to have a pleasure like to that ascribed often to the Deity, by which we enjoy our own Perfection and that of every other being[4]."

Even though the Moral Sense can make the good man a kind of ethical Narcissus, in love with his own image, and

---

[1] *Essay on the Passions*, p. 234.   [2] *Ibid.* p. 283.
[3] *Ibid.* § 5.   [4] *Ibid.* p. 159.

certain upon every disinterested excursion of a return to an atmosphere pulsating with the most "intense" and "sublime" emotion (though this is not to be the motive!), the penalty must be paid for the lack of consistency.   If the Moral Sense is to reproduce ends in hedonistic terms, all other faculties only deal with means, and in being "pleased with" particular kind affections we must run the risk of doing what is "absolutely pernicious[1]" through limitation of the affection itself.   The Sense can give no justification of its action; neither approve nor disapprove—in fact the usual Platonic arguments against Sensationalism apply.   On the other hand, if the moral decision is really made during the growth of the calm universal benevolent desire, then the Moral Sense ceases to be the power of apprehending the ultimate end and it sinks to the mere hedonistic endorsement of the discovery by a different power. These two opposite points of view run throughout the *Essay on the Passions* and Hutcheson interchanges them according to his purpose at the moment.   When virtue is to be made stable, calm Benevolence is most prominent: and, on the other hand, when, as is most usual, he is anxious "to recommend Virtue" the Moral Sense engrosses his attention.

[1] *Essay on the Passions*, p. 278.

CHAPTER XI.

PART I. HUTCHESON'S PHILOSOPHY—THIRD FORM, IN THE *SYSTEM OF MORAL PHILOSOPHY*, AND ALTERATIONS IN THE FOURTH EDITION OF THE *INQUIRY*, FROM 1730—1738. THE INFLUENCE OF ARISTOTLE.

IN the two periods of Hutcheson's thought which have been dealt with in the previous chapters, his internal development coincides with the outer chronological expression in different works. There still remain the "Compends" of Metaphysics and Morals (1742), the *System of Moral Philosophy* and *Compend of Logic*, both published after his death, and to these may be added the additions made to the *Inquiry* in the fourth edition. Here the order of publication is no longer a guide to the development of thought; for, from Hutcheson's own letters, it appears that the *System of Moral Philosophy* was finished by November, 1737, having probably been commenced from 1733—1735[1]. As the fourth edition of the *Inquiry* was published in 1738, the fresh matter it contains may be assigned to the same date as the *System*. Here however a slight complication may be noticed. The MS. remained a long time in Ireland, and, when it was returned, Hutcheson showed it to some of his friends at Glasgow—thus the time slipped away. He speaks of "being bewildered" and of "adding confusedly to a confused book all valuable remarks in a farrago[2]." Therefore to the original MS., finished in 1737, were added the "valuable" remarks upon it from various sources. Hutcheson's language

---

[1] *Supra*, Chap. VI. p. 113.   [2] *Supra*, p. 114.

seems to convey the idea that he made no attempt at systema-
tization of the new material, but simply incorporated it as
received, to refresh his memory when lecturing. Some of the
"remarks" may be detected, since they contain references to
Butler's *Analogy* which did not appear until 1737; thus there
is a note upon the passage treating of Justice, which refers to
the theory of punishment in "that excellent book Bishop
Butler's *Analogy*[1]." The proof of Immortality as well as
certain remarks on "Moral Government" read like echoes of
Butler—especially the former—though it is quite possible that
Hutcheson may have arrived at both quite independently of
the *Analogy*. But beyond isolated expressions there is nothing
in the structure of the argument that is based upon Butler's
later work, though there is much that shows a deeper comprehension of the *Sermons* than is to be found in the *Essay on the
Passions*.

It is interesting to note this influence of the Molesworth-
Shaftesbury school at Dublin upon Hutcheson's more mature
work. He specially acknowledges a "multitude" of valuable
thoughts from Wm. Bruce and Synge, besides others from
Abernethy and Rundle, Bishop of Derry, who was a friend
of Butler's[2]. To these must be added "still more in number
from some excellent hands here," of whom there is no record,
though one might conjecture Moor, who helped in the translation of Marcus Aurelius and perhaps Dunlop and Leechman.

To understand the transition from the *Essay on the Passions*
to the *System of Moral Philosophy*, it is necessary to remember
two general series of facts, the one being the remarkable output
of controversial literature during the interval, and the other
Hutcheson's own experience as a lecturer.

His return to Glasgow brought him into contact with the
academic side of the Hellenic revival; and it can readily be
imagined that after his training in Shaftesbury's Philosophy he
would be a much more enthusiastic supporter of Dunlop's
renaissance of the study of Greek Literature, than he could
have been when leaving the University in 1717. Further, he
was not merely a sympathiser with Dunlop, but an active

---

[1] *System*, I. p. 256.   [2] *Supra*, p. 114.

supporter of the same movement, even going so far as to devote
a considerable number of lectures to the exposition of Ancient
Philosophy[1].   This work had an important bearing on his own
mode of thought, and in the *System of Moral Philosophy* there
is a new wave of Classicism.   It is worthy of note too that
Hutcheson has now fallen very greatly under the influence of
Aristotle, and this shows a somewhat striking divergence from
Shaftesbury, who was rather a Platonist than an Aristotelian,
which difference of inspiration will be found to have an important bearing upon the general drift of this phase of Hutcheson's
thought.

In the second place allowance must be made for the effect
of the great mass of philosophical literature which appeared
between 1728 and 1737.   No doubt the issues debated were somewhat fluctuating and confused, besides in many instances being
confined to discussion of details rather than of principles.
Hence it is that in no other instance in the history of thought
has so much writing produced so little result, or left so slight
an impress upon the general progress of historical and rational
culture.   Just as in the development of national life, there have
been periods when factions or parties were enormously subdivided, and the efforts of each group contributed little or
nothing to the progress of the people as a whole, so here the
division of philosophical thought precluded any broad contention for or against principles of permanent importance.   Such
division was far from being an accidental phenomenon, it was
the direct result of the individualism of the age; while at the
same time, by diffusing Philosophic ideas, it aided in no small
degree the growth of the Enlightenment[2].

Yet amongst so much concentration on details certain broad
lines of historical demarcation in Moral Philosophy emerge as
a result of the various contentions—on the one hand egoistic
individualism, and on the other rational universalism, amongst
followers of Clarke.   Hutcheson was related to both and yet he

---

[1] From various references in his works, it is probable that Ancient Philosophy, with Hutcheson, meant *primarily*, but not altogether, Cicero and other
Roman Moralists (cf. Chapters XIII. and XIV.).

[2] Cf. Chapter XIII.

differed fundamentally from either tendency. His rooted belief in a macrocosm of ethical ends was entirely universalistic; and yet his epistemological point of contact was quite opposed to that of Clarke. With regard to the other group, while in so far as he accepted a hedonistic valuation of ends, he was at one with the egoists, at the same time his universalism necessarily separated him from them. Thus his hedonism and universalism drew his sympathies in two different directions, and conversely this separation of interests made him subject to two different attacks[1].

Hutcheson was better prepared to resist the assault of the egoists than that of the "Rational Moralists"; for even in the *Inquiry* and his *Letters to the Dublin Journal,* he had prepared himself against the arguments of supporters of Hobbes, and hence he had only to meet any new objections brought forward by thinkers like John Clarke of Hull or Archibald Campbell. His true weakness was upon the other flank, exposed to the assaults of the "Rational Moralists." When his beloved Moral Sense was satirized as a mere instinct, he was left without a reply, and his only answer was really an equivocation, in so far as he attempted to show that Reason and Reason alone either presupposed some emotive spring or else never effected any-thing in the moral sphere[2]. The early stages of this contro-versy present a somewhat comic picture of "one party milking the he-goat while the other held the sieve"; since the Clarke school contended that the Moral Standard was wholly a matter of reason; while Hutcheson in his early work is inclined to reply with the counter-assertion that it is wholly a matter of a "natural" emotion or feeling. However his strong common sense tends to save him from this extreme position, even at the expense of consistency; since, as has been seen in the second phase of his thought, he admits many rational elements, in the formation of the Benevolent desire. After a further considera-tion of the arguments on both sides he endeavours doubly to strengthen his position not only against followers of Clarke but also against the egoists, in the third form of his system, first by

[1] Cf. *supra* Chapter vi. pp. 103—4.
[2] Cf. *Essay on Passions. Illustrations of a Moral Sense, passim.*

making morality consist, neither altogether in feeling nor in Reason, but in the *will*, and secondly by a further revision of his theory of the Moral Sense.

To a certain extent the third period might be described as an explication of the implications of the second, since much is repeated from the *Essay on the Passions*; and the order is the same, namely beginning from the microcosm and ending with the macrocosm, whereas in the *Inquiry* this arrangement is reversed. But on the other hand there is much that is new— not merely in matter but also in theory and form. In addition to the tendency giving prominence to the position of *Will* in Morality, the ideas of Perfection and Dignity (which received mere incidental mention in the *Essay on the Passions*) now constitute an integral part of the revised system. The enume- ration of the Internal Senses is extended in several directions; and most important of all, following this fresh arrangement of the microcosm, the Moral Sense is subjected to changed con- ditions; in fact the Moral Sense of the second period is the final determinant on the side of Benevolence; but now, in its charge over a more extensive "constitution," it must be supposed at least to have acquired fresh functions, and hence the chief characteristic of the *System* is the use of the expression *Moral Faculty* as the equivalent of the Moral Sense.

The starting-point of the second phase of Hutcheson's thought was the revision of the microcosm to prove its cosmic character, and similarly the beginning of the *third* phase is also a revision of the microcosm, but in a practical rather than æsthetic interest, that is to exhibit it, not so much as a " balanced or symmetrical system " (which effort broke down in the *Essay on the Passions*) but rather as conducive to a *summum bonum* of Happiness and Perfection[1]. Hitherto the end of Hutcheson's work has been always frankly eudaemonistic, and further since Happiness was merely a sum of pleasures, it was nothing more than hedonism; now, on the contrary, Happiness and Perfection become twin ends, presumably coincident. It is true that the earlier view still maintains its ground, since

[1] *System of Moral Philosophy*, I. p. 1.

Happiness is defined as "the state of soul arising from its several grateful perceptions or modifications[1]"; elsewhere it is "the full enjoyment of all the gratifications its [i.e. "a being's"] nature desires and is capable of[2]." The point of transition is to be found in an explanation of Aristotle's celebrated definition (ἐνέργεια κατ᾽ ἀρετὴν ἀρίστην ἐν βίῳ τελείῳ) as "consisting in the compleat exercise of all these nobler virtues, especially that entire love and resignation to God, and of all the inferior virtues which do not interfere with the superior; and in the enjoyment of such external prosperity as we can consistently with virtue obtain[3]." Thus the idea of ἀρετή becomes a prominent characteristic of Hutcheson's third period, as ἁρμονία was in the second.

Joined with the notion of human Perfection, as ἐνέργεια κατ᾽ ἀρετήν, there is another which introduces quite a contrary train of thought, namely a development of Locke's "Reflection" (which began in the *Essay on the Passions*). This is now described as "an inward perception, sensation or consciousness of all the acts, passions and modifications of the mind, by which its own perceptions, judgments, reasonings, affections, feelings, may become its object, it knows them and fixes their names[4]." Apparently here the mind is *passive*, whereas the idea of excellence or perfection refers to it as *active*; and the contradiction is intensified when both these characteristics are used simultaneously, if not in the deduction of the Internal Senses, at least as rubrics, under which they are classified. From the point of view of Reflection, certain things, whether objects or actions, become causes which affect the mind, and the result is recorded by an Internal Sense which is internal because distinct from the bodily Senses. This distinction gives no clue as to how the various internal Senses are to be differentiated. From the second point of view every "natural" activity has a possibility of excellence, and when such excellence is realized the result is perceived and pleasure follows. That is, the faculty of action must be "natural"—φύσει, not either the result of association or education—its excellence is known either intuitively

---

[1] *System of Moral Philosophy*, I. p. 2.
[2] *Ibid.* I. p. 100.
[3] *Ibid.* I. p. 222.
[4] *Ibid.* I. p. 6.

or by comparison with an ideal[1], and lastly, being recognised, the pleasure resulting retains a graduated scale of dignity according to that of the realised activity[2]. While both these principles of division to all appearance diverge from the æsthetic standpoint, it is really through it that they meet. The Internal Senses as derived from Reflection, representing the attitude of the "Spectator" or observer in a picture gallery, while on the other hand, as deduced from ἐνέργεια, they find a parallel in the artist's own consciousness of success in his work—thus the former might be called static and the latter dynamic consciousness, or in the special case of Morality, the first applies primarily to approval of the acts of others, the second to each individual's approval of his own conduct. The prominence of the second principle in the *System* is important as showing that Hutcheson is now looking at action, not as externalised, but rather as expressing an energy just put forth and now completed. It must be noted however that he is by no means consistent in this position.

When the Internal Senses are to be deduced from these two opposite principles, a considerable amount of confusion is to be expected. The first group consists of a revised edition of the Sense of Beauty of the *Inquiry*, which is now called the Sense of Beauty and Harmony, which gives the "pleasures of imagination." This Sense, which Hutcheson finds difficult to name, has the following subdivisions.

(a) The perception of Beauty and consequent pleasure in all objects where "uniformity or equality of proportion among the parts is observable[3]." It is important to note that the perception of Beauty is now clearly distinguished from the subsequent pleasure—"the bare idea of Form," Hutcheson adds, "is something separable from pleasure.... Similitude, Proportion, Analogy or Equality of Proportion, are objects of the understanding and must be actually known before we know the natural causes of our pleasure[4]." Though Hutcheson after-

---

[1] In the use of natural, in this period, Hutcheson follows Aristotle whose two main uses of φύσις were (1) "the original" (2) "the ideal." *Natural Rights*, by D. G. Ritchie, M.A., Lond. 1895, p. 28.

[2] *System*, I. p. 29.   [3] *Ibid.* I. p. 15.

[4] *Inquiry*, Ed. 4, p. 10. Cf. Balguy, passages quoted, *infra*, p. 104—5.

wards partially qualifies this statement, he subsequently strengthens it in reference to the Moral Sense, when he says that the "perception of the approver, though attended with pleasure, *plainly represents something quite distinct from this pleasure,* even as the perception of external forms is attended with pleasure, and yet represents something distinct from this pleasure[1]." Secondly, it is interesting to remark that "the variety," in the oft-repeated formula of the *Inquiry,* has dropped out of the definition—the reason being that this is now a special province of the general Æsthetic Sense[2].

(*b*) The next subdivision is the perception and pleasure from the observation of imitation. These two divisions together correspond to the "Absolute and Relative Beauty" of the *Inquiry.*

(*c*) Harmony or Music calls for no special comment.

(*d*) The appreciation of Design is an important subdivision. It is rather the recognition of an end attained, than the active attaining of it. The inclusion of it under the general Æsthetic sense shows Hutcheson's conception of Beauty to have been devoid of the unconscious element in art. "In works of art," he says, "we are pleased to see intermixed the beauty of form and imitation, as far as consists with the design." The mental basis of this appreciation throws some light upon the difficulty mentioned in connection with Hutcheson's conception of Reason in his earlier works. "As we are endued with Reason to discern the fitness of means for an end and the several relations and connections of things, so there is an immediate pleasure in knowledge, distinct from the judgment itself, though naturally joined with it[3]." Elsewhere Reason is denied the power of conceiving an ultimate end, this being the function of "some sense *and* some determination of will[4]."

(*e*) It is doubtful whether Hutcheson intended to include the "grateful commotion" due to "novelty" under the Æsthetic Sense. In the *System* this pleasure is the result of a cognitive activity, subsequent upon the perception of novelty; and therefore there is no direct connection between the two. Anything

[1] *Inquiry.* Ed. 4, p. 131.   [2] *Vide infra* (*e*).
[3] *System* I. p. 16.   [4] *Ibid.* I. p. 58.

new raises a desire of further knowledge, and thus the pleasure is a pleasure following the cognitive activity. Probably the inclusion of this characteristic is an attempt to reinstate the Variety of the first period as an element in æsthetic appreciations.

(*f*) Lastly the recognition of grandeur is a further aspect or subdivision of the Æsthetic Sense.

If Novelty be omitted, it will be found that the Sense of Beauty includes Æsthetic appreciation as the Beautiful and Sublime—the former being further subdivided into Beauty in nature, art and music—and also the recognition of a realised end[1]. Of these the latter as teleological dominates the other aspects, since order or proportion of any kind is order towards some end; so that, as in the *Inquiry*, Æsthetics ultimately result in a comprehensive teleology.

In the Æsthetic Sense the point of view is that of Locke : the object, as æsthetic, is also the object of the sense. It is supposed to meet a certain determination of a passive or receptive mind which it affects, and from this contact perception and feeling result. Yet even here this attitude is not consistently maintained since the justification of our gratification by a realised end depends upon the prior consciousness of our own individual power in realising an end[2], and further the "pleasures of knowledge" resulting from "novelty" depend upon the effort, not the result[3].

After the subdivisions of the Æsthetic Sense Hutcheson next mentions what he calls the Senses of Sympathy and Congratulation, but it is difficult to see the grounds for their inclusion, else every affection would be equally a "Sense." It seems the position assigned to Sympathy is a survival from the *Essay on the Passions,* where a Public Sense was added to the two taken over from the *Inquiry*; at the same time, such a

---

[1] Hutcheson's Pleasures of Imagination result from

$$
\begin{cases}
\text{Beauty proper} \begin{cases} \textit{in Nature} \ (\text{division} \ (a) \ \text{of Sense}) \ \text{from Uniformity} \\ \textit{in Art} \quad (\quad ,, \quad (b) \quad ,, \quad) \ \text{Hutcheson's ``Imitation''} \\ \textit{in Music} \ (\quad ,, \quad (c) \quad ,, \quad) \quad ,, \quad \text{Harmony} \end{cases} \\
\text{the Sublime} \ (f) \\
[\text{Novelty}] \ (e) \\
\text{Design} \ (d).
\end{cases}
$$

[2] *System* I. pp. 16, 17.   [3] *Ibid.* I. p. 19.

concession to the divisions of the second period involves a
lack of consistency, since the perceptive element of the other
Senses is wanting here; and the same remark applies to the
parental and conjugal affections, which Hutcheson sometimes
seems inclined to admit as a Sense, because they are natural[1].

After the Sympathetic comes the Moral Sense, or "Faculty
of perceiving moral excellence[2]." Its object, as in the *Essay on
the Passions*, is "calm Benevolence," which is now attributed
to a "settled disposition of the Will." As Hutcheson puts it,
"the προαίρεσις which is necessary to virtuous actions is ὄρεξις
βουλευτική; and that virtue needs not only the λόγον ἀληθῆ
but the ὄρεξιν ὀρθήν. Those very authors who deny any affections or motions of the will to be the proper springs of sublime
Virtue, yet, inconsistently with themselves, must allow in men
of sublime virtue, and even in the Deity too, a settled disposition of Will[3]." The further consideration of the Moral Sense
or Faculty may be temporarily postponed, since, being the
crowning sense, it naturally presupposes that the table should
be complete.

Next in order is the sense of Honour, repeated from the
Essay on the Passions; and this is followed by a Sense of
Decency or decorum, which now appears for the first time. It
takes note of the excellence of any natural faculty in operation,
or of a dexterity acquired by repeated acts of will. It is
derived from the conception of φυσικαὶ ἀρεταί[4]. In the *Essay
on the Passions* Hutcheson had identified his Moral Sense with
the "Sensus Decori[5]," but he now sees that good manners,
though "the very dress of virtue[6]" are not virtue itself; but,
at the same time, he has also a tendency to subsume this Sense
under the Moral Faculty, making such natural excellences an
immediate object of moral approbation[7].

---

[1] *System*, I. p. 33. [2] *Ibid.* I. p. 53.

[3] *Inquiry*, Ed. 4, p. 195 (note). Hutcheson evidently had the following
passage before his mind as he wrote: ὥστ᾽ ἐπειδὴ ἡ ἠθικὴ ἀρετὴ ἕξις προαιρετική,
ἡ δὲ προαίρεσις ὄρεξις βουλευτική, δεῖ διὰ ταῦτα τόν τε λόγον ἀληθῆ εἶναι, καὶ τὴν
ὄρεξιν ὀρθήν, εἴπερ ἡ προαίρεσις σπουδαία, *Nic. Ethics*, VI. 2.

[4] *Ibid.* p. 197. *System*, I. p. 67.

[5] *Essay on the Passions*, p. xx. [6] *System*, I. p. 67.

[7] *Ibid.* I. p. 66. Contrast *Inquiry*, Ed. 4, p. 201.

The interaction of Aristotelian and Lockian stand-points, in distinguishing the revised list of Internal Senses, makes it difficult to obtain a general statement of Hutcheson's dominant idea. On the one hand that strange compound with Locke— the mind—which is sometimes as useful and elsewhere as un-manageable as "the child" of the modern Psychologist, is supposed to make an object of its own activities dealing with Sensation, and then adopt a passive *rôle* to observe, and, as Hutcheson says, "to know and name" what it has done. "Reflection," then, through the personalization of faculties or powers, is an observer, and so is affected by objects or its own past acts. From the other point of view each active power is capable of excellence in use, and such exercise of it is perceived in and with the activity[1]. Consequently excellence of function displaces "good" as the end of action, and strictly speaking all activities should be enumerated, and their respective excel-lences noted; but Hutcheson does not attempt this, nor does he explain how the individual excellences of the different faculties are to be synthesized; unless he intends the ideal of perfection to perform this office, in reference to the consolidated activity of the individual as a whole.

If then each faculty has its proper excellence, what is the "differentia" of moral excellence? Possibly the answer may be found in a further examination of the various excellences of the different activities. It is noteworthy that Hutcheson does not endeavour to include the Æsthetic sense under this division, except by a single incidental reference[2]; and hence, in this phase of his thought, there is less mention of the "Beauty of virtue" than in his other works.

Passing the problem of how the excellences of different faculties are united, it will be found that a threefold division is implied. First the excellence of all *cognitive faculties*, which, to a certain extent, is covered by the Sense of Novelty; though by a strange inconsistency, novelty *starts* the process, and does not, as in the case of all other senses, recognise the excellence of the result. In fact, the observation of Novelty, Hutcheson admits, produces the curiosity that Hamilton later used so

[1] *System*, i. p. 59.   [2] *Ibid.* i. p. 59.

freely, and therefore, neither the one nor the other can deal with the result. In the second place, the excellence of activities in which *will* largely preponderates is perceived by the Sense of Decorum, and finally the object of the Moral Sense or Faculty might be described as the excellence of *both* cognitive and practical activities, starting from the basis of a particular altruistic affection; and therefore it is human energy as a unit, constituting the power of the individual realized to the highest degree of discursive and practical reason. The "extensive view of the tendencies of actions" is plainly a cognitive act; and the suspense in carrying it out till the examination is complete, or the deliberative stage, followed by the "settled determination," is to be attributed to the will. Moral excellence, then, is the excellence of the whole man for the good of the macrocosm.

This line of thought naturally leads to the transition from Moral excellence to individual Perfection, which now becomes an alternative for the highest Self-Love. Yet this transition suggests the obvious difficulty as to whether it would not be probable that the desire of individual perfection of the microcosm would lead to a different valuation of natural activities from that following from the desire of moral excellence, which concerns itself with the macrocosm. To this there are three replies—first there can be no conflict, when perfection and moral excellence are rightly conceived; secondly, supposing there were a divergency of valuation of ends or activities, the Moral Sense would decide in favour of Benevolence, and it is a superior Sense just to exercise such control. Here it is obvious that, as already shown, the decision or approbation is valueless, since it depends altogether upon the *presented* scheme of conduct as benevolent; or, thirdly, Hutcheson contends that there is an inherent dignity in the exercise of different activities, and that this dignity is graduated according to the scale of faculties from the exercise of which it results, and that the highest form of it is that shown by the most extensive principle. Now such dignity is *not* an attribute of the Moral Sense, but rather of the activity, and therefore justifiable only by means of a prior justification of the examination, deliberation and determination from which the extensive principle results. Thus again the Moral Sense is a supernumerary. In fact Hutcheson was so fully aware of this that he changes the function of the Sense repeatedly. Sometimes it is one with, and indistinguisable from the activity. Excellence, and pre-eminently moral excellence, is perceivable or knowable, and the Moral Sense is nothing more than such bare recognition. Therefore, and this is a wide divergence from the *Inquiry*, it has no necessary hedonistic element. This idea is suggested upon several occasions and plainly stated as follows—" When we are under the influence of a virtuous temper, and thereby engaged in virtuous actions, *we are not always conscious of any pleasure* nor are we only pursuing private pleasures, as will appear hereafter : 'tis only by *reflex Acts* upon our Temper and Conduct that we enjoy the delights of Virtue[1]." In connection with the description of material and formal good—the former being that " which tends to the interest of the system as far as we can judge of its tendency, or to the good of some part, consistent with that of the system, whatever were the affections of the agent "; and " formal good," when " an action flows from good affections in a just proportion[2]"—the " reflex acts " become partially identified with what is called *Conscientia subsequens*, which deals with past actions in connection with the motive, abstracting from effects[3], while the *Conscientia antecedens*, being prior to action, is the true faculty of moral decision, and it invariably prefers " that which appears most conducive to the virtue and happiness of mankind[4]." In this distinction Hutcheson anticipates Mill's well-known contrast between the estimation of motive and intention[5]. The same general tendency is shown in the criticism of the Golden Rule as the sole ethical principle, which " is mistaken by some authors who, without acknowledging any prior principle of moral Reasoning or any inward immediate taste of action, would make this proposition an axiom whence they would deduce all rules of conduct "—its use being " to prepare the heart for an

---

[1] *Inquiry*, Ed. 4, p. 130.   [2] *System*, I. p. 252.
[3] *Ibid.* I. p. 253.   [4] *Ibid.*
[5] *Utilitarianism*, p. 27.

impartial discernment of what is just and honourable, and what not, by making the Selfish Passions operate a little on the other side[1]." Again, in distinguishing the threefold signification of Conscience, we find it sometimes "denotes the Moral Faculty itself," or "the judgment of the understanding concerning the springs and effects of actions, upon which the Moral Sense approves or condemns them"; or else our judgment concerning actions compared with the law[2]." The idea of law is new and requires some explanation. Here it applies to moral rules, understood as the commands of God; but, later, "the notion of a law shows how justly the practical conclusions of right reason, from the order of Nature constituted by God, and laid open to our observation, are called laws of nature and laws of God[3]." These laws further, though discovered by reason, are deemed immutable and eternal[4], as being rules relative to the permanent tendency of certain courses of conduct to the end of the macrocosm. Therefore the last two aspects of Conscience ultimately coincide with regard to their content: for both are different aspects of the same element in the moral decision, the one being the condition of the will tested by Reason, and the other—the relation to law—being the conclusions of Reason enforced upon the Will. Both then, as dealing with "material good," are different sides of the *Conscientia antecedens*, while the first (namely Conscience as denoting the moral faculty) may be identified with the *Conscientia subsequens* or "the reflex acts." If such identification be just, the Moral Sense, strictly speaking, refers only to the accidental hedonistic consequent of right conduct; and, since it is no integral part of the moral state, it cannot be the criterion. In so far as Hutcheson emphasizes moral excellence as the result of activity, this appears to be his meaning, but there is also a marked tendency to assign the work of the *Conscientia antecedens* to the Moral Sense, which is often spoken of as the hedonistic determinant of the moral decision. Thus there are many expressions, repeated from the *Inquiry*, as to virtue being recognized by a taste or relish, that "the approbation of moral

[1] *System*, ii. p. 16. [2] *Ibid.* i. p. 234.
[3] *Ibid.* i. p. 268. Cf. also i. p. 271.
[4] *Ibid.* i. p. 273.

excellence is a grateful action or sensation of the mind[1]," right conduct raises "the most joyful sensations of approbation and inward satisfaction[2]"; "we improve our moral taste by presenting larger systems to the mind[3]" and it acts through "recommending the generous part by an immediate undefinable perception[4]." Further, to provide an object for the Moral Sense independent of "moral reasoning," Hutcheson explicitly states that it "immediately approves the particular altruistic affections, irrespective of their tendency to the good of a system[5]," yet this is only a provisional approval, subject to no counter protest being entered by the principle of calm Benevolence, and so the Moral Sense in this aspect of its work is forced to borrow from the Ethics of a schoolboy, who acts as he pleases until he has received an express prohibition. So employed, the Moral Sense is reduced to Sympathy—indeed Hutcheson only escaped this identification by appealing from the instability of the latter to the permanent character imported into the moral decision by the settled determination involved in calm Benevolence. Again, he carries his distrust of cognitive elements in Morality so far that he sometimes excludes reason altogether as "too slow, too full of doubt and hesitation to serve us in every exigency," and therefore just as the external Senses are "expeditious monitors and importunate solicitors[6]" for the preservation of the body, so some such rapidity is to be found in the Moral Sense, apart from the rational and deliberative process involved in calm Benevolence or the *Conscientia antecedens*. Finally, if there be any doubt as to the Standard, "moral reasoning" is only admitted to be censured virtually for securing the "approbation" of the "Sense" upon false pretences — though, if the Moral Faculty is unable to detect any oversight in investigation of the tendencies of actions, the alleged "commanding nature" (which is "proved by appeal to our hearts[7]") is, to say the least of it, useless—and if the verdict of the heart is not accepted, Hutcheson, rather than discuss the "immutable

[1] *System*, I. p. 53. 　　　[2] *Ibid.* I. p. 24.
[3] *Ibid.* I. p. 60. 　　　　[4] *Ibid.* I. p. 77.
[5] *Ibid.* I. p. 254. 　　　[6] *Inquiry*, Ed. 4, p. 272.
[7] *System*, I. p. 61.

law of nature," derived from practical reason, appeals upon the authority of Aristotle to the "sensation of the truly good man[1]" "whose sentiments must be the last resort in intricate cases[2]."

But, while the hedonism of the moral Sense still survives in the third phase of Hutcheson's thought, he has made a distinct advance from the position of the *Essay on the Passions*. There the stability of the moral Sense depended upon the cognitive elements, presupposed in the genesis of the calm Benevolent Desire. Now, on the contrary, he has become aware of this inconsistency, and he has at least endeavoured to readjust his theory to meet it. At the same time there is still the same clinging to the "pleasures of virtue," and therefore concessions must be made, so that "moral reasoning," "the settled determination of the will," "the law of Reason," while admitted into the system, are certainly unwelcome auxiliaries; but, as in certain historical instances, the mercenaries are likely to subvert the government which they were called in to support.

The numerous additions to the list of Internal Senses proved unmanageable when it became necessary to arrange the moral constitution as a microcosm; in fact Hutcheson makes no attempt to deal with them as parts of an ordered whole. On the contrary he reverts to the method of the *Essay on the Passions* by arranging all particular affections under the headings of Self-Love and Perfection on the one side, and Calm Benevolence on the other. The addition of Perfection to Self-Love, as its highest development, makes the "balance" more symmetrical; but it leaves the theory weaker, since, if the Moral Sense is barely a hedonistic determination to be pleased with a presented end, its pleasure is unintelligible either to Self-Love or Benevolence—if, on the other hand, Moral Reasoning—the *Conscientia antecedens*—be the faculty of moral decision, it is merely a reduplication of the idea of moral excellence, which gave birth to Calm Benevolence as now understood. Indeed the apparent similarity of Perfection for the individual and Moral Excellence must have disguised the difficulty; yet, unless the presupposed harmony of the two

[1] *System*, I. p. 237. [2] *Ibid.* II. p. 140.

remains unbroken, the Perfection of the individual is in danger of losing its rights as a member of the balance, since, whether the moral faculty be rational judge or æsthetic pleader, its verdict is already pledged in favour of Benevolence.

While Hutcheson's idea of the *microcosm* was subject to changes during each stage of his thought, that of the *macrocosm* is much more constant. In the *System of Moral Philosophy*, he becomes something more of an ethical idealist by endeavouring to utilise the Moral Faculty as a connecting link in addition to the conclusions of his teleology. "The Moral Faculty," he writes, "itself seems that peculiar part of our nature most adapted to promote this correspondence of every rational mind with the great Source of our being and of all Perfection, as it immediately approves all moral excellence, and determines the soul to the love of it, and approves this love as the greatest excellence of mind, which too is the most useful to the system[1]." This use of the moral faculty, in part, accounts for the introduction of the fresh view already mentioned of its functions, since within the microcosm it is a matter of indifference how the "Sense" is conceived; whereas, if it be a connecting link with the macrocosm it must, to be serviceable, have at least one side as *Conscientia antecedens*, and all that this implies in reaction upon the theory generally.

As the Moral Faculty is, in its highest form, the best expression of all human power, excluding the Æsthetic sense, so the transition from the microcosm to the macrocosm includes, besides moral excellence, teleological considerations. When investigating the "natural" tendency towards Religion, Hutcheson finds that "as the several classes of animals and vegetables display in their whole frame exquisite mechanism and regular structure, evidencing counsel, art, and contrivance for certain ends, men of genius and attention must soon discover some intelligent beings one or more, presiding in all this comely order and magnificence[2]." Later on, teleology justifies the existence of an "intelligent artificer[3]," and the lengthy proof proceeds to establish his benevolent character. This follows

[1] *System*, I. p. 210.   [2] *Ibid*. I. p. 35.
[3] *Ibid*. I. pp. 168—174.

directly from Hutcheson's Optimism, which is now reinforced by the dignity or difference in kind of the pleasures of the higher internal Senses, and is further strengthened by the proof of the immortality of the Soul. This addition to the argument involves the abandonment of Lockian empiricism, taken over with the idea of Reflection from the *Essay on the Passions*. The soul is now conceived as "active," and as such, inconsistent with the passiveness of matter[1]. All activities of thought and will we "feel to be the immediate qualities of this *Self*, the personal excellencies in which all its true dignity consists[2]....Nature thus intimates to us a spirit distinct from the body over which it presides....Nay it intimates a greater difference or disparity of substance." Therefore, as with Butler, in the *Analogy*, the soul, "being disparate from matter, is unaffected by any change, such as death in the body," and so any possible objections to the Optimistic belief are met by the certainty "that the evils of these few years, during our mortal state, are not worthy of regard; they are not once to be compared with the happiness to ensue[3]." Therefore the "great Architect" is benevolent, and finally, following Descartes and Spinoza, the "Physico-theological" proof culminates in the Ontological, which shows that God is infinite, "uncaused," One, a Spirit, omnipotent and omnipresent[4].

Thus the whole macrocosm is graduated, according to degrees of excellence, "from the meanest animal to the infinite Deity."

To Hutcheson, however, the "system as a whole" is to be conceived rather as the social organism, and therefore the principles of Jurisprudence, Government and Economics, constitute not merely an appendix but rather an integral part of the theory. For, since the *Conscientia antecedens* deals with the tendencies of actions in reference to the public good, the general rules or maxims of estimation are at once ethical and social laws[5]. Many of Hutcheson's summaries of tendencies have "come down through Roman judicial theory from the specula-

---

[1] *System*, i. p. 200.

[2] *Ibid.* i. pp. 202, 205.

[3] *Ibid.* i. p. 201.

[4] *Ibid.* i. pp. 205, 206.

[5] *Ibid.* i. p. 227.

tions of Greece[1]," and their chief interest consists in the
ingenious manner in which he has united or "deduced" them
from the general ethical position. In fact, as Teleology has
been reduced to a system of both Universal Happiness *and*
Perfection, so now the apparently egoistic ideas of Property
and individual rights must be ranked under the same principle.

The "State of Nature" is not one of war, but of mutual
offices of good-will. " In the first state constituted by Nature
itself, we must discern abundantly, from the preceding book,
that there are many sacred rights competent to men, and many
obligations incumbent on each towards his fellows. The whole
system of the mind, especially our moral faculty, shows that we
are under natural bonds of beneficence and humanity toward all,
and under many more special tyes to some of our fellows,
binding us to many services of an higher kind than what the
rest can claim: nor need we other proofs here that this first
state, founded by nature, is so far from being that of war and
enmity, that it is a state where we are obliged by the natural
feelings of our hearts, and by many tender affections, to innocence
and beneficence toward all: and that war is one of the accidental
states arising solely from injury, when we or some of our fellows
have counteracted the dictates of their nature[2]." Thus natural
rights depend upon the moral faculty, and arise as follows—
" when a man's acting, possessing, or obtaining from another, in
these circumstances, tends to the good of Society, or to the interests of the individual consistently with the rights of others
and the general good of Society and [when] obstructing him
would have the contrary tendency[3]," and so every " proper right
is in some way conducive to the public interest and is founded
on some such tendency[4]." Thus the natural right of liberty " is
not only suggested by the selfish part of our constitution but
by many generous affections and the moral Sense, which represents our voluntary actions as the grand dignity and perfection
of our nature[5]"; and similarly the right over one's own life is
held, in trust, to be devoted to the public good, if necessary.

---

[1] *History of Political Economy*, by Rev. John Kells Ingram, p. 61.
[2] *System*, I. p. 281.   [3] *Ibid.* I. p. 253.
[4] *Ibid.* I. p. 257.   [5] *Ibid.* I. p. 295.

At the same time, the mere admission of Natural right, if only in a modified form, is sufficient to cause a 'lapse from the extreme form of Benevolence, for if the Rights of the individual are to be worthy of the name, he must hold them as his own, not merely upon behalf of the social organism as represented in his own person. To further reinforce society against the individual, Hutcheson introduces an extended scheme of rights due from the individual to the general body of his fellows[1], which are obviously intended to outweigh the claims of any single member. Even the "adventitious right" of the possession of property is to be explained upon altruistic principles. It depends upon the right of the first occupant to such "things as are fit for supporting ourselves or *those who are dear to us*[2]," and is confirmed as an incentive to industry, which contributes to the general interest. "Diligence will never be universal, unless men's own necessities and the love of families and friends excite them[3]." In this connection, Hutcheson admits that the general Benevolent disposition, which played such an important part in the earlier portion of the theory, would not be a sufficient motive to labour. Further, while the right to property is beneficial to the social system as promoting industry, the motive *of the individual*—failing calm Benevolence, which is admittedly insufficient—can only be either selfish or a narrow particular altruistic affection, which is subject to considerable suspicion from the moral point of view, until legitimated by Benevolence. Indeed Hutcheson admits that the desire for the possession of property is primarily egoistic, for the satisfaction of pressing wants, and he endeavours to offset this admission by insisting upon the duties of persons in easy circumstances, in a civilized community, to devote themselves gratuitously to aiding in movements of public utility.

[1] *System*, ii. p. 105.
[2] *Ibid.* i. p. 317.
[3] *Ibid.* i. p. 321.

CHAPTER XI. (*continued*).

PART II. HUTCHESON'S ECONOMICS AND HIS RELATION TO ADAM SMITH.

In connection with Hutcheson's remarks concerning property, as well as elsewhere in his later works, there occur some opinions upon economic principles. These possess considerable importance, when it is remembered that Adam Smith had been a student at Glasgow from 1737—1740, that he had attended Hutcheson's class and had been much impressed by the personality of his teacher.

Mr Cannan states that the discovery of Smith's *Glasgow Lectures* conclusively proves that much of the theory of the *Wealth of Nations* had been thought out and taught in class long before Smith became acquainted with the work of the Physiocrats and of Turgot in particular[1]. He further conjectures that the germ of Smith's theory is to be found in the chapter "Concerning the Values or Prices of Goods" in the *Compend of Morals*[2]. Additional information concerning Hutcheson enables one to add something to the chain of historical continuity, through connecting Smith's economic work with that of his predecessors as he found it focussed by Hutcheson. Regarding the relations of the two, Mr Cannan gives an interesting psychological account explaining the great influence of the older thinker upon the younger. "In the work of professors, as in other things, a kind of atavism is often observable. A professor has rarely been a student under his

[1] *Lectures on Justice, Police Revenues, and Arms*, by Adam Smith, edited by Edwin Cannan, Oxford, 1896, p. xxiv.

[2] Book II. ch. XII. Smith's *Glasgow Lectures, ut supra*, p. xxvi.

immediate predecessor in the chair. While he has been obtaining experience in a less dignified post, or has been absent acquiring the honour which it is proverbially difficult for a prophet to obtain in his own country, his master has died or retired and been succeeded by a man of an intermediate generation[1] and probably of intermediate views, whom he very likely regards with that slight dash of contempt which men are apt to feel for those who are older than themselves, but yet not old enough to obtain from them the respect universally and fortunately accorded to the surviving lights of a past age and an 'old school,' whose virtues have become uncommon, and whose weaknesses and eccentricities, instead of annoying or disgusting, afford kindly amusement. We should do well, therefore, to look in Adam Smith's work for important traces of the influence of Francis Hutcheson...to whom Smith acknowledged obligations and of whom he used warm words of praise[2]."

It is important to note that Mr Cannan bases his claim for the recognition of Hutcheson's influence upon Smith on the *Compend of Morals*, and the discovery of new light on Hutcheson's life and works adds additional weight to it. In the first place it has been shown that the MS. of the *System of Moral Philosophy* was used by Hutcheson for his class lectures about 1737, that is before the time Smith attended his class; therefore, as a student, the latter must have been familiar with the economic data contained in it; and, as will be shown below, these are more considerable than one would expect. Further the *System* contains many reproductions of views of Pufendorf, Grotius and Locke upon Politics and Economics. Similar passages, as Mr Cannan shows by many references, reappear in Smith's works; and Hutcheson's function was to collect and classify them, so that they were available for Smith. It might of course be contended that Smith consulted the authorities direct; but when it is remembered that he heard these very passages read and expounded in the Glasgow class-room, and

---

[1] The following are the names of Professors of Moral Philosophy at Glasgow: 1727 Gershom Carmichael, 1730 Francis Hutcheson, 1746 Thomas Craigie, 1752 Adam Smith, 1764 Thomas Reid.

[2] Smith's *Glasgow Lectures, ut supra*, p. xxv.

further that the *System* was published a few years after his
appointment to the Chair of Moral Philosophy, when he would
be preparing his own lectures, it seems only reasonable to trace
Hutcheson's influence here. Thus, in this case as elsewhere, he
belonged to the Enlightenment, preparing a thesaurus of valuable
material for his successor.

In the second place, Smith is indebted to Hutcheson for
the general philosophical position that is presupposed by his
Economics. In both thinkers we find the same natural liberty,
Optimism and Naturalism generally, with Smith as an assumption with Hutcheson as a thesis.

It is true that the same general point of view reappears
amongst the Physiocrats, and it has been pointed out that its
appearance in France was due to the influence of Shaftesbury[1].
Indeed it was this common ground that made the affiliation of
Physiocratic principles to those derived from Hutcheson possible
for Smith in the *Wealth of Nations*. But here, as in the former
case, the fortunate find of the *Glasgow Lectures* conclusively
settles the question : for these lectures might be best described
as a brilliant and original commentary upon those of the "never-
to-be-forgotten Hutcheson."

At first sight it would appear that there was little similarity
between the two sets of lectures, which by a curious coincidence
were not intended by either professor for publication. The
difference however is largely one of arrangement, Smith, as he
explicitly mentions, reversing the order of "others," therein
including Hutcheson[2].

The *System* and *Compend of Morals* are very badly divided.
The first book in each case deals with Ethics, the second begins
with Ethical investigations and continues with Rights and
Property, the third contains some economical matter and the
theory of the State. Now Smith in his lectures first dealt with
Ethics—and this part of his course is represented by the *Theory
of Moral Sentiments*—next he treated Economics separately,
giving this subject a distinct position under the head of

---

[1] *Die allgemeinen Phil. Grundlagen der von F. Quesnay und Adam Smith
begründeten Pol. Oecon.*, von W. Hasbach, p. 59.

[2] Smith's *Glasgow Lectures*, p. 8.

" Police[1]." The remainder of Hutcheson's material constitutes three groups of subjects; and, following the hint in the introduction of Smith's *Glasgow Lectures*, it will be found that Hutcheson's order is reversed. Thus the treatment of the two men runs as follows:

Hutcheson's *System*	Smith's *Glasgow Lectures*
Book II. chaps. 6—13, subject-matter treated in Part I. Division III.	
„ III. „ 1—3 „ „ „ „ „ II.	
„ III. „ 4—8 „ „ „ „ „ I.	

It need scarcely be added that, as Mr Cannan shows, Smith's work is a distinct advance upon that of Hutcheson, and here one might conjecture that Smith's admirable historical treatment may have been suggested by the example of Hume.

Notwithstanding the excellent work done in tracing out the growth of Adam Smith's theory of Economics, it would appear that Hutcheson's contribution towards its development has failed to secure sufficient notice. The importance of his influence upon Smith's *Ethics* has indeed been fully recognised, but most writers, as for instance Skarżyński, after a bare mention of Hutcheson's economic work, emphasize Smith's indebtedness to Hume[2]. Now there is not the least doubt that there is much common to Hutcheson and Hume as economists; and this may readily be accounted for by their close personal relations, and also by that great deference already mentioned which Hume showed to Hutcheson's opinions. Therefore if Smith had not known Hutcheson, nor heard his lectures, many of the views of the earlier thinker would, in all probability, have found their way into his lectures and thence to the *Wealth of Nations* through Hume. But it has already been shown that Hutcheson's work had made a great impression upon Smith and so it might have been conjectured that he would have availed himself of such material as proved suitable directly. Not only so, but in certain directions Hutcheson in Economics is closer than Hume to Adam Smith—in fact many

---

[1] Part II. Division II., "Of Cheapness and Plenty."

[2] *Adam Smith als Moralphilosoph und Schöpfer der Nationalökonomie, passim.*

of the principles used by both the later thinkers are traceable to the earlier one. To Hume Adam Smith may owe a working example of the value of historical treatment and detail, which may have led to that "copiousness of felicitous illustration," for which he is justly celebrated[1]. These characteristics, though not altogether wanting, are certainly far from prominent in the *System*.

Several writers have drawn attention to Hutcheson's chapter on the "Values of Goods in Commerce and the Nature of Coin[2]," and this is often spoken of as his sole contribution to Political Economy. As a matter of fact there are several important remarks upon economics which occur in odd and unlikely corners of the *System*. If these are read together important parallels to well-known passages in Smith's work will at once be noticed. Needless to say the *Wealth of Nations* is immensely more full of detail; but if we compare these passages in Hutcheson with the corresponding sections of "Cheapness and Plenty" in the *Glasgow Lectures*, it will appear that the difference between the latter work and Hutcheson's is no greater than between the *Lectures* and the *Wealth of Nations*.

Upon looking into the subject-matter of Hutcheson's economical work a striking example of Smith's indebtedness to his old teacher, rather than to Hume, at once becomes apparent in the order of treatment adopted. Hume, it need scarcely be remarked, dealt with economics in a series of disconnected essays, and "some have represented Smith's work as of so loose a texture and so defective in arrangement, that it may be justly described as a series of monographs[3]." It would therefore appear that the alleged discontinuity of the *Wealth of Nations* might be due to Hume's mode of expression, but a closer examination shows that the order of the topics discussed in the economic portions of Hutcheson's *System* is repeated in Smith's *Glasgow Lectures* and again in the *Wealth of Nations*. The

---

[1] *A Short History of Political Economy in England*, by L. L. Price, M.A., p. 14.

[2] *System*, ii. p. 53 ; *Intr. Mor. Phil.* p. 199.

[3] *History of Political Economy*, by John Kells Ingram, p. 93.

following table, showing the order of treatment in the three books will make this point clear, though of course the parallelism may be nothing more than coincidence.

Hutcheson's System		Subjects	Adam Smith	
			Glasgow Lectures	*Wealth of Nations*
Bk. II. Ch. IV.		Division of Labour	Pt. II. Div. II. §§ 3—5	Bk. I. Ch. 1, 2
„	VI.	"Necessaries and comforts require an universal laborious industry"	„ „	„ „ 5
„	XII.	Value	„ „	„ „ 4
„	„	Value in use and in exchange	„ § 7	„ „ „
„	„	Money medium of exchange		
„	„	Money standard of value	„ § 8	„ „ 4—5
„	„	Price	„ § 7	„ „ 7
„	„	Wages	„ § 7	„ „ 8
„	XIII.	Theory and rate of interest	„ § 14	„ „ 9—10
„	„	Explanation of Rent	„ § 16	„ „ 11
Bk. III. Ch. IX.		State and Foreign Trade	„ §§ 10–12	Book IV.
„	„	Maxims of Taxation	Part III.	Book V.

Probably the first subject mentioned (namely the Division of Labour), as being dealt with by Hutcheson, may amuse the reader, who credits writers of monographs with a more or less praiseworthy endeavour to show that their "author" has "anticipated" the largest possible number of later theories. Consequently one rather shrinks from claiming priority for Hutcheson in this case, were it not that a passage in his *System* seems to have been before the mind of Adam Smith when writing of the advantages of the organization of industry. Hutcheson, having justified the state of liberty, proceeds to show that we are indebted for comforts and conveniences of life "to the friendly aids of our fellows." "'Tis plain," he continues, "that a man in absolute solitude, though he were of mature strength, and fully instructed in all our arts of life, could scarcely procure to himself the bare necessaries of life, even in the best soils or climates; much less could he procure any grateful conveniences....The mutual aids of a few in a small family may procure most of the necessaries of life and diminish dangers, and afford room for some social joys, as well as finer pleasures.   The same advantages could still be obtained more effectually and copiously by the mutual assistance of a few such families, living in one neighbourhood, as they could execute more operose designs for the common good of all; and would furnish more joyful exercises of our social dispositions.

   " Nay 'tis well known that the produce of the labours of any given number, twenty for instance, in providing the necessaries or conveniences of life, shall be much greater by assigning to one a certain sort of work of one kind, in which he will soon acquire skill and dexterity, and to another assigning work of a different kind, than if each one of the twenty were obliged to employ himself by turns in all the different sorts of labour requisite for his subsistence, without sufficient dexterity in any. In the former method each procures a great quantity of goods of one kind, and can exchange a part of it for such goods, obtained by the labours of others as he shall stand in need of. One grows expert in tillage, another in pasture and breeding cattle, a third in masonry, a fourth in the chace, a fifth in iron-works, a sixth in the arts of the loom, and so on throughout the rest.   Thus all are supplied by means of barter with the works of complete artists.   In the other method, scarce any one could be dexterous and skilful in any one sort of labour.

   "Again some works of the highest use to multitudes can be effectually executed by the joint labours of many, which the separate labours of the same numbers could never have exe-cuted.   The joint force of many can repel dangers arising from savage beasts or bands of robbers, which might have been fatal to many individuals were they separately to encounter them. The joint labours of twenty men will cultivate forests or drain marshes for farms to each one, and provide houses for habi-tation and inclosures for their flocks, much sooner than the separate labours of the same number.   By concert and alternate relief they can keep a perpetual watch, which without concert they could not accomplish.

"Larger associations may further enlarge our means of enjoyment, and give more extensive and delightful exercise to our powers of every kind. The inventions, experience and arts of multitudes are communicated, knowledge is increased and social affections more diffused. Larger societies have force to execute greater designs of more lasting and extensive advantage[1]."

In this passage Hutcheson anticipates Adam Smith's claim for the advantages of Division of Labour in the separation of employments and the increase of dexterity, while the growth of invention and the distinction between simple and complex co-operation are also implied. What is new in Smith's *Lectures* is the direct application of the principle to existing industrial conditions.

In treating of Hutcheson's work upon the theory of Value, Mr Rae mentions that his remarks read "like a first draft of Smith's famous passage on value in use and value in exchange[2]." Further, though Hutcheson does not use Smith's terms, his language suggests them. "The natural ground of all value or price is some sort of use which goods afford in life; this is prerequisite to all estimation. But the prices or values in commerce do not at all follow the real use or importance of goods for the support or natural pleasure of life[3]." Utility or "use" means "not only a natural subserviency to our support or some natural pleasure, but any tendency to give any satisfaction by prevailing custom or fancy, as a matter of ornament or distinction[4]."

The *differentia* between utility and wealth is found in the presence of labour as an essential characteristic of the latter. Dr Bonar mentions that it was "perhaps due to Hutcheson[5]" that Smith makes "labour the real measure of the exchangeable value of all commodities"; but it should be noted that while Hutcheson emphasizes the position of labour he does not make it the sole distinguishing characteristic of wealth, for he also adds the limitation of supply and appropriation—as for

[1] *System*, I. pp. 287—290.   [2] *Life of Adam Smith*, p. 14.
[3] *System*, II. p. 53.   [4] *Ibid.* II. p. 54.
[5] *Philosophy and Political Economy*, p. 118.

instance, "the rarity or scarcity of the materials in nature, or
such accidents as prevent plentiful crops of certain fruits of the
earth; and the great ingenuity and taste requisite in the
artists to finish well some works of art, as men of such genius
are rare. The value is also raised by the dignity of station in
which, according to the custom of a country, the men must live
who provide us with certain goods or works of art[1]." It is
interesting to notice that, when this passage was revised in the
Compend of Morals, it is added that some things possessed of
utility are not separable from commodities but that they
possess value as enhancing the price of that of which they are
"appendages," as for instance "a fine prospect" increases the
price of a dwelling-house[2].

It is not contended that Hutcheson was the discoverer of
the advantages of Division of Labour, nor of the importance of
labour an an element in Wealth, only that he influenced Adam
Smith. With regard to the former, the priority of Plato has
long been recognized, but it may not be out of place to add
that Hutcheson's treatment of Labour is expanded from
Cicero's *De Officiis*[3], an indebtedness which Hutcheson himself
acknowledges[4].

Adam Smith follows Hutcheson closely in the section on
Money, except that in the more systematic treatment of the
later writer it is closely connected with Division of Labour—a
conclusion that indeed follows logically from the passage quoted
above from the *System*[5]. Hutcheson treats money as a medium
of exchange, and as a standard both of value and of deferred
payments. The following passage shows the character of his
work on this head—"The qualities requisite to the most perfect
standard are these; it must be something generally desired, so
that men are willing to take it in exchange. The very making
any sort of goods the standard will of itself give them this
quality. It must be portable; which will often be the case if
it be rare, so that small quantities are of great value. It must

---

[1] *System*, II. p. 55. With regard to appropriation, cf. *Ibid.* II. Chap. VI.
passim.

[2] *Intr. to Moral Phil.* p. 200.   [3] II. chap. 3—5.

[4] *System*, I. p. 290.   [5] *Supra*, p. 236.

be divisible without loss into small parts, so as to be suited to the values of all sorts of goods; and it must be durable, not easily wearing by use or perishing in its nature." He also investigates the effect of the production of the precious metals and concludes that "the most invariable salary would be so many days' labour of men, or a fixed quantity of goods produced by the plain inartificial labours, such goods as answer the ordinary purposes of life[1]."

Hutcheson writes on Money with a remarkable freedom from Mercantile sympathies. "Coin," he says, "is ever valued as a commodity in commerce, as well as other goods[2]," and he strongly condemns governmental interference either with the export of the precious metals or in tampering with the coinage. To debase the coinage means "cheating" the subjects of the state—and in this connection Adam Smith's expression "defrauding" will be remembered.

Quite the most significant side of Hutcheson's relation to Adam Smith appears in connection with Distribution. The *Glasgow Lectures* are almost silent upon this subject and it is more than a coincidence that the same remark applies to Hutcheson's Economic work. With reference to wages there is nothing in Hutcheson and very little in the *Glasgow Lectures*, while both Capital and Rent are treated very slightly indeed —Smith has more detail, but Hutcheson comes nearer the enunciation of principles.

Mr Cannan conjectures that the dissertations on division of labour, money, prices, &c. existed "very nearly in their present form" before Smith went to France, and that he acquired the idea of a scheme of distribution from the Physiocrats[3]. Mr Higgs is loth to accept this statement, and he shows, on the other hand, that there is "no reason for supposing Smith was entirely ignorant of French economics in 1763" by the citation of many works of the Physiocrats published before this date[4]. Still the question is not so much whether Smith might have known

---

[1] *System*, I. p. 63; cf. authorities cited by Mr Cannan, Smith's *Glasgow Lectures*, pp. 185, 186, note.

[2] *Ibid.* I. p. 57. [3] *Glasgow Lectures*, p. xxxi.

[4] *The Economic Journal*, VI. p. 611.

French work in 1763 as whether, as a matter of fact, he was mainly, *then*, under English or French influence, and secondly how the differences between the *Lectures* and the *Wealth of Nations* are to be accounted for. The second problem is outside the range of the present work; but, with regard to the first, a preliminary difficulty should be cleared up. Writers on Economics are most acquainted with Natural Liberty or Naturalism in the work of the Physiocrats, but a cursory examination of Hutcheson's Philosophy will show that he too held this view, and, at the risk of repetition, it may again be added that he was Smith's teacher. Now the Naturalism of Hutcheson and the Physiocrats had a common origin in Shaftesbury. Not even in Laputa could it be maintained that the Physiocrats influenced Hutcheson, since he was dead before they began to write; on the other side, it is quite possible that Hutcheson may have exerted some influence upon the Physiocrats, since his works were popular in France and had been translated. Therefore on the whole the evidence is convincing that Smith learnt of Natural Liberty in the Glasgow class-room.

Next, to come to points of detail, the chief matters of interest dealt with in the *Glasgow Lectures* had appeared in Hutcheson's *System* and had been spoken of long before in the class. More remarkable still there is a certain similarity between the work of the two men. As has been shown, some of what Smith has to say upon division of labour, labour as the standard of value, value in use and in exchange, money and also some of the maxims of taxation, had been anticipated by Hutcheson. So far both agree, and finally we reach something of the nature of an *instantia crucis*, when it has been found, as has been shown above, that both Smith's *Lectures* and Hutcheson's work differ from the *Wealth of Nations* in giving only the slightest possible treatment of Distribution. Therefore the main influence in the *Glasgow Lectures* must be that of Hutcheson. This does not amount to a claim for originality upon behalf of Hutcheson, many of whose views (as in his Philosophy) were borrowed.

Few as Hutcheson's remarks upon Distribution are, they are not without historical interest. "Price," presumably including wages, is resolvable into, in addition, remuneration of the employer, Rent and Interest. "Wages of Superintendence" depend upon the "labours" of the employer, "the care, attention, accounts and correspondence about them[1], and in some cases take in also the condition of the person so employed, according to the custom of our country. The expence of his station in life must be defrayed by the price of such labours, and they deserve compensation as well as any other. This additional price of their labours is the just foundation of the ordinary profits of merchants[2]." It is also worth mentioning that Hutcheson subsequently makes provision for insurance against risk of loss of capital employed in trade.

The few sentences given to the explanation of rent are interesting as showing a divergence of Smith from Hutcheson. According to the former, landlords "love to reap where they have not sowed," but Hutcheson, himself a landowner, found nothing extraordinary in this. Having established private property, as in the general interest, and also the rights of bequests and inheritance, he states "that some goods bear natural fruits or increase, as lands, flocks, herds, gardens. The grant of these fruits naturally deserves a price or rent[3]."

A consideration of some importance emerges in Hutcheson's theory of Interest which is not followed by Smith. Böhm-Bawerk mentions Turgot as the first to express the "Fructification Theory[4]." Now twenty-one years before the publication of Turgot's *Réflexions* this theory was outlined in Hutcheson's *System*, and the idea was probably given in lectures some nineteen years earlier. After the passage quoted above on Rent, Hutcheson continues—"Tho' goods have no fruits or increase, yet, if they yield great convenience in life, and have cost such labour or expence as would have acquired goods naturally fruitful, if the proprietor grants the use of them—he may justly demand a price, such as he would have had, if he had employed his money or labour on goods naturally fruitful. This is the case in the setting of houses.

---

[1] Hutcheson's letters show he had personal experience of this kind of "labour."

[2] *System*, ii. p. 63.　　　　　　　　　[3] *Ibid.* ii. p. 71.

[4] *Kapital und Kapitalzins*, Eng. Tr. p. 61.

"If, in any way of trade, men can make far greater gains by help of a large stock of money, than they could without it, 'tis but just that he who supplies them with the money—the necessary means of this gain—should have for the use of it some share of the profit he could have made by purchasing things naturally fruitful. This shows the just foundation of interest upon money lent[1]." The repetition of the word "just" suggests rather the moral *doctrinaire* than the economist; but when Hutcheson subsequently comes to discuss the rate of interest, he bases his conclusions upon Demand and Supply, and in the course of his work there is much that is repeated both by Hume and Smith.

The next economic topic that Hutcheson reaches is the relation of the State to foreign trade. Mr Price has shown that Adam Smith's position with regard to Free Trade rests on his "conception of the functions of money, combined...with his belief in the advantages of the division of labour[2]." Now both of these were in germ in Hutcheson's work, and yet when he comes to deal with international trade, it cannot be said that he has in any way anticipated Smith's deduction from the premisses common to both. Though he is not a pronounced Mercantilist, he writes of increase in wealth as due to a surplus of exports over imports. All exports should be free of duties and taxes, as well as all imported necessaries. Young industries and import of raw material should be encouraged by bounties[3].

Hutcheson's remarks upon Taxation are brief, but, more than much of his work, condensed; and one can scarcely avoid the conclusion that they suggested Adam Smith's maxims of Taxation. It is true there is no trace of the second (the certainty of the tax). "Conveniency" is contained in embryo, and may have been expanded from the expression that taxes are "most convenient which are laid on matters of luxury and splendour[4]." The fourth and first are explicitly mentioned—

---

[1] *System*, II. p. 71.

[2] *Short History of Political Economy in England*, p. 29.

[3] *System*, II. pp. 318, 319, Hutcheson also proposes that unmarried persons should pay higher taxes, and that "sloth should be punished by temporary servitude at least!"

[4] *Ibid.* II. p. 341. Cf. *Wealth of Nations*, Book v. Chap. 2, § 3.

the fourth under the head of the advantage of taxes "which can be easily raised without many expensive offices for collecting them"—and the first is specially emphasized. "But above all a just proportion to the wealth of the people should be observed in whatever is raised from them." The means by which the necessary information might be obtained are discussed. This is spoken of as a "census or estimation of all the wealth of private families at frequently recurring periods"; by such a census, "all would be burdened proportionately to their wealth[1]."

Finally, inasmuch as the plan of the present work involves the isolation of Hutcheson's works of a period later than the *System* in the following chapter, certain revisions of his economic theory, contained in the *Compend of Morals*, should logically find their place there; but since these changes are trifling it may not be out of place to conclude the present account of his economics with some mention of them—especially as a return to this subject later would involve a want of continuity of treatment. Besides the addition of "fine prospects" to individual wealth (rather than to national) the following changes may be noticed. Hutcheson appears to have anticipated Prof. Smart in making goods convertible with "*services*[2]." In restating his views on Rent, he touches the border-line of a "tenants-gain."—"As in lands all the profits of a plentiful year fall to the tenant, so he must bear the casual losses of a less fortunate one. Indeed the rarer cases of extraordinary losses, such as wars[3], inundations, pestilence, seem to be just exceptions; as the tenant cannot be presumed to have subjected himself to rents in such cases. And in most of contracts the agreements of parties alter the obligations[4]." Also he adds a stipulation to his treatment of currency, that bank-notes should be convertible—"when notes or tickets pass for money, their value depends on this, that they give good security for the payment of certain sums in gold or silver[5]."

[1] *System*, II. p. 341.

[2] *Int. to Mor. Phil.* Glas. 1753, p. 199. Cf. *Distribution of Income, passim.*

[3] *I.e.* civil wars, of which, it will be remembered, Hutcheson had personal experience.

[4] *Ibid.* p. 208.   [5] *Ibid.* II. p. 203.

CHAPTER XII.

HUTCHESON'S PHILOSOPHY—FOURTH FORM, IN THE *COMPENDS*
—THE INFLUENCE OF THE STOICS, THROUGH MARCUS
AURELIUS.

IT would seem reasonable to expect that the *Philosophiae Moralis Institutio Compendiaria* published in 1742, and afterwards translated into English as *A Short Introduction to Moral Philosophy*, would be simply a summary of the argument of the *System of Moral Philosophy*. This however is not so, as a careful comparison of the smaller with the larger work proves that, in the interval between the composition of the latter and the publication of the former, Hutcheson had again fallen under a fresh influence, which leads to a further exposition and modification of his theory. In fact these three Compends—of Morals and Metaphysics (both published in 1742) and of Logic (1756)—have been too much neglected, in expositions of Hutcheson's work; this may be, in part, due to the natural expectation that they are merely summaries of views elsewhere expressed more fully, and, in part, to their unpretentious appearance as compared with the "large paper" form, in which the *System* was published. Together they constitute three small pocket volumes, and the *Logicae Compendium* is a very thin one, and it is difficult to realize that together they contain almost as much matter as the *System*. Nor can it be maintained that the *Compend of Morals* is only a popular exposition, designed for students and the general reader; since, though dedicated "to Students in the universities," it contains more references to authorities than any other of Hutcheson's works—indeed he states that he had intended "to make references" to the more eminent writers, ancient and modern, who treated of the subject[1].

It may be thought that there is a want of historical completeness in assigning chronological priority to the *System*, upon the ground of the date of its *composition*, as compared with that of the *publication* of the "Compends"; for it could be contended that the latter works might possibly have been in MS. for a considerable time, and therefore they might be even earlier than the publications treated of in what has been called Hutcheson's "third period." But there is some external and much internal evidence against this view. With regard to the former, in the letters to Drennan, it appears that the "Compends" of Morals and Metaphysics were printed from "some loose, hastily wrote papers[2]," and that, in Oct. 1743, Hutcheson taught the third part—*De Deo*—of the *Synopsis Metaphysicae* to his class. Now in 1741 it appears he had been using the MS. of the *System* for this purpose[3], so that, though the evidence is not conclusive it seems that the two "Compends," published in 1742, were printed very soon after they had been written. This conjecture is confirmed by several internal characteristics. First, one might apply a test to Hutcheson's work, founded on the canon of Shakesperian criticism, connected with the lateness of "weak endings"; namely an increase in the number of Senses, which multiplied approximately at the rate of one for every two years. Between the *Inquiry* and the *Essay on the Passions* there is an interval of nearly four years; and, in the latter, two new Senses are added. Between the *Essay on the Passions* and the *System* there is an interval of about nine years, and there are several new Senses added; if "novelty" and "grandeur" be taken as distinct, not as aspects or subdivisions of the general Æsthetic Sense, Novelty is a distinct addition, and Grandeur might perhaps be added; "Reflection" or "Consciousness" is sometimes spoken of as a Sense, Decorum is new and also Sympathy, unless it be treated

---

[1] *Short Introduction to Moral Philosophy*, Preface.
[2] *Vide* letter quoted above, p. 115.
[3] *Vide* p. 114.

as an equivalent of the Public Sense of the *Passions*, so that though the exact number of the additions in the *System* may be uncertain, it might be averaged at from three to five, and this is proportionate to the interval of time. Now both the "Compends" agree in retaining all the Internal Senses of the *System* and besides add two new ones, the Senses of the Ridiculous and of Veracity[1]. This again corresponds with the normal rate of increase, namely two new Senses to an interval of four or five years. Needless to say, this mathematical rate of progression should not be insisted upon—it is a mere coincidence that there is a rough ratio in the growth of Hutcheson's new discoveries or analyses; but, at the same time, it is an undoubted fact that each later work shows a tendency to add to the number, and that, therefore, the presence of new senses in the "Compends" is strong evidence that they were written later than the *System*.

Secondly, it is worth mentioning that each period of Hutcheson's work contains the germ of the dominant idea of that which follows it—for instance, the *Essay on the Passions* introduces incidentally the ideas of Dignity and Perfection, which become essential in the *System*. Now the *System* similarly introduces incidentally the idea of Conscience as an alternative for the Moral Faculty, and, in the "Compends," Conscience is the regular synonym—this in all probability is due to the *Essay on Virtue*, published with Butler's *Analogy* in 1737; and, therefore, too late to affect the *System* in its structure.

In the third place, a cursory inspection of the "Compends" —and especially that of Morals—shows that there is a large increase in Stoic terminology and modes of thought, and this is explicable by the influence of Marcus Aurelius, whose works were translated by Hutcheson and Moor during the summer of 1741[2]. This characteristic, which is quite unmistakeable, con- clusively shows that the translation of Marcus Aurelius and the "Compends" belong to the same date—probably from 1740 to the beginning of 1742.

---

[1] Veracity, it need scarcely be remarked, is obviously borrowed from Butler.
[2] Letter quoted above, p. 81.

Though Hutcheson had known Aurelius before undertaking the translation—indeed he frequently owns his indebtedness in the *Inquiry* and the *Essay on the Passions*[1]—a closer acquaintance drew him nearer to the Stoic point of view. As with many other thinkers of his time, Cicero was, for him, the only historian of ancient Philosophy: and hence one finds him prone to refer rather to minor writers—such as little-known Peripatetics or Platonists—than to seek inspiration from the masters of Greek Thought. It is a curious coincidence that the same remark applies to Shaftesbury's relation to Art— he mentions Carlo Maratti as one of the painters whom he would have wished to treat the "Judgment of Hercules[2]." It is strange, too, that Hutcheson does not take his Stoicism from the fountain head, but rather adopts it directly from Marcus Aurelius, and hence one finds no reference to the theory as held by Zeno, Cleanthes and Chrysippus. Though Aurelius was the "last of the Stoics," he held the theory in a modified form; and this, added to Hutcheson's early acquaintance with it through Cicero, made its incorporation in the "Compends" possible. To the general Stoic position may be attributed the importance now assigned to the "life according to Nature" and, as against the Clarke school, "conformity to Nature" (not to Reason) the ideal of the "good man"; many references to Perfection (in the Stoic sense), the prominence of "impulse"; the position of Conscience as τὸ ἡγεμονικόν and the introduction of "right Reason"—the ὀρθὶς̄ λόγος of the Stoics, not the φρόνησις of Aristotle, as in the *System*. To Marcus Aurelius are due the special modifications that bring Stoicism near to Hutcheson's conception of the Macrocosm—the idea of all rational beings as a πολιτικὸν σύστημα; the necessity of the social affections to the good of the whole, and the claims of disinterested love of one's fellow men—ἀπὸ καρδίας φιλεῖν τοὺς ἀνθρώπους, as Marcus Aurelius expresses it[3].

Side by side with this Stoic tendency, there is another related to it. The third period is practically Utilitarian—or

---

[1] Chapters XIII. and XIV.

[2] Fowler's *Shaftesbury and Hutcheson* (*English Philosophers Series*), p. 131.

[3] Mar. Aur. VIII. 13; Zeller, *Hist. of Stoicism*, &c. (Eng. trans.), p. 314.

one of Universalistic Hedonism, in so far as the Moral Sense is
a supernumerary, apart from the *Conscientia antecedens.* Any
intuitive character it retains is but a survival from the earlier
and more hedonistic stage. With the *System*, this tendency
has reached the maximum, and in the "Compends" Hutcheson
comes nearer Butler's *Essay on Virtue* in making Conscience
approve of "kind affections and purposes[1]"—the latter expression being probably designed to include Calm Benevolence—of
which pair of objects "*kind affections*," in opposition to the
System, take precedence, the reason being, as will be seen, that
Hutcheson now takes refuge behind their naturalness. Further
he makes a fresh attempt to bring the æsthetic Sense into line
with the rest, and so, again, there is now as much to be said
about the "Beauty of Virtue," as in the earlier works.

The mode of treatment in the "Compends of Morals and
Metaphysics" closely follows that of the *System*, the main
difference being that certain distinctions and improvements
introduced late in the *System* appear earlier in the *Compend of
Morals* : while the *Synopsis Metaphysicae* repeats, in the second
and third books, the substance of Books I. and II. of the *Compend
of Morals*, the first book of the former—"De Ente et communibus
Rerum Attributis"—containing an exposition of Scholastic
principles, in the course of which Hutcheson, following Cicero,
maintains a discreet silence upon Ontological problems.

Like the *System*, the *Compend of Morals* begins with a
definition of Happiness, which strikes the key-note of the
distinction between this and the former period. The object of
Philosophy is to make man happy by leading him to "that
course of life which is most according to the intention of
Nature[2]." Just as in the *System*, the "chief good" is explained
by an expansion of Aristotle's formula, so, now in the *fourth
period*, it is expounded by an expansion of a later Stoic dictum,
namely, "that we should love and reverence the Deity with
all our soul, and have a stedfast good-will toward mankind,
and carefully improve all our powers of body and mind, by

---

[1] *Short Introduction to Moral Philosophy*, Glasgow, 1753, pp. 16, 29, 118,
128. *Synopsis Metaphysicae*, p. 120.

[2] *Introduction to Moral Philosophy, ut supra*, p. 1.

which we can promote the common interest of all—which is the *life according to Nature*[1]." Nature, the natural, the state of Nature, the Law of Nature, are now the different expressions of the ultimate end of this phase of thought—not only the end, indeed, but also the beginning, both τέλος and ἀρχή, in the different senses in which these terms may be used, and, like one of the Pre-Socratic Philosophers, Hutcheson's monotone now is "from Nature came all things and (ethically) to Nature should all return."

Hitherto "the natural" had been used as borrowed from Shaftesbury, in the loose or popular sense of Cicero. Now following Marcus Aurelius, it acquires a more precise signification, though still far from reaching the full meaning of the celebrated formula. Possibly Hutcheson's stand-point may be most readily reached by an exclusion of several Stoic interpretations. With him "life according to Nature" is not altogether that of objective reason. Readers who are accustomed to Hutcheson as one of the chief Hedonists, will be surprised at the qualification; but, as will be seen in this period, there are too many references to "right Reason" to enable one to assert that this faculty is to be wholly excluded. Conversely, pleasure is not to be wholly condemned, as by the Stoics. The aspect of self-consistency—Seneca's "unum hominem agere"—is not important, neither is the relation to Nature as a whole, apart from Nature as social. Thus Hutcheson does not insist on internal consistency of the individual nature nor on the consistency of the individual with universal Nature, except as social, and he has little preference for one epistemological connecting link rather than another.

Having excluded so much, it would appear that the formula is in danger of being left wholly without content. Still Hutcheson is thoroughly in earnest in bringing all the threads of his mode of thought under this single expression. Nature, to him, is no mere elusive will-o'-the-wisp, to be hunted but never caught. On the contrary, it is the simplest term for conveying the idea of the social constitution of the Macrocosm, reduced to its ultimate elements in relation to the Microcosm

[1] *Introduction to Moral Philosophy*, p. 56.

as its part. Thus "Nature" is the Macrocosm reduced to its "lowest terms," and anything is "natural" that directly or immediately brings the Microcosm into connection with the whole. Further, the Macrocosm being in its highest or best state, presided over by God, the *vox naturae* is the *vox Dei.* This attitude of mind leads to the important result that the function of the Microcosm is the translation of cosmic relations into its own language, conversely, ethically, in rendering what is individual into the universal; this being its cosmical value. In relation to cognition, Hutcheson nearly approaches Malebranche in holding that the source of ideas "cannot be certainly referred to any cause other than Divine power[1]," and further that "sensations are either *signals,* as it were, of new events happening to the body, of which experience and observation will show us the cause; or *marks,* settled by the Author of Nature, to show us what things are salutary, innocent or hurtful; or intimations of things not otherways discernible, which may affect our state; tho' these marks or signals bear no more resemblance to the external reality than the report of a gun or the flash of the powder bears to a ship in distress[2]." After Cicero, more than the Stoics perhaps, Hutcheson appeals to the universality of certain powers of perception, as a proof of their being inderivative or "natural"; and this argument is strengthened by frequent appeals to what "goes on in one's own breast" or "to the heart"—here it would appear that, while there is some trace of the φαντασία καταληπτική, the force of this idea, as a criterion, has been weakened owing to its filtration through the works of Marcus Aurelius; probably, too, there is a confusion with the inevitableness of the æsthetic consciousness. The latter again, being interpreted teleologically, as elsewhere, with Hutcheson—a feature to which Hume drew attention, when he wrote that your [*i.e.* Hutcheson's] definition of natural "is founded on final causes[3]"—the only criterion is a criticism of ends, which are now divided into three, namely those arising from affections tending to the "good" of the individual, all which are primarily natural and

---

[1] *Synopsis Metaphysicae,* p. 107. Cf. *System,* I. p. 14.
[2] *System,* I. p. 5.   [3] *Supra,* p. 117.

only become "unnatural," that is inconsistent with the cosmic
end, when they are too strong; secondly, affections whose end
is the advancement of the Macrocosm, and thirdly those which
result in duties towards God—neither of the latter classes can
be ever other than natural. Here then Hutcheson drifts into
Butler's specification of the natural as a distinction both of
kind and strength between the various affections and principles,
indeed in one place he draws out a table showing six grades of
the extent and power of different altruistic affections[1].

But, with Hutcheson, Nature does not mean only mental
data reduced to their lowest terms, but also expanded to the
highest. Every "natural" power acting upon another produces
a "natural" result, if only it be non-subjective or non-individual-
istic; here he would exclude accidental associations and false
systems of education. Needless to say such exclusion leaves it
an open question, what is "nature's" training, or can there be
such a thing as "natural" association? Both questions were answered in terms subversive of Hutcheson's principles, the first
by Rousseau and the second by Hume.

"Nature" then means as $\dot{a}\rho\chi\dot{\eta}$, the original, as $\tau\dot{\epsilon}\lambda o\varsigma$ the
ideal; in fact, with Hutcheson, the "ideal" absorbs "the
original" as the basis upon which it is constructed. For, in
the "Compends" there is no hint of a "Golden Age," in the
remote past; rather, as an Optimist, Hutcheson held that the
social organism is continually developing. The "original," as
with Butler[2], is given by Nature in the form "of some little
sparks, as it were, to kindle up the several virtues or a sowing
of some little seeds of them[3]." Thus, the inlet from the Macrocosm is minimised, and the outlet, through the faculties, is
magnified. Reason "proposes to us a whole plan of life[4]," "it
is a 'divine[5]' faculty, and it frames the ideal of a truly good
man[6]." Hence there is a reaction from the Utilitarianism of the
System. Virtue becomes "the natural" in conduct, and this

---

[1] *Short Introduction to Moral Philosophy, ut supra,* pp. 74, 75.
[2] "It is sufficient that the seeds of good-will be implanted in our Nature
by God," *Sermons,* p. 6.
[3] *Short Introduction to Moral Philosophy,* p. 33.
[4] *Ibid.* p. 6.   [5] *Ibid.* p. 84.   [6] *Ibid.* p. 33.

again depends upon a right or altruistic disposition of the will and affections.

As the Macrocosm is under the government of the Divine and Benevolent Architect, so the Microcosm is controlled by τὸ ἡγεμονικόν, the office of which is to *recognize* " conformity to Nature " in one of its aspects ; and, in another, to *stimulate* the powers of the individual towards this supreme end. Hutcheson himself uses the term τὸ ἡγεμονικόν in the *Philosophiae Moralis Institutio Compendiaria*, when he writes that the mind would be a strange chaos "nisi altius repetendo, nexum quendam, et ordinem a natura constitutum, et principatum deprehenderit, aut ἡγεμονικόν aliquod, ad modum caeteris ponendum idoneum." This is slightly weakened in the translation, which runs, "human nature must appear a strange chaos, until we can discover, by a closer attention, some natural connection or order, some governing principles naturally fitted to govern the rest[1]." The same idea is frequently reiterated, as the divinity, the authority, the government or judgment-seat of Conscience[2]. Hume, in reference to such expressions says, " You seem to embrace Dr Butler's opinion in his *Sermons on Human Nature* that our Moral Sense has an authority, distinct from its force and durableness—and that because we think it always ought to prevail. But this is nothing but an instinct or principle, which approves of itself upon reflection, and that is common to all of them[3]." But there is more in the thoroughgoing maintenance of the supremacy of τὸ ἡγεμονικόν, than a borrowing from Butler, since there are many important allusions to "right Reason," as the supreme principle, this being, in fact, an introduction of the Stoic ὀρθὸς λόγος. In the *System* "right Reason" meant the tact of the φρόνιμος, now it is an objective faculty, which is the source of Law. Therefore, again, such law is the Law of Nature ; and, as the affections are ' Nature's " voice, as the echo of that of God, speaking in a language half understood, so right reason interprets the will of God as a series

[1] *Introduction to Moral Philosophy*, p. 34.

[2] " Quasi de tribunali, judicium in omnia quae agunt homines exercet," *Synopsis Metaphysicae*, p. 120.

[3] Burton's *Hume, ut supra*, I. p. 149.

of distinct commands with appropriate sanctions[1]. Hutcheson oscillates between these two descriptions of his ἡγεμονικόν, as Conscience, when the Beauty, Comeliness or Loveliness of right dispositions is to be insisted upon; on the other hand, having need of the categorical rigour of "that confused word—ought" he has recourse to "right reason" as the fount of law. The importance of the transition was probably disguised, under the ambiguity of the word "ordering" which frequently occurs (for though the "Compends" were published in Latin, Hutcheson must have thought in English) "Right Reason," as categorical, is an "ordering" faculty, while Conscience, too, in so far as it comes into contact with the æsthetic Sense—"Beauty" being now, as always, Teleological—is also an ordering power, or at least one which takes note of the ordered. In fact this confusion of thought is a direct result of Æsthetic dialectic, namely the subjection of art to law; or, on the other hand, the apparent recognition of excellence intuitively.

A further difficulty complicates the determination of what is Hutcheson's ἡγεμονικόν, since all mental faculties are reduced to two—the Intellectual and Volitional[2]. Now, right reason is plainly intellectual, but what is the nature of Conscience? It is described as "destined and fitted to regulate the whole of life[3]," "since it is the *judge* of the whole of life, of all the various affections and designs, and naturally assumes a *jurisdiction* over them pronouncing that most important sentence" &c.[4]; now "ordering and commanding" are expressly stated to be "acts of Will[5]"; and consequently the Categorical function of Conscience is to be attributed to the Will. There does not appear to be any effort, in Hutcheson's later work, to obtain a synthesis that will give the moral unity of man's power towards the ends of the Macrocosm; indeed the insistence upon the share of the will in ethical decisions reintroduces an old difficulty; for, though Conscience has been given for an object "the affections of the heart and not the external effects of

---

[1] *Introduction to Moral Philosophy*, pp. 102—105.
[2] *Synopsis Metaphysicae*, p. 106.
[3] *Introduction to Moral Philosophy*, p. 35.
[4] *Ibid.* p. 22.   [5] *Ibid.* p. 38.

them," the more extensive principle of calm Benevolence
appears as the ideal—that is (highest) natural—condition of
the Will, and further a "happy course of life" requires "steady
virtue" as an habitual state, and this could not be acquired by
concentrating attention solely upon the affections irrespective
of their effects. Thus Hutcheson's last words leave it doubtful
what exactly the Moral Faculty or ἡγεμονικόν is, and also what
is its object. Both ambiguities are disguised by a return to the
æsthetic appreciation of the "Beauty" of Moral conduct; no
mental pronouncement is more absolute, *in its expression*, than
a judgment of taste; it considers the picture of life, without
undue attention to detail; it claims "inevitableness," or, in
Hutcheson's language, necessity and naturalness; it voices its
decision, as an intuition—"the taste of a finer sense"; it is, or
is intended to be, at once the harmony of a perfect government
of every faculty by a perfect governor. When there is added
to these characteristics, the same power, in its more strictly
teleological aspect, bringing the Microcosm into harmonious
relation with the Macrocosm, it changes from being the "arbiter
elegantium" to that "Divine voice" that aims at becoming
at once the *vox rationis*, the *vox naturae*, and the *vox Dei*.

The growing importance of the Will leaves one most
important problem unsolved, though contributing something
to its solution—namely Hutcheson's attitude to the Free-Will
controversy. In his early work the general drift of his opinions
is towards Determinism, as Dr Martineau proves, by quota-
tions from the *Illustrations of the Moral Sense*[1]. In the *Inquiry*,
there can be no logical escape from Determinism; but in the
second period there are the germs of a higher view—for,
while Demonstrative evidence forthwith results in action, the
"mind" has the power of withholding its assent from mere
probabilities; and therefore there is a "liberty of suspense."
In the third period, the introduction of the conception of the
Microcosm as composed of *faculties*, not bare passive powers,
the added power of intelligence, as such, in framing an ideal of
excellence, and further the description of the "Soul" as "disparate" from "Matter," as active and Spirit, all clear the way

[1] *Types of Ethical Theory*, ii. pp. 563—565.

for a libertarian position. Hutcheson's constitutional distrust of Metaphysics leads to the shelving of the problem until it faces him uncompromisingly in the *Synopsis Metaphysicae*, and, though he pronounces in favour of Liberty, it is difficult either to collect his reasons or the form in which he accepts it[1]. In fact he was painfully embarrassed by his indebtedness to Locke, for, in the "Compends," he often speaks as empirically as Condillac. Reflection is expressedly reduced to a subsequent Sensation—that is subsequent upon the direct Sensation of the external Senses[2]. If this be so, obviously the mind, as a receptacle for impressions, is no more free than a sponge absorbing water—a *tabula rasa* has no initiative. This, however, is only one side of the theory, in its later form, which in fact nominally starts from the Lockian view, and yet reaches a conception of mind as "res cogitans et actuosa[3]." As such, it is capable of commanding or ruling or "ordering" the direct Sensations and arranging them according to the ends ordained by the law of "right Reason," that is according to ends that are its own creation, not the data of "direct Sensation." Here Hutcheson's eclecticism bursts the bonds of empiricism, but at the expense of consistency. If he is really to start from "direct Sensations," there can be no conclusion but the "mental anatomy" of Hume, and Moral Philosophy, as a fine art, is a logical extravagance[4]. Further, Sensation knows nothing of cosmical or teleological predicates, for it is necessarily non-cognitive; and the flow of feeling is not even a tissue of ideas of feeling, much less can it give the "concomitant ideas" of Sensation or Primary Qualities. On the other hand, if a start be made from the *res actuosa* there can never be a return to the *tabula rasa*. Hutcheson's mode of expression is adapted to the latter stand-point, but the underlying tendency presupposes the former. There is no attempt at reconciliation, in fact each is used, according as it is most suitable for the momentary purpose—Lockian introspection—when the "natural" is understood as the universal or

---

[1] *Synopsis Metaphysicae*, pp. 74—79, 143—149.
[2] *Ibid.* p. 107. *Short Introduction to Moral Philosophy*, p. 6.
[3] *Synopsis Metaphysicae*, p. 176.
[4] *Vide supra*, correspondence with Hume quoted pp. 116—9.

uniform, and the plain man is to be invited to see the working
of the mind, "in his breast"; the other attitude, again, when
introspection has not found what it was sent to seek, and it is
necessary to obtain some light upon the metaphysical presuppositions of Ethics.   These two stand-points Hutcheson constantly interchanges; just as, in the Second period, he passed
from the moral decision, as hedonistic, to the idea of it, as a
rational estimation of values in Calm Benevolence; so now the
former ethical *volte face* is absorbed in a theoretical one.   It is
this eclecticism that makes the result obviously inconsistent,
but at the same time interesting and valuable—interesting
because Hutcheson has more surprises for the attentive reader
than the sensational novelist, one literally "never knows what
to expect next": valuable, because he is able to construct a
working scheme of ethics, that "would touch the heart," in
despite of metaphysical deficiencies; and finally most suggestive,
possibly because this is a characteristic of most eclectic modes
of thought, when the juxtaposition of different views necessarily
produces new ideas in the reader, or else because the work is so
tactfully didactic, since no one can fail to see that Hutcheson's
object is to frame an ideal, not so much as a rational unity
but as an object of endeavour—his last word is *not* "Know the
Right" but "Do it."

CHAPTER XIII.

HUTCHESON'S GENERAL INFLUENCE UPON THE "ENLIGHTENMENT" IN SCOTLAND.

THE access to fresh sources of information, concerning Hutcheson's personality and mode of thought, renders a re-valuation of his historical position and influence necessary. All thinkers of importance, who succeeded him in Scotland, left materials for exhaustive biographies behind them, and they themselves were at no small pains to characterise their relation to the problems of the age. Hutcheson's personality has been shrouded in mystery; and, in default of fact, a certain amount of fiction or myth has grown up round his contribution to the intellectual progress of his adopted country.

From the foregoing narrative of his life—wanting, though it be, in the detail that renders a biography of interest—there is no difficulty in gathering the impression, from its broad outlines, of what he conceived his message to his generation to be and the effects which resulted from it. He himself says, "I am called 'New Light' here," and this expression embodies the whole secret of his attitude to the questions of his time. He was pre-eminently the messenger of culture and opponent of Philistinism, whether in the Church, the University, or social life. In a word he was a Philosopher of the Enlightenment in Scotland. While the expression—*Aufklärung*—is a commonplace in accounts of German and French Philosophy of the last century, it has seldom, if ever, been used in reference to this country; yet the remarkable output of metaphysical and ethical works, already noticed[1], would lead one to expect

[1] Chapter VI.

some exponent of a popular philosophy which aided in preparing the way for Hume and subsequent thinkers from 1740 onwards. Indeed, since Hutcheson bore the brunt of criticisms upon the British Enlightenment, and was generally acknowledged as a leader, if not the leader of it, in his lifetime, it would be scarcely just that he should be denied the honour, such as it is, after his death.

Already many of the salient features of his popular mode of thought have been sketched; and these suggest some comparisons of interest between the Enlightenment in Scotland and that in Germany and, later, in France. In all cases there was a popularisation of knowledge, but more especially in France, owing to the tendency of the ecclesiastics to monopolise culture. Despite the general high level of learning both in Germany and Scotland, it is a remarkable fact, that it was left to Hutcheson to revive the study of Greek Literature at Glasgow, and this achievement is chronicled by his biographer, as one of his most important legacies to posterity[1]. It will have been noticed, too, that in Scotland, as in Germany, the new Philosophy was eclectic, therein differing from that of the French Enlightenment. In all three countries there is the same quest for "the natural," but though the tendencies may be generalised under this single expression, the diverse interpretations part into contraries; for, in France, in the latter half of the century, there was a tendency to accept the "natural" as man's powers expressed "in their lowest terms," while Hutcheson aimed, at least, at expanding them to the highest. Hutcheson's Philosophy of the Enlightenment, too, is thoroughly differentiated from that of Germany, by his insistency upon Benevolence as opposed to the Egoistic Idealism of the thought before Kant. Further, the cardinal position he gives to Beauty, though, as it has been shown, in a merely mathematical sense, is worthy of note. In fact, if one may risk a broad generalisation, the tendency of the French Enlightenment was egoistic and hedonistic in ethics, realistic in metaphysics, and anarchic in its theory of the State: that of Germany was also egoistic in ethics and sentimental perhaps

[1] Leechman, *ut supra*.

rather than sensuous : that in Scotland, as represented by Hutcheson, his pupils and followers, was altruistic and æsthetic in ethics,—what it was in metaphysics, in view of current contradictory estimates, must be postponed for future consideration.

The Enlightenment in Scotland, as expounded by Hutcheson, has certain features of interest, when one remembers that he was a follower of Shaftesbury and the Hellenism of the latter with his protest against the unloveliness of Puritanism. Omitting for the moment Hutcheson's applications of these in minor matters, the question remains, what was his position to these foci of Shaftesbury's system? Did he return to Scotland, the home of the Puritan spirit, as a deserter or as a repentant prodigal? Possibly the answer that would be truest was that he was partly one, partly the other; though he certainly conceived himself as in opposition to the "zealots" —a soldier in the liberation war of humanity—as Heine expresses it. Yet there was such a persistence in the Puritan spirit, that it leavens the descendants of all those who have participated in it (as Hutcheson's ancestors had), and this inheritance runs through and determines his whole outlook. It is to be remembered also that he was a "child of the manse," in fact, doubly so, since both his grandfather and father were Presbyterian ministers, and there is no doubt that his early training left indelible traces upon his mind. Consequently, however thorough he imagined his revolt to be, it was still Puritanism modified from within, not revolutionised from without, and this fact probably explains the leverage that gave him much of his influence in Scotland. At no point is Hutcheson's difference, when compared with Shaftesbury, more marked than here. The Hellenism of the latter was, at least, an endeavour to reproduce the broad outlines of the Greek Ideal of life ; while Hutcheson, on the contrary, evidently found it wanting in moral earnestness, and hence he draws his inspiration from Cicero and the Stoic moralists of the Roman Empire.

Thus we find that, while Hutcheson protests against Classical literature being placed upon a Puritan "index" of prohibited books, this same Puritanism determines his choice of

authors in a manner exclusive of the main end which dictated
Shaftesbury's Hellenic revival. This characteristic has several
important consequences. In the first place it inevitably adds
to the already large amount of Eclecticism Hutcheson had
learnt from Shaftesbury. Starting from Cicero, as he explicitly
states in his first work, he has a natural tendency to avoid all
metaphysical problems, and there are few writers who more
persistently evade supplying answers, or, when one is imperative, give the perplexed reader a larger number to choose
from. Further, Shaftesbury aimed at a renaissance rather of
the Greek Ideal than of Greek Philosophy as such; while
Hutcheson's Classicism being derived from Philosophical
writers inevitably tends to revive many of their opinions.
When it is added that his favourite authorities were Cicero,
Seneca, Epictetus and Marcus Aurelius, it is easy to see that
his debt to "the Antients" resembles a mosaic, in being
composed of separate borrowings from many sources. Further,
Hutcheson, like Shaftesbury, differed from the Cambridge
Platonists, in endeavouring to come to terms with contemporary thought; and here, again, his procedure was eclectic.
He borrows alike from Descartes, Locke, Wolff and Berkeley,
so that the final result is an eclectic treatment of modern
Philosophy, superimposed upon Ancient Eclecticism. Such
a type of thought could not be expected to be consistent, but
it was eminently popular and educational, and therefore served
its purpose as a philosophic enlightenment.

In the second place, Hutcheson's modification of Shaftesbury's Hellenism is of importance in stamping his preference
for one of the two answers to national needs already indicated[1];
with him, when his Stoic training is remembered, Benevolence
takes precedence of Beauty, and, thus an explanation is found
for his concentration of attention upon the former, and for
the practical ignoring of the essential features of the latter.
This is all the more curious, since, through the accident of
his having written a separate treatise on Beauty, Hutcheson
is often named as the founder of modern æsthetics, though
either Shaftesbury or Arbuckle might be mentioned, as having

[1] Chapter viii, pp. 148—155.

more adequately treated the subject, the former earlier and the latter at the same time as Hutcheson[1].

In the third place, such Classicism was obviously imperfect, and it failed in that there was a tendency to introduce Greek literature through Latin reproductions, and this, though in a smaller degree, was precisely the same rock upon which Scholasticism had struck. The number of editions and translations of the later Stoics, mentioned above, during the first half of last century was remarkable, and though Hutcheson was prominent in popularising their opinions, he was little more than the spokesman of a broad tendency both here and in Germany.

It is interesting to note how one of the many movements originating from Hutcheson swings round to precisely the opposite point from which he started. As already mentioned his Classicism begins with Cicero, who became for that generation—and indeed long remained—the entrance way to Greek Philosophy. This tendency continued, but quite apart from the general line of historical development, and it may be taken to culminate in the eccentric Lord Monboddo, who was in the habit of replying to the questions of his correspondents by sending them long extracts from Plato or Aristotle, sometimes amounting to four or five pages of ordinary type; and, on one occasion, he expressly declares that Latin writers on Philosophy are "contemptible," and he would even advise every student to read Roman History only in the works of Greek writers.

One of the difficulties in dealing with an eclectic writer, such as Hutcheson, is that one is forced to proceed by digressions, and granting that he was the prototype of the Scottish Enlightenment, it is necessary to investigate the claim adduced on more than one occasion that he was the father or founder of the " Scottish School" or of "Scottish Philosophy." If it were only possible to ascertain what these expressions were intended to convey, the whole matter could be disposed of in a few lines. Unfortunately there is no unanimity or fixed definition, and therefore it is somewhat wearisome to disen-

[1] *James Arbuckle* in *Mind*, N. S. vol. VIII. No. 30 (April, 1899).

tangle the exact signification each writer intends to give his reader. Obviously "Scottish Philosophy" may mean two very different things, either (a) Philosophy produced in Scotland or by Scotsmen, or (b) the special type of thought expounded by Reid, which is also known as the Common Sense School, or Natural Realism. It might scarcely be credited that the former interpretation would be used, since it introduces an utterly false principle of classification, that of mere "provincialism"; and to say that Hutcheson was the founder of Scottish Philosophy in this sense, is to pay a very poor compliment to the state of learning in the country prior to 1730; besides ignoring the claims of very many thinkers, whose work, if not profoundly original, was at least of sufficient importance to deserve some mention in any chronicle of the country's speculative achievements. Yet this is exactly the line of argument that the late Dr McCosh appears to adopt. To secure inclusion in his volume on *The Scottish Philosophy*, apparently, a writer should have prefaced his work with a condensed family-tree to show that he was "connected with Scotland[1]." Such a phrase suggests sufficiently wide possibilities and yet it is not wide enough to include all homogeneous thinkers, else how comes it that Cousin (who, according to McCosh has written "a most faultless historical disquisition upon Scottish Philosophy") is excluded? One step more is needed, namely to follow the example of certain unfortunate societies for persons belonging to some county or clan, and to offer membership not only to those with Scottish connections, but also with Scottish sympathies. Not only is there an error in the inclusion, but also in the exclusion, else how comes *Kant* to be omitted and *Shaftesbury* to be included?

Upon closer enquiry, however, it will be found that McCosh has a somewhat lengthy test to propose before he admits persons as members of the Scottish "school" or "fraternity." They must "proceed inductively," "employing self-consciousness as the instrument of observation," and thereby "reach principles prior to and independent of experience[2]." If only this test had been fairly applied, the size of the volume would

---

[1] p. 7.   [2] *Scottish Philosophy*, pp. 2—6.

have been reduced by one-half. How can the last clause be
stretched to admit Hume, or the Associationalists such as
Brown and James Mill, and why if the latter be admitted is
his son excluded ?

It would be an exceedingly difficult thesis to maintain
that Hutcheson conformed to all these conditions, but suppose
his claim were admitted, obviously Shaftesbury has a better
title to be the " founder," and again, every passage that was
admitted as satisfying the test could be traced back to Cicero
and other Eclectics, and here we should find the true origin
of the tendency. In fact the supposition that Hutcheson had
any new Philosophy or any new Philosophical method does
violence to the whole texture of historical continuity. Could
there be anything more farcical than to represent one of the
most eclectically minded of men as founding a new school,
a title which he himself invariably disclaimed in his own day
while he even quoted the sources whence he had borrowed his
leading ideas ? Therefore if the term " Scottish Philosophy "
be taken in the widest possible sense, Hutcheson was not the
founder, but merely the *importer* of it, and we are left with
the paradox that " Scottish philosophy " is very far from being
a product of Scotland : in fact it traces its origin back to the
Moralists of the Roman Empire, and thence to the Stoics, and
from them to Socrates.

In contradistinction to this extended signification of the
term, it is also found to imply adherence to the group of
thinkers, called by Hamilton " Natural Realists," a signification
which excludes every great Scotsman in Philosophy, except
Reid. Now, Hutcheson was not the founder of the Scottish
School in this sense, for the simple reason that he was not
a Natural Realist. The more exact chronology of the composition of his works determined in the preceding chapters
proves that all the works of his first three periods were written
prior to the appearance of Hume's *Treatise*, and the " Compends " so soon afterwards that Hutcheson had not time to
grasp the true drift of Hume's scepticism. Therefore, as with
other pre-Humian thinkers, the theory of perception was far
from being the central point of a Philosophy, and thus we

find Hutcheson sometimes speaking as an Occasionalist, sometimes even as a follower of Berkeley. If further evidence
were needed it would be found in the fact that neither Reid
nor Hamilton mentions Hutcheson as an adherent of the
theory; nor does Prof. A. Seth Pringle-Pattison in his work
on *Scottish Philosophy*, and the reason is sufficiently obvious.
Since Natural Realism was the answer to a question pro-
pounded by Hume, it would be absurd to expect Hutcheson to
have answered it before it was asked! In this sense we may
accept Prof. James Seth's expression, "If Hutcheson is the
founder of Scottish Philosophy, Reid is its second founder[1]."
At the same time a protest must be entered against the
following summary: "in the characteristic features of his
thought, in his theory of the 'Moral Sense,' and in his doctrine
of Benevolence, he is profoundly original[2]." With regard to
the Moral Sense, Hutcheson may be allowed to speak for himself. "Some have, by a mistake, made a compliment to the
author, which does not belong to him; as if the world were any
way indebted to him for this discovery [*i.e.* of a Moral Sense].
He has too often met with the Sensus Decori et Honesti and
with the δύναμις ἀγαθοειδής to assume any such thing to
himself[3]." This is no isolated expression; in each of his works
Hutcheson similarly disclaims originality. For instance, on the
title-page of the *Inquiry*, in the early editions, he says, "the
ideas of Moral Good and Evil are established, according to the
Sentiments of the Antient Moralists"; and, in the Preface to
the later editions, he adds that "he took the first hints from
some of the greatest writers of antiquity, so the more he has
conversed with them, he finds his illustrations the more conformable to their sentiments[4]." Again, in his *Compend of
Morals*, he writes, "the learned will at once discern how much
of this 'Compend' is taken from the writings of others, from
Cicero and Aristotle[5]."

Similarly, Hutcheson's whole teaching upon Benevolence

---

[1] *The Scottish Contribution to Moral Philosophy*, 1898, p. 31.
[2] *Ibid.* p. 8.
[3] *Essay on the Passions*, p. xx.   [4] Ed. 4, p. xxi.
[5] *A Short Introduction to Moral Philosophy*, 1753, p. v.

may be traced back through Shaftesbury to Cicero, reinforced by his own borrowings from the Stoics already mentioned. Instances of this will be found in the discussion of his positive contribution to Universalistic Hedonism in the next chapter.

Truly, if one prophet is without honour in his own country, another is in danger of receiving too much. Hume, "the Sceptic," is an instance of the former, and Hutcheson, the quasi-orthodox, of the latter ; or rather the elder thinker is honoured for what he did not attempt, and his real achievements, as a Philosopher of the Enlightenment, are ignored. Is it not strange, that in Germany, Hume's claim to have drawn a dividing line across the development of modern Philosophy is admitted, while, in his own country, it is practically ignored ? Hume was the critic of the Philosophy of his time and the result of his criticism was a legacy of denials which his successors had to find some means of escaping. Hutcheson's work was practically finished before Hume began to write, therefore he cannot have anticipated the solutions of problems he had never heard raised. Further, as has been shown, he was an Eclectic, and Hume's thought was too profound to be disposed of by an eclecticism. Thus chronology, the genesis and content of Hutcheson's thought, dispose of this supposition.

If it cannot be maintained that Hutcheson answered Hume before the latter had spoken, it is by no means to be concluded that he is without a place in the chain of historical development. Though he was neither the first inductive, introspective, intuitional thinker, and though he was not a "natural Realist," an important place belongs to him as the prototype of the Scottish Enlightenment, that is, the diffusion of philosophic ideas in Scotland and the encouragement of speculative tastes amongst the men of culture of the generation following his own. Rather than claim for him the earliest place amongst a group of some half-dozen thinkers, is it not a higher honour to have put the last touch to the work of an earlier period, to have generalised its conclusions and illustrated them by the light of antiquity, thereby preparing the way alike for Hume, Reid, Adam Smith, and Brown ? In fine, Hutcheson

not only trained the new thinkers who were to follow him—
for Smith was his pupil, he corresponded with Hume, and
one of his works first started Reid as a thinker—but also
prepared an audience for them. This could only be effected,
as it was in fact effected, by a popular Philosophy and therefore Hutcheson may be taken as the leader of the Enlightenment. If then Scepticism be accepted as the close of an epoch
of thought, and if Scepticism is generally preceded by an
Enlightenment, this order holds good in Britain in the first
half of last century. The Realism and Empirical Idealism of
the eighteenth century alike, had reached their final development. Hutcheson, with many others, constitute the " Enlightenment," and the period rounds itself off in the Scepticism
of Hume, who turns the arguments of either tendency against
the other in order to disprove the presuppositions of both.
The thinkers who endeavoured to answer Hume, as for instance
Kant and Reid, belong to a new period.

This view of the historical order is liable to be misunderstood without a few words of explanation. So far Hutcheson
has been represented as a leader in the Scottish Enlightenment,
but he is both more and less than this. It will be remembered
that in the second period of his work, which was completed
prior to his arrival in Scotland, he had begun to borrow from
Butler, who may be taken as representing the same movement
in England. Therefore, not only was the Scottish Enlightenment conditioned by Classical ideas, but also it proceeded in
line with, and under the impetus of a similar tendency in
England. In other words, it was in no sense distinctively
Scottish, except in so far as the ferment of ideas took place
north, as well as south, of the Border, and the fact that the
former produced larger results than the latter, in no wise
affects the common origin of either. Yet the very importance
of the outcome of the movement should not be risked by
provincialising the basis upon which it rests ; and to represent
Hutcheson's Enlightenment as exclusively Scottish is to cut
off all its results from their continuity with past history.
A " kail-yard " school of fiction within reasonable limits is an
addition to contemporary literature, but a kail-yard Philosophy

verges perilously near a contradiction in terms.   Further, while
Hutcheson introduced outside ideas into Scotland, his influence
by no means remained there.   The British Enlightenment
takes chronological precedence of those in Germany and France
and therefore Hutcheson became a powerful force in the German movement which began about the middle of last century.
From this date until the recognition of the importance of
Kant's system his influence in Germany was very marked.
The eclectic nature of his work led to his admirers abroad
adopting a different starting-point from that of his disciples
at home.   In Germany, the ethical value of Perfection, which
first appears in the Second Period of his work and acquires
greater prominence in the third, reinforced the failing authority
of the Wolffian School, and thus Hutcheson's grafting of
Wolff's Perfection upon that of the Stoics repaid the original
debt with interest[1].

Another qualification is to be added to this interpretation
of Hutcheson's position.   In saying that as a leader of the
Enlightenment he belongs to the period that Hume closes, it
is not to be understood that there is a distinct and fixed
severance between periods in the history of Philosophy; or
that none of his ideas were repeated by his successors.   Such
a view is as naive as that of the child who expected to see
meridians of longitude drawn on the sea or the sky, just as
on his globes at school.   Upon the contrary, Hutcheson's successors were indebted to him for much, but the criterion that
separates them in the new period from him in the old is not
what they took but what they left.   It will have been noticed
how much all British writers of last century are indebted to
Hutcheson—Intuitionalists and Associationalists alike—and
the very fact that he has so much in common with all his
successors shows that he is not the master of any one of them.
His thought is a mine of borrowings from his predecessors,
inconsistent as between the parts, and varying as a whole
from time to time.   Between Hutcheson and his successors
Hume had intervened and taught them the paramount neces-

[1] *Einfluss der Englischen Philosophen seit Bacon auf die Deutsche Philosophie
des 18 Jahrhunderts*, von Dr G. Zart, Berlin, 1881, *passim*.

sity of consistency of thought, and hence it is that the criterion
of the new period consists in the fact that thinkers after Hume,
while borrowing from Hutcheson, at the same time endeavoured
to systematise their indebtedness, rejecting much of his work
on account of its inconsistencies with the remainder.

An instance of this is to be found in the relation of Reid
to Hutcheson, though inasmuch as it constitutes something
of a positive contribution to Philosophy, its place would rather,
strictly speaking, be in the next chapter. In so far as
Hutcheson has any principle or system, he finds a criterion
in "the natural," and this, it need scarcely be mentioned, is
traceable to the later Stoics. From his optimistic point of
view, not "whatever is, is right," as Pope expresses it, but the
non-conventionalised is the primary form and the archetype,
of which actually existing things, into which anything artificial
enters, are but imperfect reproductions. Thus the hyposta-
tisation of "the natural" is reached, which might be described
as the ideal in regress, rather than the ideal towards which
progress is to be made. Even Hutcheson never claimed any
intuition of the natural, it was the element that remained as
the residuum of Psychological analysis[1]. He was too far from
realising Hume's advance upon his own position to recognise
why the younger thinker should require any definition of the
term, and still more why he should find fault with a definition
when provided. Further, Hutcheson is by no means consistent
in the use of his shibboleth and therefore no thinker who
borrows it from him is likely to benefit by the loan. Yet this
is what Reid has done. How often does he speak of "natural
signs," "natural beliefs," "natural desires"? Indeed, no account
of his work that fails to record the Stoic signification of these
terms, through Hutcheson and Butler, does justice either to
Reid or the historical evolution of his thought. To be fair

---

[1] It is curious to find this derivation of the moral sense reappearing in the
modern novel. Mr George Moore writes, "A sense which eludes all the other
senses, and which is not apprehensible to Reason, governs the world, all the
rest is circumstantial, ephemeral! Were man stripped, one by one, of all his
attributes, his intelligence, his knowledge, his industry, as each of these shucks
was broken up and cast aside, the kernel about which they had gathered would
be a moral sense." *Evelyn Innes*, p. 327.

to him it should be added that his procedure is vastly different from Hutcheson's, for, if the word or its equivalents were removed from the works of both, Reid's argument would remain, though weakened; Hutcheson's, it is to be feared, would be only assertion, if not paradox. The same survival is to be found in Hamilton's phrase *Natural* Realism, and not to multiply examples still persists in the following passage of Dr Martineau's: "This is but the return to what it has been customary, in the esoteric schools, to call the 'common consciousness': in ignorance of any other, and unable to find myself in the sublimer experiences of the closet philosopher, I cannot withdraw my *natural* trust from a guide that has never deceived me. By all means let illusions be banished, provided the eviction be not effected, like that of an exorcised devil, by another stronger than itself. But the idealist's superior airs towards the *natural* postulates and the direct working of the honestly trained understanding, are seldom unattended by intellectual error and moral wrong....The first condition of a sound mind is to plant a firm trust on all beliefs and feelings involved in the exercise of the *natural* faculties, and the collapse of this condition opens the way to illimitable aberrations[1]."

Both the origin and the results of what has been called Hutcheson's "Naturalism" suggest some curious reflections. Prof. Sorley defines Naturalism as "a theory according to which man is essentially a sensitive subject"...whose " constitution is explained without attributing to reason any spontaneous or productive function[2]." Now, subject to the qualifications resulting from Hutcheson's Eclecticism, this definition holds good of much of his work, and we have the Paradox of the Naturalism of the Enlightenment, which, founded upon Stoic teaching, yet diametrically reverses the Stoic order of the faculties. The explanation is not far to seek; Hutcheson, like many Naturalists, was influenced by Eclectics and later Stoics, by whom the rigid outlines of the early form of the theory had been worn down and all but effaced. Moreover,

---

[1] *A Study of Religion*, I. pp. 75, 76. The italics are added.
[2] *Ethics of Naturalism*, pp. 16, 17.

it has been shown that Shaftesbury's Hellenism resulted in an over-valuation of feeling upon the analogy of the æsthetic sentiments; and thus, the Greek spirit Hutcheson had inherited from Shaftesbury is at war with the Roman interpretation of it, that appealed to the Puritan side of his character.

This inconsistency, strange to say, was popular at the time, and more especially in France. Montesquieu, Rousseau, and Madame de Staël preferred the Romans to the Greeks. With far different aims they agreed in this with Hutcheson; for the artistic impulses of the Hellenic spirit were a sealed book alike to the Professor-Preacher and to the advance-guard of the Revolution. The Greeks, as Madame de Staël expressed it, were neither "sensitive nor sad"; indeed they were "non-moral"; and with Hutcheson too, his openly expressed preference for the Romans is a tacit reproach to true classicism. This point of contact with French thought, during the latter half of last century, led to Hutcheson's works having a considerable circulation in France, though his influence is to a large extent merged in that of Shaftesbury[1].

---

[1] Cf. *Jean Jacques Rousseau*, by Joseph Texte, Book III. chaps. 3 and 4.

CHAPTER XIV.

HUTCHESON'S POSITIVE CONTRIBUTION TO PHILOSOPHY.

THE more the evidence is investigated the truer it will be found that Hutcheson's best contribution to the Philosophy of his time consisted in the place he held as a leader of the Enlightenment. This was rather a diffusion of philosophic ideas than a system proper; and, as such, should be differentiated from constructive modes of thought. If the enquiry be extended farther, and a search is made for his positive contributions to the development of thought, most readers of philosophy would probably be inclined to instance his supposed foundation of Natural Realism and his Intuitionalism. His claims to the former have been shown to be devoid of foundation, and a similar remark applies, but with considerable qualifications, to the latter. No doubt Hutcheson speaks most frequently as an Intuitionalist, he never tires of entreating or even commanding his reader to consult " his heart " and observe what happens " in his breast." His catalogue of Internal Senses might also be mentioned in this connection; but, if so, it is to be remembered that, too often, his " senses " are intuitional in name, but non-intuitional in use. Indeed it is difficult to find that Hutcheson has made any marked advance upon Cicero, whose Intuitionalism is but little removed from that of the non-metaphysical person. The unreflective mental attitude is generally intuitional; and it is upon this foundation that Cicero builds. Hutcheson adds something here and there, but he never seriously sets himself to improve the stability of the edifice. A striking instance of this has already been noticed, namely, that he seems unaware of the value of the Stoic φαντασία καταληπτική, and hence he has no criterion for the discovery of his senses, or for the discrimination of a new sense from other mental data or faculties. In fact, when as in his third period he attempts any deduction, he is thrown back either on a teleology involving his own theory of the Cosmos, which generates the Sense and at the same time is proved by it, or else he works from the notion of the "excellence of mental activities," which gives Senses as a recognition of the idea or of approximations towards perfection of function. Needless to say this is not Intuitionalism as it was understood after him in Scotland. At the same time, his expressions contain the germ of much that is found in Reid, but it is a germ that needs no little culture. Thus the appeal to Introspection, with Cicero's defence of the internal Senses, from the "consensus gentium" and the structure of language, are specific cases in which Hutcheson influenced later thought. What is his own, here, is not the message (which, after all, he only repeats) but rather the emphasis and insistency with which he expresses it.

A much more definite contribution to later thought will be found in Hutcheson's relation to Universalistic Hedonism. This fact has been disguised by the prevalent idea that Hutcheson was a consistent Intuitionalist; but, if the view of the function of the *Conscientia Antecedens* and the *Conscientia Subsequens*, in the preceding pages is even approximately correct, his third Period is simply Utilitarianism as Mill understood it, except that Hutcheson is even less Intuitional than Mill, since, needless to say, the *Conscientia Antecedens*, in its calculating process, cannot avail itself of the quasi-intuitionalism borrowed from Evolution. This being so, the *Conscientia Subsequens* becomes the Moral Sanction, and neither Bentham nor Mill would be likely to object to Hutcheson's expressions regarding its effects, though they would doubtless claim to have simplified the account of its origin.

Hutcheson's most remarkable anticipation of Universalistic Hedonism was his discovery of its formula, "the greatest Happiness of the greatest number," though, as will be seen, it is only one of many variants with him. From Hutcheson to Bentham the history of the phrase may be traced by two curious by-ways.

Mr Leslie Stephen has noted that Bentham himself admits that it was either from Priestley or Beccaria that he learnt the principle of the "greatest Happiness of the greatest number[1]." In reference to the former, Bentham says that it was in an early pamphlet (the *Treatise on Civil Government*, 1768) that he found this formula, the discovery of which "caused him the sensations of Archimedes[2]." Now Priestley, owing to his controversy with Reid, Beattie and Oswald, was acquainted with Hutcheson's works[3], so that here the line of descent from Hutcheson to Bentham, through Priestley, is complete. Bentham seems more inclined to admit his indebtedness to Priestley than to Beccaria. "Priestley was the first" he says "(unless it was Beccaria) who taught my mouth to pronounce this sacred truth[4]." "The sacred truth" appears in the introduction of *Dei Delitti e delle Pene* (1764), where Beccaria expressly states his obligation to the "philosopher, who, from his study had the courage to scatter amongst the multitude the seeds of useful truth, so long unfruitful[5]." The general tenour of this reference shows that Beccaria directly traced the expression to a "philosopher," and the concluding phrase suggests that he was fully conscious that Hutcheson was the originator of the formula, since between the first expression of it in the *Inquiry* and the date at which Beccaria wrote, an interval of forty years had elapsed. That Beccaria had read Hutcheson's *Inquiry* through the French Translation of 1749, would appear to be probable, since he says in one of his letters, that he owes everything to French books, especially in fostering his feelings towards humanity at large[6]. Inasmuch as he expressly mentions Hume amongst these "French" works, that influenced him, it would appear highly probable that he read Hutcheson in the French

[1] *English Thought in the Eighteenth Century*, II. p. 61.
[2] *Bentham's Works*, x. pp. 79, 80.
[3] *An Examination of Dr Reid's Inquiry*, &c., London, 1767.
[4] *Works*, x. p. 142.
[5] *On Crimes and Punishments*, London, 1767.
[6] *Cesare Beccaria et L'Abolizione della Pena di Morte*, Milan, 1872, p. 17.

translation; so that, both through Priestley and Beccaria, the greatest happiness formula may be traced back to Hutcheson.

Though the expression—"the greatest Happiness of the greatest number"—found its way into English thought through Hutcheson, it does not, by any means, follow that he was the "inventor" or originator of it. This formula, now the watchword of the Universalistic Hedonist, is ultimately traceable back to the Stoic "citizenship of the World," through Hutcheson, to his favourite authors, the eclectic Stoics, Cicero, Seneca, Epictetus and Marcus Aurelius Antoninus. The celebrated phrase itself is plainly foreshadowed in Cicero's *De Finibus*, which Hutcheson quotes from frequently, and which he expressly mentions as an exceptionally valuable work[1]. Cicero, when speaking of friendship, says that one should wish his friend " bonis affici *quam maximis*[2]." Here we find the " greatest Happiness " of the formula foreshadowed ; and, a little later, a phrase occurs, which suggests " the greatest number," when he writes, "Impellimur autem naturâ, ut prodesse velimus quam plurimis[3]." Further, he says that his purpose in composing the *De Divinatione* was " prodesse quam plurimis[4]" ; and again in the *De Officiis*, from which Hutcheson frequently quotes, the two "maxima" occur almost together, when it is stated that the ideal condition of society would be found— " si, ut quisquis erit coniunctissimus, ita in eum *benignitatis plurimum* conferetur[5]"; and, in the next book, we find that care is to be taken, " ut iis beneficiis *quam plurimos* adficiamus[6]." Seneca, too, expresses himself in somewhat similar terms— " Hoc nempe ab homine exigitur, ut prosit hominibus, si fieri potest multis, si minus paucis[7]." A still more remarkable anticipation is to be found in a passage from the Commentary of Simplicius upon Epictetus, where the two halves of the formula, in universalized form, occur in the same sentence[8]. Since Hutcheson himself quotes from the works mentioned, it would seem probable that the celebrated dictum is a repro-

---

[1] *Introduction to Moral Philosophy*, p. vi.
[2] *De Finibus*, II. 24.
[3] *Ibid.* III. 20.
[4] II. 1.
[5] *De Officiis*, I. 16.
[6] *Ibid.* II. 18, cf. II. 4.
[7] *De Otio*, 3.
[8] *Vide infra*, 276.

duction of Cicero; and it seems likely that it was reached in the following manner. Though "the greatest happiness of the greatest number" is the expression that has since become a philosophical "party cry," it is only one of many variants used by Hutcheson, the generic type of which was the "Universal Happiness" or the "general good of all"; and, it is worthy of note, that on two occasions, when these expressions are used, he refers to Marcus Aurelius "in many places[1]." When Hutcheson's fondness for "moral algebra" is remembered, it can easily be understood, that, when he works from such reproductions of later Stoicism, he easily reaches the formula of Utilitarianism. The following expression, to use a Kantian phrase, may be called the deduction of this ideal of Universalistic Hedonism. "In comparing the moral qualities of actions, in order to regulate our election, among various actions proposed...we are led by our Moral Sense of Virtue to judge thus, that in equal degrees of Happiness, expected to proceed from the action, the virtue is in proportion to the number of persons to whom the happiness shall extend...and in equal numbers is as the quantity of the Happiness or natural good; or that the Virtue is in a compound ratio of the quantity of good and number of enjoyers[2]...so that, *That action is best which procures the greatest Happiness for the greatest numbers; and that worst, which in like manner occasions misery[3].*"

Whether Hutcheson adopted "the greatest Happiness principle" from the expressions of Cicero, already quoted, or worked it out from the idea of "universal good" of the later Stoics, there is no doubt that the latter form of expression, converted into eudæmonistic terms, occurs most frequently in his works. For instance, he speaks of "the Happiness of mankind being desirable, or good to the Supreme Cause[4]." The moral ideal is "Universal Happiness[5]," "the general good of all[6]," "good

[1] *Essay on the Passions*, p. 44. *System*, I. p. 94.
[2] Cf. *Essay on the Passions*, p. 42.
[3] *Inquiry*, "Essay on Moral Good," III. § 8, Edition 4, pp. 180, 181.
[4] *Ibid.* p. 65.   [5] *Essay on the Passions*, p. 44.
[6] *Introduction to Moral Philosophy*, I. p. 117: and his letter to his father quoted *supra*, p. 42.

will to all[1]," "Universal good will to all[2]," "the common interest of all[3]." Such expressions are echoes, indeed, often translations, from the Moralists of the Roman Empire. Simplicius, commenting upon the query of Epictetus as to what position the wise man will hold in the state[4], says that he will co-operate in all good for all men[5]. With Antoninus, too, the ideal is to show good will to all, to love mankind, to care for all men (κήδεσθαι πάντων ἀνθρώπων[6]). According to Seneca no type of thought manifests a greater love of man or is more attentive to the common good than his own[7]. Similarly, the wise man is "in commune auxilium natus ac publicum bonum[8]"; and, in aiding others, he advances the common interest (commune agit negotium[9]). This is the teaching of nature, for "homo in adiutorium mutuum genitus est[10]," or, as he expresses the same thought elsewhere, "Hominibus natura me iubet prodesse....Ubicunque homo est ibi beneficii locus est[11]." Cicero too speaks of the "caritas generis humani[12]," and Epictetus says that just as nothing is more paltry than love of gain and love of pleasure, so nothing is more sublime than the love of mankind[13]. So Antoninus writes that the ideal of the general good is always before his mind[14], and one of his maxims is φίλησον τὸ ἀνθρώπινον γένος[15]; and, in similar terms, Epictetus, though a stricter Stoic than Antoninus, speaks of the care of Zeus to make all men happy as far as possible[16], and he elsewhere adds that the wise man

---

[1] *System*, i. p. 94.   [2] *Ibid.* p. 69.
[3] *Introduction to Moral Philosophy*, i. 56, 64, 76.
[4] Epict. *Enchir.* chap. 24.
[5] The wise man is κοινός τε πάντων ἔσται πατὴρ καὶ παιδαγωγός, διορθωτής τε καὶ σύμβουλος, καὶ κηδεμονικὸν πᾶσιν ἑαυτὸν παρέχων, καὶ συνεργὸς ὢν παντὸς ἀγαθοῦ· τοῖς μὲν εὐημεροῦσι συνηδόμενος, τοῖς δὲ λυπουμένοις συνταλαιπωρῶν, καὶ παραμυθούμενος αὐτούς· καὶ ἁπλῶς ἐκεῖνα πράξει, ἅπερ ὁ νομίζων ἔργον ἴδιον ἔχειν καὶ χώραν ἐν τῇ πόλει τὴν πάντων ἀνθρώπων εὐποιητικὴν ἐπιμέλειαν, ἐφ' ὅσον δύναται. Simpl. in Ep. *Enchir.* Cap. xxiv.
[6] Marc. Aur. iii. 4.   [7] *De Clementia*, ii. 5.
[8] *Ibid.* ii. 6.   [9] *De Otio*, 3.
[10] *De Ira*, i. 5.   [11] *Vit. Beat.* 24.
[12] *De Finibus*, v. 23.
[13] οὐδὲν κρεῖσσον...φιλανθρωπίας καὶ εὐποιΐας, Frag. li. (Ed. Fred. Dübner).
[14] E.g. πράσσω τι; πράσσω ἐπ' ἀνθρώπων εὐποιΐαν ἀναφέρων, viii. 23.
[15] *Ibid.* vii. 31.   [16] *Diss.* iii. 24.

should imitate the gods[1]. Similarly the idea that Hutcheson expresses as a regard for "the common interest" is expressed by Antoninus in the maxim, μήτε ἀκοινώνητος ἐνέργει[2], or in another form, καθ᾽ ἕτερον μὲν λόγον ἡμῖν ἐστιν οἰκειότατον ἄνθρωπος, καθ᾽ ὅσον εὖ ποιητέον αὐτούς[3].

Another form of the same idea is met with in passages where Hutcheson introduces the conception of a "system," or, translating literally, "of a whole." Thus he speaks of "the good of the greatest *whole* or of all beings[4]"; or "the good of some more abstracted or general community, such as a species or *system*"; or again, "the greatest or most perfect good is that whole series or scheme of events, which contains a greater aggregate of Happiness *in the whole*[5]," or, "the greatest Happiness and Perfection of the *largest system* within our knowledge[6]." Here, being nearest to the Stoic "Citizenship of the world," Hutcheson does little more than translate from his authorities. Seneca, in a well-known passage, writes "Membra sumus corporis magni...haec [sc. natura] nobis amorem indidit mutuum et sociabiles fecit.... Ex illius constitutione, miserius est nocere quam laedi. Ex illius imperio, paratae sint iuvantis manus. Ille versus et in pectore et in ore sit

Homo sum, humani nihil a me alienum puto[7]."

With more literal identity to the expressions quoted from Hutcheson, Antoninus says, καλὸν δὲ ἀεὶ πᾶν τὸ συμφέρον τῷ ὅλῳ[8]: so too Zeus would not have created anything εἰ μὴ τῷ ὅλῳ συνέφερεν[9]. Similarly πράξεις κοινωνικαί are due from us by the constitution or system of our nature (κατὰ τὴν κατασκευήν)[10] and in another place he expresses the same thought, using the expression σύστημα[11]. With Epictetus man

---

[1] *Diss.* II. 14, 16.　　　　　　[2] III. 5, cf. I. 16, &c.
[3] *Ibid.* v. 20.　　　　　　　　[4] *Inquiry*, p. 44.
[5] *Essay on the Passions*, p. 37.
[6] *System*, I. p. 10, cf. I. p. 161.
[7] *Epist.* Lib. xv. 52 (95). The verse is quoted also by Cicero. The reference is Terence *Heauton*. Act. I. Sc. 1.
[8] *Marc. Aur.* XII. 23, also III. 11, &c., cf. Seneca *De Ira*, II. 31.
[9] *Ibid.* v. 8.　　　　　　　　[10] *Ibid.* VIII. 12.
[11] ὥσπερ αὐτὸς σὺ πολιτικοῦ συστήματος συμπληρωτικὸς εἶ, οὕτως καὶ πᾶσα πρᾶξίς σου συμπληρωτικὴ ἔστω ζωῆς πολιτικῆς. *Ibid.* IX. 23, cf. also III. 11, VII. 13.

is a part of the social organism (μέρος πόλεως[1]), like hands
and feet to the body, or interwoven with the others, like one
thread, amongst the many, that make the piece[2]. Even this
mode of expression is not sufficiently precise for Antoninus,
who, for μέρος, would say μέλος, thereby implying that men
are not merely parts of a social whole, but members of a social
organism[3]; and all the later Stoics are rich in metaphors to
emphasise the vital nature of this membership.

Lastly, Hutcheson has two other closely related formulae
for expressing his moral ideal. The first being the definition
of the best action as " that which secures the greatest and most
extensive happiness of all the *rational* agents to whom our
action may extend," and the other similar in form, but with
the substitution of "sensitive" instead of rational—e.g. "Universal good is what tends to the whole system of *sensitive*
beings[4]," and in one instance both the rational and the
sensitive boundaries of the action appear together[5]. When
the importance of reason, even in later Stoicism, is remembered, the appearance of the former type of this form of the
principle is explained[6]; and the second is deducible, as an
alternative, from Hutcheson's contempt for Reason and from
the Hedonism that colours his whole system. Even in this
instance he has failed to add anything to his favourite author,
since Marcus Aurelius, when stating that men, as participating
in Reason, should be used κοινωνικῶς, expressly pleads for
generous treatment for all animals[7].

It is to be noted that there is a logical order amongst these
different formulæ of the principle. The most abstract is the
universal good or happiness. The second is the universal
happiness of the system or "good of the whole." The third
interprets the system as one of sensitive beings, and the fourth
as of rational beings. Finally, the most concrete is that which

---

[1] *Diss.* II. 5.   [2] *Ibid.* I. 2.
[3] *Ibid.* VII. 13, cf. St Paul, Romans xii. 4—5.
[4] *Essay on the Passions*, p. 203, cf. p. 191, p. 35. *System*, I. p. 50, p. 160.
Introduction to Moral Philosophy, p. 20.
[5] *Essay on the Passions*, p. 200.
[6] E.g. Marc. Ant. IV. 4, 24. Epict. *Diss.* I. 9, II. 10.
[7] *Ibid.* VI. 23.

has become the formula of Utilitarianism—not universal happiness nor the greatest happiness of all—but "the greatest happiness of the greatest numbers."

To prevent misconception it should perhaps be added that this logical order should not be interpreted chronologically, that is, no such order can be distinguished as between the different periods in Hutcheson's work. On the contrary, instances of each of the five formulæ might be quoted from the *Inquiry*; and all that can be said is, that the second and third forms of his Philosophy contain most references to the greatest happiness of all *sensitive* beings; while in the last, under the Stoic influence already mentioned, he is rather inclined to return to the more general expressions, reducible to "universal happiness," or "the general good of all."

It would have been unpardonable to have tried the reader's patience with this long digression were it not necessary to establish the genealogy of the formula of Utilitarianism; and it is a strange instance of the irony of history, that the Stoics —the bitter opponents of all pleasure-theories—should have provided a rallying-cry for Hedonism, long after their school had passed away. Yet the continuity is complete. The Stoic "Citizenship of the World" is so interpreted by Cicero, Seneca, Antoninus and Epictetus, that expressions such as those quoted above are to be found in their works. These were repeated by Hutcheson in a different spirit and with a different meaning, and we have the greatest happiness principle as accepted by Bentham.

Here, when Hutcheson not only anticipates the thought but even the very words of the Universalistic Hedonist, it is to be noticed that he introduces alternatives, which were developed earlier in other directions. Thus, the statement of the formula, which interprets the system as one of rational Beings, would doubtless have appealed to Adam Smith, and it may have suggested the rationality of the "Impartial Spectator." Much of Hutcheson's language in this connection, presents a striking similarity to Kant's "system of Rational Beings" and the "kingdom of ends," since Hutcheson's "system" is to be conceived teleologically. Still beneath the similarity of language there is a wide contrast of meaning, especially in Kant's clear-cut determination of the "system," as such, because rational; and the "ends" as synthesized in a kingdom, because they are self-given, as emanating from reason. Hutcheson's "system," being really borrowed from the Stoics, as a conclusion without its premisses[1], is, according to the line of argument already indicated, either no system at all or else interpolated[2]; and his position with regard to "rational" beings is exactly the same—either he knows nothing of rationality or else his Hedonism must go. Again, the other side of the same formula, the happiness of *all sensitive* beings, is a summary of many of Hume's moral conclusions. In fact, Hume does little more than adopt Hutcheson's Philosophy of the third period and make it consistent, in the light of this aspect of the principle; and so Hume's Moral Philosophy betrays the influence of Hutcheson's recommendation of virtue, at the expense of consistency with the remainder of the *Treatise*[3].

To return to Hutcheson's relation to Utilitarianism, the citation of the greatest happiness principle by no means exhausts its debt to him. It is strange to remark that the positions of *both* Bentham and Mill upon the valuation of pleasures are anticipated by Hutcheson. At first he adopted the point of view, afterwards maintained by Bentham, that pleasures differ only in quantity, afterwards having introduced, or given greater prominence to, the notion of dignity he holds that there is a difference of kind; and it is worth mentioning, that in each case, namely in Hutcheson's mental development and also in Mill's modification of Bentham, the recognition of a difference in kind comes last. Whether this is mere coincidence or a necessity of thought would open up a wide vista for investigation.

[1] It is interesting to compare this case of suppressed premisses with that mentioned below (p. 282), in the case of the missing link of Mill's proof of Utilitarianism, where the missing premiss is partly due to Hutcheson.

[2] *Supra*, chap. x.

[3] Green's *Works*, II. pp. 333—371. Cf. *Hume* by Prof. W. Knight, *Blackwood's Phil. Series*, "The admissions made in his ethical Philosophy are inconsistent with, and indeed undermine his intellectual system," p. 197.

Further, Hutcheson has anticipated the teaching of Bentham and Mill upon the distinction, in moral value, between motive and intention. In fact, Hutcheson is more explicit than Mill upon what he calls the "material goodness" of action, which corresponds to the intention—"that is what the agent wills to do[1]"—of the Utilitarian. "An action is called materially good," according to the earlier writer, "when, in fact, it tends to the interest of the system, as far as we can judge of its tendency; or to the good of some part consistent with that system, *whatever were the affections of the agent*....A good man, deliberating[2] which of several actions proposed he shall choose, *regards and compares the material goodness of them*[3]." The "motive," with Hutcheson, is represented by what he calls "formal goodness," which is equivalent to the *Conscientia subsequens*, and this is a bare "accessory after the fact," having to do, as Mill expresses it, with "our moral estimation of the agent," or, according to Hutcheson, with "the agent's own valuation of his character as a whole." Obviously, this is a wide departure from the earlier naive view of the moral sense, and it is partially withdrawn in the teaching of the last period. At the same time it is worthy of note, that the formula of Universalistic Hedonism and its distinctive tenets, such as the distinction between motive and intention as well as the problem of the valuation of pleasures, are all anticipated by Hutcheson.

Not only has Hutcheson anticipated some of the cardinal doctrines of Utilitarianism, but one of its most remarkable fallacies—namely that of "Composition," in Mill's so-called proof of the principle—may be traced to Hutcheson. "No reason can be given," Mill writes, "why the general happiness is desirable, except that each person, so far as he believes it to be attainable, desires his own happiness...each person's happiness is a good to that person, and the general happiness, therefore, is a good to the aggregate of all persons[4]." *Logically*, there is a premiss omitted here, which is the joint production of Shaftesbury, Hutcheson, and Adam Smith. According to

[1] *Utilitarianism*, p. 27, note.   [2] *Conscientia antecedens.*
[3] *System*, I. p. 252.   [4] *Utilitarianism*, p. 53.

the Economics of the latter, perfect competition, where each man seeks his own greatest good, results in the greatest public good, through a beneficent natural order, in which private interest is "led by an invisible hand" to eventuate in general well-being. This postulate, in Political Economy, again, is a metaphysical thesis of the Optimism of Shaftesbury and Hutcheson. Ethically, Self-Love may be open to suspicion, but, as already indicated in the concrete case of sociology, Hutcheson is forced to provide it with a quasi-justification to enable his teaching to proceed. If all is for the best, then legitimate efforts for self-advancement must not only be permissible but contribute to the general interest. Thus, Smith's economic assumption depends upon Hutcheson, and it only needs a further step in the confusion of material with eudæmonistic well-being to obtain a suppressed premiss which would justify Mill's argument from the logical point of view—a transition which is facilitated by his use of the word "good." It need scarcely be added that, in meaning, the gap remains as wide as ever, since Mill has to prove that the general Happiness is *desired* by the individual, not that the attainment of the "good" of the individual incidentally aids in the advancement of the "general good."

It may perhaps be said that a striking difference between the Universalistic Hedonism of Hutcheson, in some of his moods, and that of Mill, is to be found in the criticism of the association of ideas by the former and its acceptance by the latter. No doubt Hutcheson frequently criticises this principle, but the point here rather is that he establishes an Universalistic Hedonism without the aid either of Intuitionalism or of Association of Ideas, and the introduction of the latter by Mill is a concession to criticisms of thinkers between Hutcheson and himself.

Further, Hutcheson's relation to the Associationalistic Psychology has both an inner and an outer side. The latter is one of hostility; he distrusts its arbitrariness and conventionality and refuses to believe that it can account for any "sense." Upon the inner side, again, it has been shown that Hutcheson has no real criterion of a "sense," and he is driven back upon a plea for its universality. But he is met with contrary cases and exceptions, and to escape this difficulty he uses "Associations of Ideas." Any variation from his own standpoint is due to "some association." If then, association can explain the exceptions why may it not account for the rule? Or, if the Sense is but a psychological residuum that Association cannot disintegrate, may not an improvement or an extension of the method resolve the refractory mental remnant? This view was urged by John Clark of Hull, and there is no doubt that Hutcheson's vacillating attitude, in this connection, joined with the frequent concessions he made, did much to encourage the Associationalists. If the principle could do so much for *him*, how much more might it not achieve for *them*? If one of the leading opponents of the method had been forced to abandon so much territory, might not a more vigorous onslaught conquer the whole of it?

In addition to this negative impetus to Associationalism, it is worthy of remark that Hutcheson, the supposed bulwark of Intuitionalism, actually on some occasions admits the whole contention of the Associationalist. For instance, he says in one place, that "Association represents actions as good or evil[1]," after which admission, it would appear, there is nothing left to contend for by either side. There could be no stronger proof of Hutcheson's Eclecticism than this.

Another positive contribution, made by Hutcheson to Philosophy, will be found in his additions to Æsthetics and Teleology. He undoubtedly wrote the first modern *Treatise* upon the former subject, as distinguished from Arbuckle's articles in the *Dublin Journal*, which again were anticipated by Addison in the *Spectator*. This formula, too, of "Uniformity amidst variety," is a slight advance upon Shaftesbury's "order," "proportion," "harmony." It is to be added, however, that Hutcheson himself foregoes much of this development upon his teacher, since, as already shown, he is inclined in his later work to drop the "variety"—which becomes rather cognitive than æsthetic. It is needless to repeat that Hutcheson's conception of "Beauty" is altogether formal, and that his definition

[1] *System*, i. p. 30.

required a content from others, such as Henry Home (Lord Kames) and Edmund Burke, from whom it passed, as modified, to the German thinkers of the Enlightenment, and from them to Kant[1].

In fact, Hutcheson's "Beauty" is nothing more than the most abstract expression of the union of ends in any system. This is the true "original" of the uniformity. The primary type is the Macrocosm, which according to Hutcheson's point of view is capable of division—or rather perhaps is perceived as divided—into a number of parts, each of which again is a "cosmos." Thus, Hutcheson's sole Category is the idea of End, and inconsistencies arising out of his admission of it have already been indicated, yet without it he cannot advance a single step.

The renaissance of Teleology which also appeared in the system of Leibniz was a reaction against the mechanism of the general drift of thought prior to the last few years of the seventeenth century. It is quite impossible to disentangle the influence of Hutcheson from that of Shaftesbury and the Wolffian School. One instance may however be to some extent isolated, namely, Hutcheson's share in building up the proof of the existence of a personal God from "Final Causes." It has often been shown that Leibniz vacillated considerably upon the relation of God to the Monads, and very little can be expected of Shaftesbury who spoke of his God as "It." Here it is plain that the Physico-Theological Proof owes very much indeed to Hutcheson. He collected data and systematised them, leaving a collection of material likely to be convincing to the "plain man," though vitiated for the metaphysician by his inconsistencies.

---

[1] A practical contribution to the general æsthetic development will be found in Hutcheson's influence upon the Foulises, which doubtless led to the foundation of the ill-fated Glasgow Academy, which was one of the earliest provincial institutions for the encouragement of the practical study of Art. It is interesting to note this actual outcome of Hutcheson's æsthetic teaching, especially as it constitutes, to some extent, the remote origin of the modern "Glasgow School." Information relative to the Glasgow Academy will be found in *Notices and Documents Illustrative of the Literary History of Glasgow*, Glasgow, 1839, *passim*.

CONCLUSION.

THE account of Hutcheson's position in the previous pages must seem very iconoclastic, when his kindly disposition as a man and his modest claims as a thinker are remembered. Yet the estimate of his work very nearly coincides with his own; and the criticism is the unavoidable result of injudicious appraisals of his admirers, who have felicitated him either upon his borrowings or else upon what he did not attempt. It is no great compliment to a person's appearance to praise the fit of a borrowed coat or to congratulate a rider upon the hard knees of a horse hired for the day! If Cleanthes or Aristo had known the "base uses"—as they would have considered them—to which their ideas were applied by Hutcheson, they would probably have longed for a vested interest in philosophical principles.

Hutcheson's strength lay in his personality. He was a preacher, not a system builder. His personal magnetism and method of lecturing were his main influences. The first brought him his audience, the second taught it. Shaftesbury had enlightened the Upper Classes in England; through Hutcheson the same movement extended from the University to the masses. Thus Philosophy was brought home to the people and formed a part of the culture of every educated man. That Hutcheson was a Philosopher of the Enlightenment constitutes his chief claim upon posterity. This single title unites his liberalising influence in the University, his efforts towards a higher standard of culture amongst the clergy, and his eclectically popular type of thought. These characteristics centre round and gain impetus from the magnetism of his character and fascinating personality. He not only popularised

Philosophy but made it attractive—indeed to the stern Calvinistic spirit of his time it appeared that he made right living too alluring, and that rectitude manifesting itself "in a lovely form" was a dangerous concession to human weakness. But the popularisation of abstract thought by an uninteresting person is far from stimulating. Research, however rude or repellant in expression, possesses a certain charm as bringing with it contact with the library or laboratory. The writer, in this case, holds the reader at his mercy, and the latter must bear with vices of style as the price to be paid for the fruition of the discoveries they record. The lecturer or writer, who endeavours to popularise his subject, occupies a totally different position. The bait he must offer to attract an audience is to be interesting. All contemporary evidence points to the fact that Hutcheson succeeded in this, both personally and as a lecturer. So much so indeed that he impressed his ideal of the teaching of Moral Philosophy upon the Scottish Universities and, strange to say, it has persisted almost down to the present.

The didactic element in Hutcheson's lectures cannot be too strongly insisted upon. His aim was not to give his students a system of morality which would bear the searchlight of keen logical scrutiny, but rather to saturate them with a code of ethics, by which they could live—or, if need be, die by. In his own words he aimed at "touching the heart" and raising "an enthusiasm for the cause of virtue." Thus he never intended, in all probability, to systematise his indebtedness to his predecessors, in fact his borrowings were rather texts adopted for special occasions[1]. He was the sworn foe of every degraded or degrading estimate of human nature, and, like any man of generous and impulsive temperament, seeing a wrong done to humanity, he snatched at the first weapon that came to his hand. So, when Mandeville obliterated the line dividing right from wrong, he caught at Platonic and Stoic arguments

---

[1] It has been shown that Leechman actually endeavoured to supply a methodology for Eclectic procedure in his Synod Sermon. If he was indebted to Hutcheson for material, the sentences quoted (p. 87) would constitute Hutcheson's own justification of his method.

as well as the vague Hellenic impressions of Shaftesbury. To expect consistency under these conditions is to misconceive the circumstances and the man. Enthusiasm sweeps beyond the bounds of the logical syllogism, and enthusiasm was Hutcheson's goal. If the expression may be used, he was an *artistic* lecturer, whose whole attention was concentrated upon the result, not upon the logical steps by which it was attained. In fine, to repeat a word used by Shaftesbury, he was primarily a "maker" of moral men, not a constructive thinker.

This very weakness of thought, when compared with the greater systems, was precisely his strength in his own day, when reinforced by a personal charm and moral earnestness, such as his. Neither the time nor the country was ripe for a thoroughly consistent and coherent system. If this statement be questioned, it is only necessary to refer to the chilling reception given to Hume's *Treatise*, even after the way had been prepared by Hutcheson. Just as Shaftesbury's mission was to make Art indigenous in England, so it was Hutcheson's to make Philosophy indigenous in Scotland. How much greater success attended his efforts as compared with those of Shaftesbury, may be gathered from a comparison of modern British Art and Philosophy. Thus, in fact, Hutcheson is a prominent figure in the renaissance of speculative enquiry in Scotland; and, to his honour be it recorded, that this "taste," which does not appear in his list of senses, has remained more permanent than any of the others—it has even been asserted to be "natural" to the Scottish character[1].

To foster the taste for Philosophy was Hutcheson's main work. It would be unreasonable to expect that he also created a Philosophy. On the contrary, he did something better under the peculiar circumstances. By compiling an anthology of the "golden thoughts," both of ancient and modern Philosophy, he left his successors a legacy, which contained much that was best in past thought, and thereby forced them to enter upon their work in continuity with ancient speculation. Indeed, instead of starting the new impetus of·thought in Scotland, as has been too often represented, upon a provincial basis, his aim

[1] Mackintosh *Dissertation*, p. 207, note.

was exactly the opposite; and, as a matter of fact, solely
through his exertions and his eclectic teaching, the material
he provided was more cosmopolitan than the similar work
undertaken later in Germany and France—or indeed than any
other of last century.

When thoroughly realised, this achievement is a greater one
than any of those with which Hutcheson's name is generally
associated. He possessed unique gifts—not those of a system
builder—which made a fresh departure in British thought
possible. For this he prepared the way. He gathered very
many seeds, from practically unknown granaries of thought,
and sowed them broadcast, only caring that they should
germinate and that the crop should be luxuriant. To winnow
the harvest and divide the wheat from the tares, the useful
from the merely ornamental, was the work he bequeathed to
his successors.

INDEX.